BEYOND CHARITY

BEYOND CHARITY

U.S. Voluntary Aid for a
Changing Third World

John G. Sommer

Overseas Development Council

©Overseas Development Council 1977
Library of Congress Card Catalog No. 77-89276

Cover design by Artwork Unlimited, Inc.
Cover photo courtesy of CARE. Photo depicts a CARE staff member demonstrating pruning and fertilizing techniques combined with terrace farming to Indians in the Altiplano region of Guatemala.

The views expressed in this volume are those of the author and do not necessarily represent the views of the Overseas Development Council, its directors, officers, or staff.

Contents

Foreword	*by Hubert H. Humphrey*	vii
Chapter 1	A Future for Charity?	1
Chapter 2	A History of Good Deeds: For Better and for Worse	12
Chapter 3	Poverty at Home: How Is It Relevant?	31
Chapter 4	How Humane Is Relief?	39
Chapter 5	The Many Faces of Development Assistance	52
Chapter 6	Measuring Success and Failure	80
Chapter 7	Uncle Sam and the Voluntary Ethos	94
Chapter 8	Where Do the American People Stand?	122
Chapter 9	Beyond Charity	141
Annex A	Facts of Interest about the Private and Voluntary Organizations	159
Annex B	Private and Voluntary Organization Program Criteria	171
	About the Overseas Development Council and the Author	177

Acknowledgments

This book could not have been written without the friendly and valuable assistance of literally hundreds of people who cooperated in the several phases of its evolution—the private and voluntary organization executives and concerned development specialists who encouraged the effort and served on an ODC advisory task force for it; the voluntary agency staff members working both at U.S. headquarters and throughout the Third World who, in long and short conversations at frequently odd hours of day or night, contributed their perspectives, hopes, and frustrations; the officials of donor governments, both North American and European, and of multilateral aid agencies who added their particular views; and the many beneficiaries of U.S. private and voluntary assistance—citizens of some one dozen countries of Asia, Africa, and Latin America whom I had the privilege of visiting in their villages and capitals, offices and homes, during the course of the research.

Nor could this book have been written without the encouragement, critiques, and broader perspectives brought to bear by my colleagues of the Overseas Development Council and particularly by James P. Grant, its President. The book's ultimate readability has been greatly enhanced by Nancy Krekeler's skillful editing and, at an earlier phase, by Margaret Jameson's cheerful deciphering and typing of numerous drafts. The total effort has benefited from the encouragement of Landrum Bolling and James Morris of the Lilly Endowment, which provided the financial support for this project.

To all these friends and colleagues, many sincere thanks.

John G. Sommer
August 1977

Foreword

The record of our American private and voluntary organizations overseas has been a truly remarkable one. Since well before the U.S. government began providing humanitarian assistance to other countries, Americans, through literally hundreds of spontaneously organized voluntary associations, have been sending relief to people suffering from natural calamities and the effects of war in far-flung parts of the world. In recent years, many of these groups have turned their attention to combating the root causes of poverty, disease, and ignorance.

The problems these groups are trying to solve are as old and difficult as human civilization itself. Yet the private and voluntary organizations are enjoying considerable success—largely unheralded, not even widely known, but real nevertheless. They operate, in a sense, at the cutting edge of history, both in geographic terms—in remote areas of the globe where few outsiders are willing to tread—and in program terms—through innovative and creative new approaches to development. These organizations represent the finest tradition of our American people and society concerned with individual liberty, equality of opportunity, and a better life for all.

I have been an ardent supporter of these efforts for many years. In 1961, when I introduced legislation on the floor of the U.S. Senate to establish the Peace Corps, it was the experience of some of our private and voluntary organizations that gave us the confidence to know that the Peace Corps was an idea whose time had come. We knew that there were many Americans of all ages and all across our land who had significant technical skills to contribute in assisting the new nations of Africa, Asia, and Latin America achieve social and economic as well as political independence. We also knew that they had the human sensitivity to understand the tensions faced by individuals in those countries—people emerging from colonial status and training themselves for the new roles required of independent nation-states trying to better the lot of their own poor.

In 1973, when we introduced the "new directions" legislation into the U.S. foreign aid bill—insisting that significantly increased priority be placed by our government on providing aid for the poorer groups in the developing countries—we stipulated that private and voluntary agencies be increasingly encouraged to assist in this effort. We knew that whereas government-to-government programs were often effective in the capital assistance and large-scale training aspects of development, people-to-people initiatives were often more successful in ensuring that the benefits of any kind of aid were shared by those most in need in the world's villages and slums.

As our country now emerges from the unfortunate period of national disillusionment overseas of the 1960s and early 1970s, as the nature of our global interdependence is becoming ever clearer, and as the poor countries are making considerable progress already, it is important for us to reexamine the changing roles and activities of our American private and voluntary organizations. This book by John Sommer of the Overseas Development Council comes as a most timely and thoughtful contribution—really the first one of its kind—to our thinking here and to our planning for the future. We need to better understand both the strengths and weaknesses of the voluntary sector in grappling with the new demands of development, as well as the most desirable roles for private initiative not just for the usual one, two, or five years of budget-planning cycles, but for the rest of this century.

Whether or not one agrees with all of Mr. Sommer's specific observations and conclusions, this book helps greatly in clarifying the critical issues. It goes beyond this, too, by giving concrete recommendations for how private and voluntary assistance can be made more effective oveaseas as well as at home in the United States. It also contains a number of useful suggestions for reorganizing and improving both U.S. government and U.S. private sector support for this broad range of development activities.

I hope that all these suggestions will be seriously considered and will stimulate the further initiatives we so urgently need if we are to be more effective in ameliorating the curse of global poverty. In a world that has seen enough of paternalism and that is striving to meet both basic human needs and essential demands for dignity and equality, this issue of how we Americans relate to other peoples becomes even more sensitive and important than in the past. As the Peace Corps experience has demonstrated, we have much to learn from our voluntary interactions with other societies and cultures.

I certainly intend to stay close to these efforts of the private and voluntary organizations and to contribute in every way I can. .

August 1977

Hubert H. Humphrey
United States Senate

BEYOND CHARITY

Chapter 1

A Future for Charity?

Americans generally like to do the right thing. They are compassionate toward other people less fortunate than themselves. They like to perform good deeds both at home and abroad. They like to do this, as John F. Kennedy declared, "because it is right." It is right to send food and clothing for victims of disasters. It is good to help bring education, better health, and increased agricultural production to other countries. Or is it?

It is a sign of the times that good deeds currently are being viewed with an increasing degree of skepticism, even suspicion. Some argue that there is an inherent contradiction between a nation interested in maintaining preeminent world power status and one committed to good deeds; politics, the argument goes, does not bestow power on those who are merely kind and charitable. The argument, indeed, extends beyond the governmental sector to U.S. private and voluntary organizations. Is this unfair? Perhaps not, inasmuch as it would be reasonable to expect that many of the same values and character traits run constant throughout American society at large. Yet to many private organizations, proud of their independent status, the thought that they are motivated by anything other than compassion and altruism, and that their effectiveness is anything other than positive, is alien indeed. Good deeds are, by definition, good.

The enormous diversity and scale of assistance provided by U.S. private and voluntary organizations overseas are impressive. Traveling along the ruttiest dirt trail, across mountains, deserts, or swamps, miles from the beaten track, one is constantly struck to find there some isolated American doing his or her bit to help other people. There seems no place too remote and no cause too marginal to deter these missionaries for modernity. In fact, the more difficult the assignment the greater their commitment. The countries of the Third World have in a sense become the new frontier, as if manifest destiny had been extended from the American West to the world at large. Problems to be solved? Americans are there.

This is often good. Millions of lives have been saved as a result of American private assistance overseas; Herbert Hoover once estimated, no doubt overzealously, that one billion lives were saved during roughly the first half of the current century alone.[1] Americans helped prove that famine could be defeated, that the prospects for genocide could be vastly diminished, and that universal responses to both natural and man-made disasters could be made a fact of life. Besides this, large numbers of new schools, roads, and irrigation facilities have been built, new agricultural crops and livestock practices introduced, numerous diseases virtually wiped out, and a variety of useful local developmental experiments innovated. More importantly, and a point which statistics and generalizations hide, hundreds of thousands of people—probably millions—have been given significant new cause for hope in improving their own lives in the future.

Were it only Americans who were now calling these achievements into question, one might perhaps attribute their uncertainty to a heightened across-the-board sensitivity and soul-searching induced by the recent Vietnam and Watergate experiences and Bicentennial reflections. But Third World observers are also questioning the record of private and voluntary organizations and are being increasingly outspoken about what they want and do not want in the future. Their criticism is rooted partly in ideological concerns about hidden motivations; partly in observed experience with insensitive and poorly trained individual foreigners; and partly in social and economic concerns that the proffered assistance is not always helping the people most in need—indeed, that it often strengthens the entrenched power elites at the expense of the downtrodden poor.

The numbers of the poor are, in fact, increasing in the world today, largely, but perhaps not entirely, as a result of the multiplying global population. While their poverty cannot be adequately described in aggregate terms or statistics, it is generally accepted that up to two billion people—one half of the world's population of four billion—are now poor. The World Bank describes one billion of these people as "individuals [who] subsist on incomes of less than $75 a year in an environment of squalor, hunger, and hopelessness. They are the absolute poor, living in situations so deprived as to be below any rational definition of human decency. Absolute poverty is a condition of life so limited by illiteracy, malnutrition, disease, high infant-mortality, and low life-expectancy as to deny its victims the very potential of the genes with which they are born. In effect, it is life at the margin of existence."[2] For the other billion poor who are living slightly above this absolute poverty level, life is nearly as joyless and has improved little if at all through decades of "development" efforts; these people are living in a still serious state of *relative* poverty, a condition that, by virtue of its injustice, is nearly as deplorable. It should be noted that the half of the earth's people who live in poverty do not all live in the Third World, although most of them do. Indeed, the fact of poverty within the United States itself forces one to

---

[1]Merle Curti, *American Philanthropy Abroad* (New Brunswick, N.J.: Rutgers University Press, 1963), p. 627.

[2]Robert S. McNamara, *Address to the Board of Governors,* Washington, D.C., September 1, 1975 (Washington, D.C.: World Bank, 1975), p. 13.

sharpen one's examination of the values and development strategies Americans tend to export overseas.

New Perceptions of Development

Customarily it is assumed that the solution to poverty is "development." One speaks of the "underdeveloped" countries or, more recently (out of politeness), the "developing" countries.[3] But the titles, in a sense, are as misleading as the basic assumption. "Development," after all, is not so much an end goal as a *process* of history in which all peoples are engaged in multifaceted dimensions—social and cultural dimensions as well as the more commonly articulated economic and material ones. In this sense the United States is as much a developing country as Bangladesh; indeed, as Gunnar Myrdal has pointed out, the United States is developing at a faster comparative rate than the poor countries and, as is increasingly recognized, not necessarily for the better. Yet not to be "developing" would be cause for alarm, for the alternative is social, economic, and cultural stagnancy. A further complication is that "development" has become linked with modernization, which usually—and inaptly—is articulated as synonymous with Westernization; this is because it was the West that modernized first and defined today's development vocabulary.

These definitions are now changing to a considerable extent, as will be examined in the pages that follow. Years of experience with efforts described as "developmental" have led to increasing sensitivity about cultural diversity and to culturally specific definitions of what development is all about. It has become increasingly clear that economic well-being is not a sufficient goal and that measuring development on the materialistic basis of per capita gross national product is inadequate and often misleading. Gross national product, in fact, reflects only the monetary value of designated goods and services entering the market economy; it thus excludes virtually the entire output of subsistence economies and, as American housewives rightly observe, it also excludes essential sectors of Western economic activity. Furthermore, the GNP measure obfuscates the critical question of internal income distribution. Many argue, therefore, that a new, less ethnocentric measure of development is needed, one that measures more widely accepted basic goals such as the provision of minimum human needs and overall physical quality of life. Indeed, a tentative new measure along these lines—a physical quality of life index (PQLI)—was introduced by the Overseas Development Council in 1977. The PQLI is a composite measure of life expectancy, infant mortality, and literacy—attributes which not only are important in their own right but which also reflect levels of nutritional and health well-being. The PQLI has somewhat startling implications, suggest-

---

[3]Because of the conceptual constraints of the terms "developed" and "developing" countries, the "West" (construed to include Japan) and the "Third World" will be the distinguishing terminology used throughout this volume.

ing, as it does, that countries that are poor in the traditional GNP sense can enjoy very high physical qualities of life, and vice versa.[4] Viewing development in this broader way, it becomes even clearer that alternative strategies of development are needed and that both new values and revitalization of old values must be sought. Traditions may stand in the way of a preferred direction of development in some settings and facilitate and enrich its advance in others.

What is also clear is that the psychological degradation of being *relatively* poor is often as serious as the physical degradation of existing in *absolute* poverty.[5] That is, the satisfaction of basic physical needs is not enough. Any individual human being has a variety of needs, of which the minimum *physiological demands* of food, shelter, and health care are only the most elemental for sustenance of life. There are also requirements for *safety and security* and for *self-respect*, achieved in part through employment and job participation and the ability to control one's individual physical destiny. Then, too, one may become interested in greater *wealth and material well-being* to enjoy better standards of living; in *intellectual freedoms* to express oneself religiously and politically; and ultimately in the spiritual and cultural freedom to exploit one's full range of talents for greater *self-actualization*.[6]

One reason for the changing perceptions of development lies in the evolving configuration of international power politics. As recently as five years ago, power was derived from military muscle and gross national product. While this is still true to a significant extent, moral suasion and selective economic pressures have come into their own as forces with which to reckon. One has only to observe the change in voting patterns in the U.N. General Assembly and the enormous impact of the Organization of Petroleum Exporting Countries oil cartel to conclude that the world is no longer the same as it was. Even if the dramatic impact of these developments may have been exaggerated in the recent past, the trend line clearly suggests that the majority of nations representing the majority of the world's people will have an increasing say in how this planet's resources are distributed and used in the future.

---

[4]See John W. Sewell and the staff of the Overseas Development Council, *The United States and World Development: Agenda 1977* (New York: Praeger Publishers, Inc., 1977), pp. 147-52.

[5]For an analysis of English perceptions of these issues see W. G. Runciman, *Relative Deprivation and Social Justice* (Berkeley and Los Angeles: University of California Press, 1966).

[6]Abraham Maslow, in his book, *Motivation and Personality* (New York: Harper & Row, Publishers, 1954), formulates these needs on a hierarchical basis and has been criticized for a degree of ethnocentricity in doing so. His formulation also places more emphasis on the individual than on the community, a difference of significance when applying the framework to many Third World societies. A nonhierarchical form of the Maslow scheme is presented here because of this difference and because many non-Western societies may pursue "higher" levels of needs before "lower" ones, even though it is difficult to imagine a large degree of creativity being possible in cases where people are severely deprived of minimum physiological requirements such as food and shelter.

This is not to suggest that one can necessarily equate the poor *nations* with the poor *people* of the world; the former, after all, now include a growing number of high-income families. Indeed, one of the sobering lessons of past development experience has been the frequent failure of aid transfers to the so-called developing countries to actually affect in a positive way the lives of the poorest people in those countries. Thus the means, as well as the ends, of development were often misperceived. The predominent development theory in the past was that economic growth initiated on national levels would "trickle down" to create more and better jobs and thus enhanced incomes for all. But what often resulted instead was the enrichment of the upper classes and an enlargement of the gap between rich and poor, that is, little or no trickle-down. This happened primarily because the social and political barriers to development for the poor—mainly class barriers that restrict equality of access to resources—were not fully taken into account. These barriers can be a strong influence in any social setting, but they were particularly so when Third World elites, consciously or subconsciously, felt that they had broken the shackles of colonialism and that they truly represented their people's aspirations. These elites did not always appreciate or admit the extent of the class barriers that were usually traditional to their cultures and that were further strengthened by the patterns of colonial administrations. The elites were reinforced in their narrower class interests by the classical Western development doctrine (in which they also had been trained), which called for increasing the size of the economic pie (to encourage savings for further investment) before dividing it up. The options of increasing and dividing the pie had traditionally been perceived—rightly or wrongly—as mutually contradictory. Thus in the interests of "efficient growth," the equity interests of the poorest people of their countries, insofar as one had or took the time to really think about them, could wait until later.[7] Self-reliance, social justice, liberation—these were all terms that were applied mainly on an *inter*national, not an *intra*national basis.

During the mid-1970s, it has become increasingly clear that new development goals and strategies are needed and that the first goal must be nothing less than the defeat of poverty. Given the extent of global financial resources, this goal no longer appears unrealistic—*if* the hard political choices and commitments can be made, the necessary resources creatively brought to bear, and the appropriate strategies found. According to one estimate, $10-$15 billion in additional annual expenditures could enable the entire population of the world to meet its basic human needs at the level of a country like Sri Lanka—a country that enjoys one of the highest physical qualities of life of any country defined as poor by traditional measures of GNP alone.[8] (This amount is roughly the same as that spent annually in the

---

[7]For an excellent analysis of the trade-offs in development between equality and efficiency, see A.M. Okun, *Equality and Efficiency: The Big Tradeoff* (Washington, D.C.: Brookings Institution, 1975).

[8]See Sewell et al., *Agenda 1977*, p. 120.

United States on household cleaning and polishing preparations and approximately half as much as is spent on alcoholic beverages.) In the absence of vastly strengthened efforts, millions of people will continue to die needlessly every year, while still more millions will suffer from malnutrition and disease. In an era when the issue of human rights has increasingly come to the forefront of public discussion, this denial of minimum human needs in the face of available solutions is tantamount to a form of violence as severe as that of war; Mahatma Gandhi and his followers called it structural violence.

What Future for U.S. Voluntary Aid?

What is the role of private and voluntary organizations at this critical stage of rethinking both the ends and the means of development? What is their role in the face of the larger forces of structural violence? Surely it would be naive to believe that these organizations could solve the poverty problem —an effort that would require not only the just-mentioned increased financial expenditures but also an enormous amount of political effort and global bargaining to make sure that the funds were applied as intended. Yet private and voluntary organizations enjoy two special qualities that have been their strengths in the past and could continue to be in the future. First, they have shown high motivation and frequent creativity in activating the development efforts of others. Second, their roots among the American people are strong. In an era of increasing populism and national self-confidence, these organizations could be further developed to express the best of essential American values for a more humane development process at home and abroad. Indeed, it was the private and voluntary organizations —particularly those of the United States—that took the lead in demonstrating the need for helping the poorest groups of Third World people directly at the grass-roots level. It was they who pioneered many of the efforts and approaches that are now being adopted by governmental and multilateral assistance agencies. It was a recognition of their special capability and role—and a disillusionment with governmental foreign aid—that led the U.S. public and the U.S. Congress to reinforce the role of private organizations through proportionately larger monetary contributions and to give them a special place in the congressional foreign aid legislation of 1973 and 1975. Furthermore, during a period when the United States has declined from top ranking to twelfth ranking among the seventeen member nations of the OECD Development Assistance Committee in terms of governmental aid as a percentage of gross national product, the United States has held steady in its percentage of GNP for *private* aid, ranking third only to Switzerland and Sweden.[9] Equally significant is the fact that while the trend of overall U.S. philanthropic giving has been decreasing in recent years,

---

[9]See Annex A, Table 1.

giving for international assistance has generally increased—a denial of the common wisdom that in the aftermath of the Vietnam experience Americans have turned inward, even isolationist.[10] U.S. private assistance to the Third World—to the extent reliable figures are available—now totals approximately $1 billion annually.[11]

The purpose of this volume is 1) to examine the impact of different types of U.S. private and voluntary organizations overseas; 2) to analyze the historical direction in which private assistance appears to be moving in a rapidly changing international social, political, and economic order; and 3) to formulate recommendations for improvement of these activities, both for the benefit of the poor majority in the Third World and—perhaps equally important—for greater understanding and sensitivity within the United States itself. If there are any underlying assumptions in this study, they are, first, that private contributions to development, while substantial and impressive, are now being outpaced by the increasing magnitude of the problems; second, that the requirements of an increasingly interdependent world demand more informed involvement and interaction among people in the United States and abroad; and third, that the private and voluntary sector, whatever its individual shortcomings, is a unique source of hope and promise as the people of the United States strive to reassert a constructive role in tomorrow's world.

It is worth pausing here to indicate how the private and voluntary organizations fit into the larger context of development assistance, and to specify which kinds of organizations are considered here as falling under the rubric of "private and voluntary." Viewed in the larger context of development spending, U.S. private aid appears quite modest. In terms of overall developmental efforts in the Third World, the largest expenditures are clearly made by Third World governments themselves. In Asia and Africa this has

---

[10]See Annex A, Table 2.

[11]This means that in 1975 the amount of U.S. private overseas aid was approximately the same as that of U.S. government bilateral development aid (excluding security supporting assistance). The $1 billion approximation for aid channeled through private organizations is derived from two sources: *First*, according to the U.S. Department of Commerce, which monitors U.S. dollar *outflows*, private and voluntary organization contributions to overseas aid averaged $815 million annually, exclusive of U.S. government contributions, during the period 1973-1975. These figures are based on some 700 reporting organizations including foundations, missionary societies, and private U.S. contributions to UNICEF. If one were to add to this $815 million the average amount of $274 million the U.S. government contributed to the 94 agencies registered with the Advisory Committee on Voluntary Foreign Aid of the U.S. Agency for International Development over the same period, the total would approach $1.1 billion. *Second*, according to the Advisory Committee on Voluntary Foreign Aid, the total average *income* figure for its 94 agencies was $860 million annually during the agencies' fiscal years reported for the period 1973-1975 and $951 million in 1975 alone. These figures account for all of the largest and most of the major U.S. organizations and include the $274 million in U.S. government contributions; they exclude foundations, missionary societies, UNICEF, and a number of other groups counted by the Department of Commerce. (See Annex A, Table 4 for a breakdown of income by agency reported during 1975. Preliminary private and voluntary aid figures for 1976 suggest a slight decrease in outflows and income from 1975 figures but no significant trend changes.)

been the case since the individual nations achieved independence beginning in the late 1940s and continuing into the 1960s. In Latin America, where political independence had been achieved as early as the 1820s, it took the anticlerical movements of the late nineteenth century for governments to begin to accept development responsibilities; the church, however, is still instrumental when it comes to efforts for the poorest groups. The next largest expenditures come under the heading of official development assistance. This includes bilateral aid programs, including those of the United States, Western Europe, and Japan; the U.S.S.R., Eastern Europe, and the People's Republic of China; the Middle Eastern OPEC countries (largely confined to helping Middle Eastern neighbors); and, in a beginning sense, countries like India (which gives assistance to smaller neighbors such as Nepal and Sri Lanka), and Nigeria and Venezuela (OPEC members which help other poorer countries in their respective regions). Also included in official development assistance are resources that flow through the multilateral institutions, for instance, the World Bank, regional development banks, and the various organizations of the U.N. system. Official development assistance through both bilateral and multilateral channels totaled $17.1 billion in 1975, some $4 billion of which was from the United States. An additional $1.3 billion was given by private organizations, nearly $1 billion of which was from U.S. groups.[12] The total world GNP, by way of perspective, was about $5.6 trillion in 1975.

While it is necessary to be realistic about the limited potential impact of these relatively small amounts of overseas private assistance, it should also be borne in mind that the voluntary agency figures are artificially diminished—perhaps by as much as one half—by the uncounted volunteer component and other factors.[13] Furthermore, in the private sector it is often the qualitative impact that is critical and that may enhance the value suggested by the monetary figures alone. Some would go as far as to argue that the low absorptive capacities of some of the poorest countries ensure that, barring the sort of prior voluntary agency training of local people that makes progress possible, large-scale government aid programs will be relatively ineffectual.[14]

Because the term "private and voluntary agencies" is open to varying interpretations, it is important to clarify which kinds of groups will be considered in this study. *First,* and primary in consideration here, are the "voluntary agencies," a rubric so broad and inclusive as to nearly defy any attempt at generalization. In legal terms—and to qualify for tax exemption status—a voluntary agency is considered loosely to be a nonprofit organization established to fill a public "charitable" (though undefined) purpose. It is

---

[12]Sewell et al., *Agenda 1977,* pp. 230 and 236.
[13]See Jørgen Lissner, *The Politics of Altruism* (Geneva: Lutheran World Federation, 1977), pp. 46–51.
[14]Ibid., p. 52.

more illustrative, however, to characterize the world of voluntary agencies by way of examples. For the purposes of this study, emphasis will be on those professing development as one of their major goals. The best known in the United States are no doubt CARE and the large church consortia such as Catholic Relief Services, Church World Service, and the various Jewish agencies.[15] Voluntary agencies also include child sponsorship programs such as Christian Children's Fund and Foster Parents Plan, largely supported, like the church groups, by constituency contributions. Less widely known but at least as effective are the smaller, more technically oriented groups such as World Education, Volunteers in Technical Assistance (VITA), International Voluntary Services, and Technoserve; these particular agencies are joined together in a consortium called Private Agencies Collaborating Together (PACT), just as a number of church denominations and other groupings are joined together in Coordination in Development (CODEL). The list does not end here. Various associations of U.S. cooperatives are also often included among "voluntary agencies," as are other private nonprofit bodies such as the Asia Foundation and the International Executive Service Corps.[16]

Each of the organizations described in the following pages tends to have its particular strengths, its particular operating style, and its particular sources of support. Many rely on contributions from the U.S. public, and it is the nature of their relationships with the public that is of special interest here. Others, however, are quite dependent on U.S. government funding or on private foundation support. Very few engage "volunteers" in the strictest sense of the term, though almost all function at lower levels of staff remuneration and overhead than other kinds of organizations, relying, rather, on the high levels of motivation of their individual members.

Second—and secondary in consideration in this study—are the endowed independent foundations. The ones with Third World development programs range from those with resident overseas staffs (largely the Ford Foundation and Rockefeller Foundation) to those (such as the Lilly Endowment) that have made overseas grants from their U.S. headquarters, whether directly to Third World recipients or to U.S. or other intermediary organizations such as voluntary agencies and university groups.[17] Sometimes included in this category are the foundations that are still closely allied with their immediate corporate benefactors. Yet they are more properly

---

[15]Because the Jewish agencies in many ways constitute a separate category of their own—specializing in massive aid to Israel and to Jewish communities elsewhere—they are discussed little in this volume. It should also be noted that an entire category of agencies effectively specializing in refugee and migration affairs and in transnational child adoptions are excluded from this study.

[16]For an annotated listing of some 400 private and U.S. voluntary organizations having overseas activities, see *U.S. Non-Profit Organizations in Development Assistance Abroad* (New York: Technical Assistance Information Clearing House of the American Council of Voluntary Agencies for Foreign Service, Inc., 1971).

[17]See Annex A, Table 3 for a listing of U.S. foundations making the largest grants for Third World activities.

included under the rubric of business philanthropy and thus are not discussed here.[18]

Third, there are university groups that execute programs overseas. However, since they are almost exclusively dependent on foundation and government contracts and grants, and since they are not in the same sense independent program–initiating agencies, they are not included in this study.

What are some of the approaches taken by private and voluntary organizations to development in the Third World? They have ranged from basic infrastructure development—mainly building and running schools and hospitals during the early missionary days—to what the Catholics call "corporal works of mercy": emergency relief efforts in the aftermath of natural and man-made disasters, World War II being the most notable example. They have ranged, too, from the more secular concentrations on technology transfer, people-to-people interactions, economic infrastructure, and agricultural development to the more recent quasi-spiritual concentrations, particularly in Latin America, on consciousness-raising aimed at enabling liberation from oppressive political, economic, and social structures. Small as the overall impact of these programs may have been on development as a whole, local impact appears to have been significant in many cases, particularly where the programs have had demonstration effects that could be absorbed thereafter into broader governmental, private, or larger development agency programs. One of the chief problems, however, lies in being able to separate the particular contribution of the foreign voluntary intervention from all the other influences on the general development process. To a large extent, it must be admitted, one does not know whether and to what degree private assistance actually has contributed to improving the lives of the poorest two billion of the world's population.

Some argue that it is not particularly important to know. Voluntary assistance, they say, is in the main an expression of the American public's need for self-fulfillment rather than a means for helping the poor. By projecting American compassion onto others who are deemed less privileged, Americans demonstrate either a secularized missionary zeal for ego gratification or a need to expiate their feelings of responsibility—even guilt—arising from "our" richness and good fortune compared with "their" deprivation. This leads to a moral paradox whereby Americans feel they must act, whether or not it is in the recipient's best interests. The distinguishing feature of private and voluntary assistance, as compared with official assistance mechanisms, is that the former often represents a direct constituency and thus to a somewhat greater extent expresses the many states of mind of various groups of American people at any given point in time.

---

[18]For a discussion of grants made by business corporations, see John G. Sommer, "The Rich, the Poor, and American Private Philanthropy," to be published in the Program for Studies of the Modern Corporation series at Columbia University Graduate School of Business (New York: Macmillan, Inc., forthcoming in 1978).

Some people, however, question whether private and voluntary organizations even do that properly. They argue that these private channels have themselves become bogged down in bureaucratic procedure, becoming interested primarily in justifying and extending their existence, clamoring for grants from any source, and appealing to the lowest common denominator in their fund-raising appeals—in short operating like any vested business interest but under the guise of goodwill. To the extent that many agencies say they are able to raise funds only by making emotional appeals—by showing, for example, the image of a tearful child who can be "saved"—they may be further widening the gap between Americans and people of Third World countries, perpetuating paternalism and dependency, and rendering more difficult both balanced understanding and the inevitable trend toward increasing global interdependence.

There are no easy answers to these problems, questions, indeed dilemmas, of private and voluntary assistance overseas. They are of great and continuing concern to people in the agencies themselves. Many of these questions and problems are endemic, in fact, to the development process, and it is perhaps only because one expects more of the altruistic voluntary sector that the dilemmas relating to them become that much more pointed. The heart of the issue is to judge developmental effectiveness with integrity for both givers and receivers—and this within a context of reducing as soon as possible the blatant inequities between them. For if private and voluntary organizations cannot be effective in this critical domain, one must ask the overarching questions: How ultimately humane is private humanitarian assistance? And is there a future for charity?

Chapter 2

A History of Good Deeds: For Better and for Worse

> Americans of all ages, all conditions, and all dispositions constantly form associations. They have not only commercial and manufacturing companies, in which all take part, but associations of a thousand other kinds, religious, moral, serious, futile, general or restricted, enormous or diminutive. The Americans make associations to give entertainments, to found seminaries, to build inns, to construct churches, to diffuse books, to send missionaries to the antipodes; in this manner they found hospitals, prisons, and schools. If it is proposed to inculcate some truth or to foster some feeling by the encouragement of a great example, they form a society. Wherever at the head of some new undertaking you see the government in France, or a man of rank in England, in the United States you will be sure to find an association.[1]
>
> *Alexis de Tocqueville, 1840*

While de Tocqueville would have found similar inclinations to form associations in Asia and parts of the world besides the United States, it is certainly true that no non-Anglo-Saxon society has so merged ideological convictions with a multiplicity of organizational channels and devices for spreading those convictions around the world. While U.S. history texts have romanticized the motivational purity of America's early settlers from Europe, the United States did begin primarily as a land of refuge for Europeans seeking freedom of religion, enhanced economic opportunity, and other freedoms found lacking in the Old World. If the founding fathers were not ardent democrats in the current definition of the term (the fate of American Indians and African slaves attests to that), by the standards of their day they were at least imbued with a relative sense of government of, by, and for the people. Certainly the United States began on more auspi-

---

[1]Alexis de Tocqueville, *Democracy in America*, Vol. 2 (New York: Vintage Books, 1945), p. 114.

cious foundations than did other countries colonized by Europeans, who were more concerned with escaping the law or plundering for gold.

And what a continent this was: the prototypical land of milk and honey with vast expanses of fertile land waiting to be exploited, with mighty rivers, virgin forests, and mineral and other natural resource wealth. Small wonder that despite the vicissitudes of settling the North American continent, the people of the newly established United States were full of energy, ebullience, and optimism. Necessity became the mother of success as people traversed the prairies and deserts and organized to tame the land. The dual fact that communities existed long before large government and that so many of the immigrants came in order to escape the rigidities of the Old World placed a premium on individual initiative and inventiveness. The further fact that the American experiment proved to be viable and, by the turn of the twentieth century, a pronounced success (at least for white Americans) reinforced this optimism, the "can-do" attitude, and, whatever the individual modesty, an understandable pride in the achievements already made. It became America's manifest destiny to absorb not only the entire continental territory but also large numbers of immigrants from Europe, Asia, and (under less fortuitous circumstances) Africa, until the United States became a classic human mosaic.

American Philanthropy at Home and Abroad

In the context of this historical background, it is not surprising to find what de Tocqueville observed nearly a century and a half ago. Pluralism and individual initiative are a part of the American fabric and explain in large part the plethora of privately controlled and voluntarily supported institutions observed then and today—institutions ranging from some of the world's leading educational and cultural institutions to local garden clubs, from politically powerful national associations to local block associations. The Commission on Private Philanthropy and Public Needs, in an exhaustive study of U.S. philanthropy, estimated that in 1975 there may have been as many as six million organizations in America's voluntary sector, employing one out of every ten service workers and one out of every six professional workers in the United States, and (if one includes labor unions and chambers of commerce) owning one ninth of all property.[2] The Commission further estimated that overall revenues—including both government and private funds—of these charitable, religious, scientific, literary, and educational organizations added up to some $80 billion annually and,

---

[2]*Giving in America,* Report of the Commission on Private Philanthropy and Public Needs (Washington, D.C., 1975). The Commission was established in 1973 to study the role of philanthropic giving in the United States and to make recommendations to the voluntary sector, to Congress, and to the American public concerning ways in which private giving can be made more effective.

including non-money resources such as volunteer work and free corporate services, amounted to some $100 billion in annual value. Half of this, or $50 billion, is estimated to have come from individuals alone, with about half of that amount (some $26 billion) in money and the other half in the value of volunteer time; one out of every four Americans over the age of 13 does some form of volunteer work.[3]

The 1972-1974 Watergate experience, which shook the public's confidence in government in a particularly pointed way, served to illustrate the importance of pluralism and of maintaining private structures such as the voluntary organizations as alternatives to those of government alone for filling public needs. Besides this, the increasing automation and impersonality of the giant governmental and corporate institutions on which American life is increasingly based underscores the need for smaller, more personal arenas in which individual Americans can exercise personal initiative and make their influence felt on the course of events concerning them.

In addition to these factors which favor the U.S. private sector, government itself has built in certain inducements to promote pluralism. The chief inducement is a tax policy that allows contributions to recognized private organizations to be deducted from the taxable income of both individuals and corporations. The government, in effect, is thus subsidizing private agencies to the extent of tax receipts foregone. While this provision may appear to render somewhat less noble the intended largesse of private gifts, the Commission on Private Philanthropy and Public Needs suggests its practical value: approximately one quarter of all giving is induced by the charitable deduction provision, and for each dollar of government tax revenue lost, some $1.15-$1.29 in additional contributions to charitable organizations are made.

During the past half century, there has been a fundamental shift in the relative size of private philanthropic spending and U.S. government spending. In terms of medical and health services, for example, the federal government in 1930 was spending only 15 per cent more than private philanthropy; in 1973 it was spending nearly 700 per cent more. In higher education, all public funds accounted for only 10 per cent of income a century ago, while private giving accounted for 60 per cent (the remainder being tuition); today the 10 per cent and 60 per cent figures are reversed.[4] Indeed, just in the past twenty-five years, the proportion of all U.S. students enrolled in private institutions of higher learning fell from more than half to less than a fourth.

Two opposite forces are at work here. Government health, education, and welfare spending have, of course, dramatically increased under the

---

[3]The $26 billion cash value is comprised roughly of $10.3 billion for organized religion; $4.4 billion for education; $3.9 billion for health; $2.1 billion for social welfare; $1.7 billion for arts, humanities, civic, and public causes; and $3.2 billion for others. Ibid., pp. 14, 15, and 73.

[4]Ibid., pp. 90-91.

impetus of the social welfare legislation of the 1930s, the GI Bill of World War II, and a host of new programs introduced in the 1960s. During the same time, however, private giving did not keep pace with the growth of the economy, and in recent years, when discounted for inflation, it significantly declined.[5] During the 1960-1974 period alone, the government's "philanthropist" role (which the Commission equates roughly with nondefense spending) quadrupled while private giving increased only two and a half times. Government "philanthropic" spending thus expanded in the process from nine times that of private giving to fourteen and a half times as much.

All this may be cause for little concern if one's objective is to see that basic social and economic needs are met, whatever the source. But it is cause for substantial concern over the long run if one believes that a plurality of approaches and flexible innovations are required to keep American society vibrant and forward-looking. In addition to private philanthropy's complementary role in ameliorating social and economic problems is its role as an independent advocate and critic of government. Increasingly it is argued that the voluntary agencies' role is "not primarily to serve as an alternative to government, but instead, to help keep government honest and responsible. The primary role of voluntary associations in American life is to continually shape and reshape the vision of a more just social order, to propose programs which might lead to the manifestation of that vision, to argue for them with other contenders in the public arena, and to press for adoption and implementation.[6] Indeed, it is often forgotten that some of the most effective volunteering in the United States has been directed at influencing the government on political issues. Such efforts include those of Jane Addams and Dorothea Dix, for example—whose unpopular activism ultimately reformed child labor practices, prisons, and mental hospitals—and, more recently, those of Dr. Martin Luther King and the many others active in the civil rights movement.

Within the context of relative decline in philanthropic giving, it is interesting to note that as a proportion of personal income, giving by individuals also has dropped—by about 15 per cent between 1960 and 1972—with the greatest decrease being evident in the $10,000 to $25,000 income ranges. Yet it is important to realize that the overall decrease has affected some areas more than others. Contributions for religion have declined the most (falling from 49 per cent of all giving in 1964 to 43 per cent in 1974), whereas donations to civic and cultural causes and volunteer work have actually risen. Indeed, one of the most striking points to emerge from the Commission's study of U.S. philanthropy is that "the success of some causes in regularly raising large sums suggests that the spirit of giving may

---

[5]Ibid., p. 15.
[6]Paul H. Sherry, quoted in Brian O'Connell, "Voluntary Agencies Must Ask: What Price Independence?" *Foundation News* (July-August 1976), p. 17.

not be fading so much as shifting its focus, even if the level of giving, of money at least, clearly has declined, by virtually every barometer.[7]

The point of shifting focus is significant because theoretically the primary virtue of private organizations lies in their ability to innovate without excessive concern for the political and bureaucratic risks of failure. The Commission on Private Philanthropy and Public Needs correctly suggests that the diminishing level of giving to the more traditional philanthropic sectors of health and education may be due precisely to the increase of governmental expenditures in those sectors and to the public's feeling that their tax contributions are contribution enough—the notion that "we gave to the IRS." It may not be a negative commentary, therefore, that private spending is decreasing relative to government spending if the reason is that private efforts have paved the way for larger-scale governmental efforts helping a larger proportion of an expanding needy population.

It would be highly unfortunate, however, if innovative programs aimed at problems such as those of needy minorities and other poverty groups in the United States were being cut and ignored. Indeed, recent study and action associations have decried traditional philanthropy's relative neglect of the problems of these groups and have advocated a considerable reorientation of priorities.[8] The fact is that such innovative efforts *are* endangered. This is partly due to the fact that the fastest-rising costs in the United States today are the very wage costs that—given the labor-intensity and lack of economies of scale in pioneering new approaches to social problems—tend to comprise the largest share of philanthropic expenditures.

On balance, therefore, the Commission found American philanthropy overall to be in a crisis state because "the prevailing financial pattern of the nonprofit sector has become one of uncommonly higher costs, more resources required for old problems and new solutions, more users needing greater aggregate subsidies for traditional services and new, less traditional groups adding their claim to the philanthropic pie. And it has been, in terms of private support, a barely growing pie all this time, not growing at all of late in terms of the real purchasing power of private contributions."[9]

American Philanthropy Abroad

Against this background, the international side of the philanthropy equation is all the more significant. Belying both the overall declining trend of private philanthropy and the common wisdom that America has been looking increasingly inward in recent years is the fact that during this same period

---

[7]*Giving in America*, pp. 15–16.

[8]See *U.S. Foundations and Minority Group Interests,* prepared for the National Science Foundation by the U.S. Human Resources Corporation (San Antonio, Texas: Mexican American Cultural Center, 1975); and *Private Philanthropy: Vital and Innovative? Or Passive and Irrelevant?* (Washington, D.C.: National Committee for Responsive Philanthropy, 1975).

[9]*Giving in America*, p. 87.

American philanthropy *abroad* has been *increasing*. While the increase is barely sufficient for it to hold steady as a percentage of GNP (0.05-0.07 per cent), it is noteworthy in comparison to the private domestic and public overseas declines noted above. It would be premature to be too confident in projecting a long-run trend from this phenomenon, however, in part because the data for such a diverse grouping of organizations are less than perfect and in part because the past few years have witnessed what is perhaps an unprecedented series of unique events that inspired additional giving: the 1973 Middle East War, which caused Jewish contributions for Israel to double over those of the previous year; unprecedented droughts and famines in South Asia and Sahelian Africa; and an energy crisis and recession which, having made themselves deeply felt in the United States itself, were, for those who cared to extrapolate, that much worse for Third World people. Furthermore, this was a period when television had the capability of bringing these crises into every American home.

The history of U.S. private assistance abroad might be divided roughly into three periods. The *first* (until about 1900) comprised the early missionary efforts, the development of the American Red Cross in 1882, and a large array of ad hoc responses to particular events. During the *second* period (1900-1945), increasing amounts of assistance were given in accordance with the emerging role of the United States as a great power; furthermore, attention began to be directed toward the causes of poverty rather than to just its effects. The *third* period (1945 to the present) has been a time in which both public and private aid became better defined within the context of national policies; it also embraced labor, corporate, and university extensions abroad, and increasingly encouraged local articulation of needs, self-help participation, and self-reliance.

In the seventeenth and eighteenth centuries, the fledgling American colonies were, understandably, the recipients rather than the donors of international aid. The British, in the early days, offered considerable philanthropic support to missionaries and to schools for Indians, Negroes, and poor whites, as well as to colleges and learned societies. One of the earliest recorded examples of foreign aid to North America was a shipment of food sent to New England in 1647 by Irish Protestants "to the poor distressed by the late war with the Indians."[10]

With Americans sharing the same religious and humanitarian values as the Europeans, it was natural that Americans, in turn, should help others as soon as they felt able. Indeed, de Tocqueville advanced an argument that might lead one to expect Americans to be more generous: the particular American weakening of barriers of class and privilege, he suggested, fostered special feelings of compassion for all members of the human race. In spite of the enormous early developmental needs of America itself, not to

---

[10]Merle Curti, *American Philanthropy Abroad* (New Brunswick, N.J.: Rutgers University Press, 1963), p. 3.

mention subsequent needs arising from Civil War tragedies and from fires and floods, Americans soon found enough to spare for occasional gifts to social welfare and relief causes in Europe and elsewhere. In 1793 private assistance was provided for thousands of Santo Domingans fleeing to U.S. cities from revolutionary turmoil on their island. In 1812 U.S. government help was sent for the first time (not without consideration of U.S. commercial interests in the Caribbean) for victims of a Venezuelan earthquake. In the 1820s, in the first major instance of relief becoming intertwined with political issues, Americans aided the Greeks during their fight against the Ottomans. And in 1847, during the Great Irish Famine, an editorial in the Washington *Daily Union* exhorted, "We trust that the whole country will rise up, and that America . . . will present the full bosom of her plenty and luxuriance to the lips of the famished Irishman."[11] America did help, though the fear was expressed, as it still is 130 years later, that the magnitude of the charity might keep "the lower orders of peasantry" from returning to work. Throughout the nineteenth century, Americans continued to respond to overseas needs, whether to famines in Russia and India or to other hardships. All of this help—with the exception of a special congressional appropriation in the Venezuelan case and the occasional provision of U.S. naval ships for transporting supplies—was given through private channels, the belief being that the U.S. Constitution did not give Congress the power to use public funds for foreign relief.

The second period of American private aid began around the turn of the century, when the United States—having assumed the position and perceived responsibilities of world power status—found itself with an additional range of motivations for both overseas assistance and direct governmental involvement therein. In the aftermath of World War I, government-owned food and other surplus goods were allocated to private agencies for war victims. During the Spanish Civil War (1936-1939), after much discussion about the relationship between the U.S. government interest in preserving official neutrality on the one hand and the private agency impulse to respond to human needs (with frequent political implications) on the other, government began to require the federal registering and supervision of U.S. private overseas aid. Also during this period the Red Cross and various missionary groups found themselves joined by other private organizations such as the American Jewish Joint Distribution Committee, the American Friends Service Committee, the Rockefeller and Near East Foundations, and the Carnegie Corporation. Inherent in the establishment of these new bodies was the institutionalization, for the first time, of a cadre of trained administrators and overseas field workers. Given the consequently increased exposure to and knowledge of overseas conditions, it is not surprising that U.S. efforts then tended to aim at root causes

---

[11]Ibid., p. 53.

of suffering as well as at pure relief. An exemplary case was in the 1920s in China, where famines began to be combated by work projects for flood control, irrigation, reclamation, and reforestation. At the same time, the Rockefeller Foundation introduced modern medical education. The Near East Foundation, significantly renamed from its original title, Near East Relief, modified for overseas use such tested American rural development practices as demonstration farms, 4-H Clubs, and county extension agents, and thus stimulated self-help in agriculture, health, homemaking, and community activities.

These tendencies were reinforced during the third period, which began in the aftermath of World War II and came to comprise the heyday of both public and private overseas assistance. Whereas overseas aid had declined after the immediate post-World War I relief efforts had been met, World War II set the stage for continuing quantum jumps in aid. On the public side, the entire United Nations family of agencies, the World Bank, and the Bank's associated International Development Association were born. In addition all the major U.S. governmental bilateral aid bureaucracies came into being, beginning with the U.S. Point Four program, which was subsequently copied in various shapes and forms by the European countries, Canada, and Japan. On the private side—except for the Jewish agencies newly established to help Israel—the Ford Foundation ultimately became the largest single spender for international causes, followed by a handful of other foundations. The newly consolidated Catholic and Protestant church relief organizations, CARE, and a variety of others were also very active. The major focus of U.S. aid increasingly shifted during this period from Europe to Latin America and to the newly independent countries in Asia and Africa.[12] In those areas there were new challenges, new needs and, not surprisingly, new problems.

Of course foreign assistance was always replete with problems. Sometimes the aid did not reach those for whom it was intended, partly due in the early years to pirates on the high seas, and in later years to their functional equivalents in corrupt bureaucracies. The struggle to raise the necessary funds at home or to requisition shipping facilities to send supplies abroad often ended in inaction and failure to help at all. Sometimes this was due to political reasons, including a quite logical concern for preserving official American neutrality in a period when peace was considered essential for national survival; sometimes it was rooted in the argument that continues to run through American politics, namely, that domestic needs outweigh foreign ones. Not surprisingly, the motivations for U.S. assistance abroad always have been mixed, including, as they have, Judeo-Christian compassion and charity, a more secular humanitarianism, gratitude and solidarity growing out of earlier common bonds with various European groups, commercial interests, and political muscle-flexing. What Emerson once

---

[12]See Annex A, Table 5, for the shift in geographic focus of U.S. aid from 1946 to 1975.

wrote about altruists applied here: "Take egotism out, and you would castrate the benefactors."[13]

The churches alone have passed through a long and significant period of change since the early missionary days. This change was dramatized by the achievement of independence by most of the Asian and African countries in which the missionaries had been serving. As a result, the role of the missionary effectively changed from that of a representative of the rulers to that of a guest of the new rulers—a guest who was sometimes welcome, sometimes not, or welcome in some roles and not in others. This applied not only to American church people, of course, but to Europeans as well. And as the new, postcolonial governments increasingly made development and nationalism their call words and were usually suspicious of attempts at religious conversion, the missionaries were forced to increase their concentration on temporal welfare in order to justify their continuing presence. The correspondence between the Protestant missionary Ziegenbalg writing from India and his Danish Mission Board secretary, Christian Wendt, in the early eighteenth century provides both a historical perspective and a sense of flavor of the continuing dichotomy faced then—and now—by the missionaries. A twentieth century commentator described their exchange thus:

> Wendt's ideal was an apostolic mission. He took offence at the externals in the mission activity and thought he noticed too little actual work among souls. He feared that the missionaries permitted the externals to keep them away from their real missionary task. Wendt felt that Jesus had given his disciples a different example. Should further money be sent from Europe for all the churches and schools and for all those employed in them, and for food and drink? "In externals," he said, "Asia must be able to help itself without Europe and must receive from Europe only the divine and godly life." He blamed Ziegenbalg for having acquired a house and garden and for having built a church for many thousands. "But what will come out of it? A European Christendom!"[14]

Ziegenbalg's response, dated August 15, 1718, stated that "as the body is bound to the soul, so precisely is the service of the body connected with the service of the soul, and these cannot be separated from each other. This work demands the service of the whole man." On the Roman Catholic side, Pope John XXIII's 1961 papal letter, "Mater et Magistra," strengthened the hand of those missionaries who were interested in temporal concerns at least as much as in proselytizing: "Though the first care of the Church must be for souls, how can she sanctify them and share in the gifts of heaven if she does

---

[13]Curti, *American Philanthropy Abroad*, p. 23.
[14]A. Lehmann, "It Began At Tranquebar" (Madras: CLS, 1956), pp. 86–87; cited in Yngve Frykholm, "Christian Churches as Agents of Socio-Economic Development in India," mimeographed (Stockholm: World Council of Churches, 1969), pp. 28–29.

not concern herself also with the exigencies of man's daily life, with his livelihood and education, and his general, temporal welfare and prosperity?"

Quite aside from the missionary efforts, the period of immediate relief and rehabilitiation in the aftermath of World War II marked, in a sense, the high point of Catholic and Protestant assistance to date. Both Catholic Relief Services and Church World Service were founded in response to the extreme needs of the time, and both aided in the resettlement of refugees and sent considerable amounts of food, clothing, and financial assistance to Europe. With the establishment of the state of Israel in 1948, U.S. Jewish aid—at least to Israel—also became a major force. Important for religionists of all three faiths was the fact that so many of the American contributors were related to those in need in both Europe and Israel. Some two out of three American Jewish families are reported to have lost family members in Europe during the war, and a trend was beginning where by 1975 one half of all American Jewish families were said to have relatives in Israel. Small wonder that American Jews—whose co-religionists have been buffeted throughout history—felt a keen sense of identification with the fate of that country.

CARE, which first stood for Cooperative for American Remittances to Europe, was also founded during the post-World War II period and was soon deluged with contributions destined for the relatives of Americans suffering in postwar Europe. As a CARE report of the period stated,

> The six most destructive years in world history closed in summer, 1945. Great cities were rubble; factories charred junk-heaps; farms, railroads, shipping in ruins; the means of production wrecked; 30 million producers dead; the survivors drained of hope and energy; ragged, hungry, homeless by the millions. Thus, the issue of war having been resolved, the postwar issue had to be faced. It had two parts: for economists, scientists, governments, a task of rebuilding that would occupy at least the next generation; for a man and his family—the next meal. . . .
>
> From all over America, people clamored: how can I get help directly, quickly, surely, to my aged parents in Poland, my uncles in Germany, my cousins in France, my old teacher in Czechoslovakia, my friends in Finland? For the President of the United States and the humblest citizen, CARE was the answer.[15]

CARE differed in a real sense from all the other voluntary agencies known to date. It was organized by representatives of Catholic Relief Services, the Cooperative League of the USA, and the American Friends Service Committee, among others, to meet a special and temporary postwar need. It had no well-defined constituency as the religious groups had. Rather, it suc-

---

[15]*Three Years of CARE* (New York: The Advertising Council, undated), pp. 2-4.

ceeded by capitalizing on the skillful use of mass media and by meeting human needs to such a degree that in many minds it was, and still is, identified with all American overseas relief. It began in a period when the needs were clear and direct. Food, clothing, and supplies available *here* were needed *there*. The recipients, if not family members or friends of the donors, had at least been of kindred cultural backgrounds. Besides that, they represented industrial nations with highly trained human infrastructures which needed only some breathing time and capital investment to attain again the economic levels they had enjoyed earlier. Because of both the humanitarian need and the likelihood that any aid would prove effective, the impulse was strong to help.

These special factors are worth highlighting because they contrast sharply with the situation in which private assistance organizations were increasingly to find themselves thereafter in newly independent countries of the Third World. Not only were the same personal and family relationships and identifications no longer applicable, but the economic and cultural backgrounds of these people were so different that a fundamentally different process was required from that of the earlier postwar and other postdisaster rehabilitation efforts. As if this were not enough of an adjustment to have to make, the cold war also developed during this period, profoundly influencing the U.S. perception of its role overseas as well as the Third World's perception of that role. While selfish motivations were not entirely absent from earlier foreign assistance efforts, the cold war struggle brought them very much to the forefront. Given the temper of those times and the fact that two very opposed political systems emerged as victors from the debris of World War II, competition was probably inevitable. And it was equally inevitable that that competition would spill over from the more traditional political arena into the overall comportment of Americans both at home and overseas.[16]

If American efforts abroad had always reflected a certain missionary zeal in trying to spread Western standard-of-living notions to other peoples, the new superimposition of cold war politics intensified that zeal. Thus Americans were not only helping others to enjoy "the better life"; they were also proclaiming that the way to achieve that life was within the context of "freedom" rather than "communism" or, worse yet, *atheist* communism! The fact that most Third World societies had known neither freedom nor communism in the Western sense of the terms was less relevant than the fear that if they did not now begin to follow the American way, the communists would impose *theirs*—as they had done in Eastern Europe, North Korea, and China. In fact, Americans saw economic development as contributing to political development. Just as the former was defined in terms of growth of

---

[16]One is reminded of the intensity of the cold war period today when "expiring" civil defense biscuits left over from the days of household and community nuclear bomb shelters are being offered by voluntary organizations overseas as part of the U.S. surplus food program.

per capita product, so the latter was defined in terms of stability, democracy, anticommunism, "world community," peace, and pro-Americanism. Thus the directly political purposes of U.S. economic aid. As at least one analyst has noted, the American attempt to promote liberal constitutionalism is often both unrealistic from the point of view of feasibility and ethnocentric from the point of view of desirability.

> The ethnocentricity inheres partly in the American tendency to define democracy mainly or exclusively in political terms, whereas many people in the Third World define democracy in economic and social terms as well, often giving greater weight to the latter. Also, American democracy is exclusively linked to the norm of gradualism, to the idea of reform and evolution within a "moving equilibrium"; it does not admit the appropriateness under some circumstances of radical or revolutionary patterns of political change. Finally, exporting democracy is ethnocentric insofar as it fails to take into account the possibility that the political systems of the Third World may be, and quite possibly should be, changing in ways that are different from those that have come before, but which may be more appropriate in those settings than any "developed" patterns they might emulate.[17]

Although American representatives of voluntary agencies were doctrinally as anticommunist as the U.S. government, it must also be noted that their organizations frequently have been willing to assist people in communist-governed countries. CARE, for example, notes that it regretfully pulled out of Romania in 1947 only because the new communist government there began impeding the flow of CARE packages. Catholic Relief Services remained at work in Poland, Czechoslovakia, Hungary, and Romania about one and a half years after the communist takeovers; however, in the different circumstances of North Vietnam some years later, they were forced to leave immediately at the time of independence. The larger practical point, though, is not so much whether U.S. organizations are or are not willing to assist countries governed by communist governments as whether those highly centralized political systems are willing to accept such assistance. Sometimes they do not perceive any distinction between the U.S. government on the one hand and the plurality of the U.S. private sector on the other. Sometimes they fear the inevitable intrusion of foreign values that accompanies any aid. And sometimes they may simply feel that their need is not so great that they are willing to accept the outside supervision that accountability to contributors within the United States normally demands. This question of acceptability leads to the key point of how U.S. private and voluntary organizations

---

[17]Robert A. Packenham, *Liberal America and the Third World* (Princeton: Princeton University Press, 1973), pp. 189-90. Also on the subject of national traits carried into overseas behavior, see the chapter entitled "National Style" in Stanley Hoffman, *Gulliver's Troubles, or the Setting of American Foreign Policy* (New York: McGraw-Hill, Inc., 1968).

are perceived outside the United States, a point which reflects as much upon the image of the American people as upon that of their well-meaning organizations.

America's Image Abroad

The American image overseas is inevitably shaped by the individual observer's reaction to the United States as a superpower. If the superpower status of the United States is less preeminent today due to the diffusion of power since the quarter century following World War II, it is still a reality. Although the renewed American emphasis on promoting human rights around the world may be welcomed by many, it may also be suspect in the minds of others. To many in the Third World—and not only to the far left ideologues—any and all American involvement overseas is part and parcel of an overall extension of U.S. power and influence; the inflammatory term for this is neocolonialism. It is assumed that having achieved preeminence, the United States will continually be engaged in preserving it. If the United States is engaged in this preservation, these people continue, it is logical to assume that Americans would not aspire to one set of political and economic goals as a government and to another set as groups of private citizens. Americans, after all, are Americans, and the same values that permeate national policy must surely derive from the people who, in the final analysis, formulate that policy through their elected representatives. Thus, they reason, the U.S. government aims to create and preserve favorable conditions for U.S. corporate investment. This is seen, in turn, as inevitably strengthening the status quo of certain local Third World power elites at the expense of others and certainly of the majority of their populations. American foundations and voluntary organizations—frequently controlled by the same elites who control the government and the large corporations—are seen as agencies designed to create favorable internal climates for this continued American exploitative presence. While it is easy to discount out-of-hand this rationale—after all, voluntary organizations exist for philanthropic purposes!—doing so risks shutting one off from a prevailing world opinion, one that is particularly strong in Latin America but that is also evident in Asia and Africa.

Indeed, there is at least a quantum of truth in this position. Americans *do* feel free to roam the world, applying their entrepreneurial spirit and initiative abroad as readily as at home, extending the capitalist reach in individual ways but with cumulatively far-reaching effects, as the recent disclosures on multinational corporations have demonstrated. On the humanitarian side, compassion and magnanimity have also been freely shown, with both favorable and less-than-favorable implications. For all the virtues of this largesse, there are inevitably counterreactions, whether born of jealousy about the "rich brother" or suspicion as to presumed ulterior motives. After all, no other society in history has been so generous without motivation, so why should anyone be so naive as to believe the United States is acting free of other designs?

While philanthropy, by definition, means "love of mankind," in practice it implies inequality. While many sensitive Americans would like to proclaim equality for all—after all, the Declaration of Independence does so—others know it does not exist. For America is rich and the Third World countries are largely poor. The fact that poverty exists in America itself is generally not discussed in the context of overseas programs. Consequently, many aid recipients in the Third World are unaware of American poverty. Among those who are aware, some justifiably wonder how Americans can presume to alleviate Third World problems when they have yet to solve their own at home.

In a sense, relationships between the West and the Third World might be compared with those between a psychoanalyst and his or her patient.[18] The patient wants to be cured (the Third World recipient wants "development") and the analyst (the West) wants to cure him. Simultaneously, however, a contradictory force is at work: whether consciously or subconsciously, the analyst also may want to keep a hold on the patient, and the patient may, quite in spite of himself, feel irresistably drawn to the protective powers of the analyst. The result, of course, is a mutual dependence rooted in inequality and likely to continue until the patient is sufficiently strong to feel confident in separating himself from the analyst.

While theories of psychoanalysis may seem remote from the subject at hand, it is nevertheless clear that the colonial period of the past gave vent to a complex range of overlapping and contradictory reactions with which the world is still living today; because traditionally the West ruled over most of the Third World, it is assumed by many that the desire to rule remains. From the West's point of view, lingering illusions from that period—illusions of superiority if not still of grandeur—would be quite natural. During Daniel Patrick Moynihan's brief tenure as U.S. Ambassador to the United Nations, many criticized his insensitive and insulting behavior toward Third World countries as he railed against their various anti-American vituperations. Others argued that since primarily the big powers, led by the United States, had established the U.N. system on their own terms and had used it for their own purposes for so many years, it was only just that the Third World countries should express themselves now that they had finally achieved even as modest a platform as the halls of the U.N. afford. Yet if Moynihan was guilty of the arrogance of the pot calling the kettle black, it was only fair that he should respond to Third World criticisms openly, directly, and in kind, thus implying a relative sense of intellectual equality by not sitting back and "sensitively absorbing" the "understandable" Third World reactions to a history of Western rule. By the same token, aid, too, whether

---

[18]In the West, a parent-child analogy is more commonly cited to describe these relationships, leading to understandable resentment in the Third World.

public or private, may be better appreciated and better utilized if the motivations for giving it—and receiving it—are more clearly understood, more openly expressed on all sides, and not disguised by unbelieved (in their entirety) explanations of compassion and humanitarian goodwill alone. For aid, no matter how much one possesses purely humanitarian motives, is also culture-bound—thus political—and carries its own values, self-rationalizations, and impetus for self-perpetuation that can too easily, unless one is careful, corrupt both recipients and donors.

In addition to these more philosophical and ideological concerns, two practical criticisms are frequently leveled against the voluntary agencies: their failures in continuity and their excesses in overhead and style. The same problems, to be sure, are found in all kinds of development agencies. Continuity is a problem in that, for all the good short-term effects of voluntary assistance, there is often insufficient follow-up by local participants and thus little to show for the foreign efforts some months or years later. Even some sympathetic observers have gone so far as to suggest that a large majority of voluntary agency activities have little or no net effect over the long term. The continuity problem is one that especially reflects the social and political constraints to development, constraints that the more traditional humanitarian agencies feel least equipped to tackle and that will be considered in more detail later.

The second criticism, that of overhead and style, is a more surprising one, inasmuch as voluntary agencies are known for their commitment and for the willingness of some of their employees to work for wages that are very modest in Western terms—a sense of sacrifice that is particularly striking when compared to the salary profiles of government and multilateral organizations. Yet one hears of the voluntary agencies' "high style" abroad and at worst of "soldiers of fortune" who hear of a disaster and flock to help, staying in expensive hotels, eating well, and living, in short, better than they could afford to at home.[19] While these kinds of excesses are hardly unknown, the problem is often one of definition. As noted earlier, a voluntary agency need not be a *volunteer* agency; there is nothing in the definition to suggest that professional staffs cannot be paid the going professional wage. Standards also vary; because the cost of living is generally lower in Third World countries, a volunteer by Western standards may be indulging in a high standard of living by Third World measures.[20] Perhaps more fundamental than this type of criticism, therefore, is the occasional criticism of paternalistic attitudes, lack of professionalism, and a certain parochialism that is evidenced in overestimating the significance of one's own small programs and in competitiveness over asserting individual

---

[19] See, for example, Eugene Linden, *The Alms Race* (New York: Random House, Inc., 1976).

[20] In this context, the term "nongovernmental organization" used by the United Nations is clearer in that it avoids the confusion between a *voluntary organization* and a *volunteer worker*.

identities above what are sometimes the better interests of the potential recipients. At its worst, this leads to arrogance—an arrogance illustrated in the internal report of one U.S. voluntary organization that, having described its efforts to sell an African country on the virtues of its proposed assistance program, concluded that "the priorities of the local government are not the same as ours, and the first step in development work is to make the government and the local agencies straighten up their scale of values."

The problem is perhaps best stated directly in the words of one Third World individual:

> For us, we do not look on U.S. aid as humanitarian or given out of guilt or pity, but rather as an attribute of pride and arrogance. It seems that in an overseas setting one tends to depend upon one's own native culture. Yet we would prefer to die in our poverty than to live like Americans. Take your agriculturalist who knows agriculture and the Bible and who feels it is his God-given duty to teach others to be like him. But who wants to be like the U.S., with your breakdown of the family system, with your missionaries who teach brotherhood, yet do not act like brothers—indeed, who tell the local children playing with their children to go home at lunchtime so that they themselves can eat, rather than, as is our custom, sharing their food with whomever is there at the time? Then, too, the American concepts of organization, evaluation, and time itself which are all different from ours. An American understands time by the clock, but we understand it by establishing personal relationships which are not timebound; the American, to begin with, comes to us, with his aid, on a seventeen-day excursion ticket! But then, since no project lasts more than three years, we can afford to humor our donors.[21]

This critic and others agree that American sensitivity is now increasing and that there is a greater willingness to engage in two-way exchanges. "But even then," he says, "our people are often turned off by their excessive desire to 'identify.'"

Research suggests that aid recipients are extremely concerned about the intentions of the donors. In a study on foreign aid conducted by two Swarthmore College professors, 80 per cent of donor-country foreign aid officials interviewed singled out donors' motives as an important influencing factor in shaping recipients' reactions to aid. Views of the American character further colored recipients' opinions of aid from the United States, as there is "a strong human tendency to see things in emotionally consistent ways, so that 'bad' people can't be expected to engage in any 'good' act even if the act appears to be a helping hand." Reactions to aid were also influenced by the characteristics of the aid itself and by the psychological

---

[21]Oral testimony of a Third World voluntary agency director during an informal 1975 Overseas Development Council discussion of U.S. private aid.

state of the recipient. "No obligation to repay tends to imply inferiority, whereas the obligation to repay with interest smacks of exploitation." Finally, nine out of ten foreign aid officials interviewed felt that "foreign aid tends to succeed or fail, psychologically and materially, depending on whether the aid relationship strengthens or weakens the recipients' self-esteem."[22]

Third World voluntary organizations share in the responsibility for donor-donee misunderstanding and frictions. An open letter appearing in the newsletter of the Asian Cultural Forum on Development put it this way:

> We continue to tolerate being treated in a condescending manner. Let's face it. Some of us don't mind such treatment, so long as the money comes in. We remain pacified and contented if we can manage to ensure the growth of our projects, programmes and institutions. Often we are more concerned with expansion, with the physical development of campuses, complexes, offices, equipment and the usual paraphernalia of prestigious institutions. With our sights set on achieving recognition—social or institutional—it is not rarely that we give less importance to consolidation as opposed to expansion. That's when the money becomes indispensable. And that is when we unwittingly gag and deprive ourselves of available options by kowtowing before powerful funding organisations or their agents and brokers.
>
> NGOs [non-governmental organizations] often suffer from false illusions about being non-bureaucratic, more humanistic and more innovative in their approach to development work. Sometimes they form an even more warped opinion about themselves; that they are closer to the poor people than the institutions of commerce, industry, and government. But is this really so in the case of all the NGOs? Can the disparate heterogeneous NGO sector in all honesty consider itself to be the people's sector? . . .
>
> Don't we have a tendency of going a little too far in attaching a halo around our work? We seldom fail to hold forth on our dedicated volunteerism, on our spirit of self-sacrifice, public service and other self-effacing attitudes. If only there could be more honest self-introspection and mutual criticism about our modes and even our motives for work! The sad truth is that too much of the volunteerism we have is scarcely distinguishable from career professionalism. Voluntary work should of course be professionally competent, but does it have to be also marked by the same jockeying for positions, politicking for power and bargaining for privileges? Even more serious than some of these shortcomings are other serious lapses such as the squandering of funds, nepotism, corruption and sheer incompetence. There is a

---

[22]Kenneth and Mary Gergen, "What Other Nations Hear When the Eagle Screams," *Psychology Today* (June 1974), p. 54.

need, therefore, to separate the grain from the chaff from within ourselves in order to qualify more to be what we claim to be.[23]

Given the many Third World criticisms of private and voluntary organizations, and also given the relatively small percentage of development assistance provided through these agencies, it is noteworthy that a disproportionately large amount of appreciation is felt for private and voluntary efforts in the Third World. While most aid recipients would be positively inclined toward their own donors, their general impression is indeed that voluntary agencies exhibit high levels of dedication, honesty, flexibility, promptness of action, willingness to go into remote and needy areas, and ability to experiment and coordinate with other related efforts—all these virtues placing voluntary agencies at an advantage over the host governments themselves, as well as over official bilateral and multilateral aid programs. In Niger in 1975, for example, government officials noted that voluntary organizations contributed only 7 per cent of that country's total foreign aid, but an important 7 per cent for the reasons just cited. The government of India, which has a tendency to downplay programs aimed at any number of people less than the 620 million for whom it must ultimately be concerned, has expressed similar appreciation for the role of private and voluntary agencies, even during the recent period of severely strained relations between India and the U.S. The types of programs most often cited by enlightened government administrators are those that experiment successfully with a particular approach that, theoretically at any rate, can then be adopted for broader replication; the fact that the programs receive international assistance makes them more visible and thus more likely to be accepted and replicated. Examples would include the multiple cropping and management training programs for local cooperative workers introduced in Bangladesh by the Mennonites and CARE, respectively; the polytechnical vocational schools established in Kenya by the local, though Western church-supported, National Christian Council; and the pump sets given by Africare in Senegal that enabled the opening of newly irrigated lands in that country.

A very different type of example is that of what may be the least criticized American organization overseas: the American Friends Service Committee, indeed, the Quaker movement generally. The Friends themselves tend to be bemused by their popularity, though, when forced to speculate, they attribute it to the quality of the staff they are able to attract, their explicitness about their true motivations, and their willingness to be supervised, in effect, by their Third World peers (within the terms of reference mutually agreed to at the outset of their setting up a program). The Quakers do support a number of relatively traditional development projects. Yet the real reason for their reputation may be that their program originates,

---

[23]"Two Open Letters," *Asian Action* (March/April 1976), pp. 1-2.

significantly, not from a traditional emphasis on development and its attendant values but from a shared concern for peace and human relationships. Thus the Quakers are more concerned with providing opportunities for people from different settings to dialogue together on their own cultural terms than with "development" in an exclusively materialistic sense. One may argue, of course, the extent to which this starting point and methodology permit them to profoundly affect living standards of the Third World poor or even, in the final analysis, to affect the prospects for peace itself. This would be difficult—if not impossible—to assess.

This aspect of the Quaker experience, viewed in conjunction with general feelings expressed in the Third World about U.S. voluntary organizations, suggests the deeper dilemma of the Third World: its people are impelled to "development" but resent the dislocations and inequities caused by the Western approach to it. Indeed, the Western assumption of universally applicable stages of economic growth and of a universal path to development is increasingly open to serious question. Today's poorest countries are not just "slow starters" in the development process; rather, they are in a substantially different position from that of the United States and Western Europe at comparable stages of history. Their structures are different and their poverty is pervasive in a way that was never true of today's rich. There is also reason to believe that countries like Turkey, Brazil, and the OPEC countries—often included among Third World nations—have been sufficiently different in the relative modernity of their economic structures and in their overall growth records that their development experiences are not completely relevant for today's poorest countries. For the latter, the problem is really one of *pervasive* poverty, not simply of minority poverty pockets, serious as those may be. Because of this essential difference, it is quite possible that for them totally new development strategies must be discovered, building on indigenous social patterns in order to minimize undesired intrusions of foreign values and influence. If all too little attention has been paid to such alternative approaches in the past, voluntary agencies, at least, have tended at local levels to be more sympathetic to the need for them. While voluntary agency efforts abroad will be the subject of the following chapters, it will be useful first to survey recent antipoverty experiences in the United States to observe to what extent—if any—the lessons from these experiences can be applied in other countries.

Chapter 3

Poverty at Home: How Is It Relevant?

One of the astonishing facts about international development assistance is that it is planned and given with so little regard to equivalent U.S. experience with poverty at home. In a way, this is a good sign, since an opposite tendency to copy abroad what has been done at home would be unwise and even risky. On the other hand, the total divorce deprives planners and activists on both sides of the benefit of considerable enriching experience. Rare is the overseas field worker who does not have to admit virtually total ignorance of the strategies and effectiveness of poverty programs in the United States itself; the converse, for that matter, is also true.

There are two major differences between American poverty and that of the Third World. One is qualitative. Most poverty-striken Americans have running water and electric lights, and perhaps even a car and a color television, symbols of unimaginable luxury in the Third World. The other is quantitative in that the poverty percentages are reversed.[1] Poor people in the United States are in the minority and declining, whereas in the Third World they are generally in the majority and increasing in numbers. In the United States, therefore, integration into the larger social and economic system tends more obviously to be the prescribed formula for combating poverty, while in the Third World the plight of the majority of society itself is at issue.

There is always debate, at home and abroad, as to which types of policies are best in ameliorating poverty conditions: those aimed at increasing the size of the economic pie—by encouraging overall industrial expansion, for example, which could trickle down to absorb more of the poor into the economy's mainstream—or those focusing specifically on the hard-core unemployed through such programs as job training. Still others feel that

---

[1]According to a 1976 Gallup global public opinion survey, one person in four in North America and Western Europe worries most or all of the time about making ends meet; in Third World countries, two persons out of three share this level of constant concern.

31

only profound structural changes in allocations of power will enable sufficient solutions to the problems. For all the rhetoric on various sides, the answer is inevitably a combination of all three approaches, whether the setting is that of the majority poor of the Third World or the minority poor of America.[2] Yet the realization of the importance of multifaceted programs specifically targeted toward the poor is recent and seems to have come almost simultaneously in both settings. The inadequacies of the trickle-down strategy in the Third World began to become accepted as fact at virtually the same time that President Lyndon Johnson's Great Society initiatives were being implemented at home. Thus Americans are not transferring proven antipoverty techniques and wisdom from the United States to the Third World. Rather, the simultaneous search for solutions to a similar problem continues on both sides. This observation carries some implications for one's attitudes and expectations for success.

For example, it comes as a surprise to many that well after the Depression and as recently as thirty years ago, 45 million people, or nearly a third of the U.S. population, were living below the poverty line as defined by the U.S. government.[3] This number was reduced during the early 1950s by about 1 million annually, with some 39 million Americans under the poverty line throughout the recession period of the late 1950s and early 1960s. The number further declined during the 1962-1969 period of strong economic advance by about 2 million persons annually, fluctuating up and down during the early 1970s. In 1975, some 26 million persons, or 12 per cent of the U.S. population, were under the poverty line. If one includes the cash value of in-kind aid (most notably food stamps), only about half that number are considered under the line.[4] On the other hand, such arguments, based as they are on gross figures, disguise the fact that the antipoverty system is sometimes inequitable and inefficient, with benefits sometimes going to the wrong people. Furthermore, the basic-needs standards adopted more than a decade ago to measure poverty are less applicable today because the living standards of the general population have risen substantially. Thus for many individuals in the United States, poverty remains a scourge. And for many others, it persists in terms of *relative* misery, lack of opportunity,

---

[2] An example from Appalachia shows how direct targeting of aid and overall economic growth each, in turn, exerts an influence. The poverty gap between poor Appalachian whites and U.S. society in general narrowed during the period of governmental antipoverty initiatives in the mid-1960s, only to widen thereafter and to narrow again more recently due to the macroeconomic consequences of the new demand for coal as an energy source.

[3] The poverty line—about which there is much dispute—is defined by the government at approximately $5,500 annual income in 1975 prices for a nonfarm family of four. See Robert J. Lampman, "What Does It Do for the Poor? A New Test for National Policy,"*The Public Interest,* No. 34, special issue entitled *The Great Society: Lessons for the Future* (winter 1974), p. 67. Some argue that the line should be defined at a higher level, which would mean a substantially larger number of poor Americans for all years cited. See, for example, Mariellen Procopio and Frederick J. Perella, Jr., *Poverty Profile USA* (New York: Paulist Press, 1976).

[4] "Study Finds 50% Fewer Poor People," *Washington Post,* January 16, 1977, p. 1.

and deprivation. Indeed, the relative distribution of family income has changed very little in the past generation,[5] and the percentage gaps between rich and poor have essentially remained constant.

Because the Great Society programs were initiated during the period of generally strong economic advance of the 1960s, it is difficult, if not impossible, to isolate their specific targeting effects from the effects of the broader process of economic growth. Yet the initiation of these programs added a fundamentally new element to the U.S. government's stance on domestic poverty and to U.S. thinking generally; clearly the programs had some impact. The New Deal legislation of the 1930s, after all, had dealt more with the aged, the physically disabled, and the industrial working class affected by the transitory effects of the Depression than with the root causes of poverty among a significant segment of the population. American Indians, for example, received scarcely any attention until the 1960s. Until the founding of the Office of Economic Opportunity (OEO) in 1965, native Americans could look for assistance to only the Bureau of Indian Affairs (BIA) and the churches. Ironically, until 1973 the BIA was under the Bureau of Public Land Management in the Department of the Interior, hardly a logical supporting organization for the substance of minority group development needs. (Before 1849, the Bureau was under the War Department.) Compounding the problem was the fact that development programs were initiated for the Indians from outside, without their local participation, frequently resulting in new social problems being created even as old ones began to be solved.[6]

Participation, indeed, became one of the hallmarks in the OEO panoply of programs, along with the understood need to improve services such as education and health care. Participation took on a measure of prominence because of the feeling that income increases alone would not be sufficient to permanently solve the poverty problem. Indeed, "only with the participation of the poor in the planning and execution of antipoverty programs would the other aspects of poverty be overcome. . . . Participation is advocated as both a preferred means and a desired end."[7] Yet participation, as both means and end, is difficult to achieve. Organizational structures can be—and were—created, yet to what extent can one encourage people to participate in them? Is it sufficient simply to abolish discriminatory barriers to political activity? How does one go beyond this without arousing the ire of either the intended beneficiaries or the established elites? These are hardly trivial questions, whether posed at home or abroad.

---

[5]A.M. Okun, *Equality and Efficiency: The Big Tradeoff* (Washington, D.C.: Brookings Institution, 1975), p. 69.

[6]For a complete account of U.S. government programs for American Indians—whose condition is probably more closely akin to that of the Third World poor than that of any other minority group in the United States—see Sar A. Levitan and William B. Johnston, *Indian Giving: Federal Programs for Native Americans* (Baltimore: Johns Hopkins University Press, 1975).

[7]Lampman, "What Does It Do For the Poor?" p. 79.

The case of American blacks, recently researched in depth at the George Washington University Center for Manpower Policy Studies, is illustrative of the state of the "development art" on the U.S. scene.[8] While blacks account for only about 30 per cent of the total number of people living below the poverty line today, their changing status and conditions are not atypical of those of other poor Americans.[9] The studies show, to begin with, that substantial gains have been made by blacks since 1960. Between 1960 and 1972, black wage and salary incomes nearly tripled with 1) the long-delayed entrance of black males into more skilled and better-paying jobs, 2) the rapid equalization of black and white women, and 3) the massive impact of government aid. The ratio of black to white median incomes rose from 53 per cent to 62 per cent for men and from 62 per cent to 96 per cent for women; the 1972 figures are some 5 per cent higher still if one adds increases in federal in-kind aid to the relative income of blacks. But in spite of this progress, blacks still have not been escaping poverty as fast as whites, and the number of poor blacks actually rose in the early 1970s. The relative gains disguise the fact that there is a widening absolute dollar gap between blacks and whites, a widening of $853 in median family income between 1960 and 1972.[10]

Still more serious is the fact that much of the registered improvement turns out to have come from non-self-sustaining initiatives. More than half of the income of poor blacks in 1972 came from government sources, compared with a fourth in 1959. Very little black income originates from property revenues or from self-employment, and blacks still control but a small fraction of the country's income-producing assets and seldom own their own businesses. Neither of these facts changed during the 1960s. In short,

> Whatever gains blacks have made, they have not won control over the sources of wealth which can be passed on from one generation to the next. . . . The gains resulted from a unique combination of social consensus, government commitment, and economic expansion. Even if the favorable conditions could be maintained and rates of gain sustained, it would take at least two generations before blacks would reach economic equality with whites. And no matter how one reads the conflicting evidence on relative gains, the fact remains that blacks still receive only about three-fifths as much income as whites and that millions of blacks remain locked in poverty.[11]

---

[8]Sar A. Levitan, Robert Taggart, and William B. Johnston, *Still a Dream: The Changing Status of Blacks Since 1960* (Cambridge: Harvard University Press, 1975).

[9]Sar A. Levitan and Robert Taggart, *The Promise of Greatness* (Cambridge: Harvard University Press, 1976).

[10]Levitan, Taggart, and Johnston, *Still a Dream,* pp. 41-43.

[11]Ibid., p. 43.

Analyses of specific quality-of-life indicators show roughly similar trends. While opportunities for better education, health care, and housing have significantly increased for blacks, these opportunities are still insufficient and inferior to those available to whites. Programs such as Head Start, providing schooling for disadvantaged preschool children; Follow-Through, an experimental program to determine the best ways of educating students in grades 1-3; Upward Bound, providing remedial programs and counseling to selected students in grades 10-11; the Neighborhood Youth Corps and the Job Corps; and a variety of other efforts of the 1960s have led to some small but still helpful improvements. Yet neither compensatory education nor vocational training has begun to develop much of the untapped human resources of blacks. If national evaluations reveal that the problems have not been solved, they reflect more the enormity of the task of bringing about greater equity in human resource development than failures of design or implementation of federal programs.[12]

Not surprisingly—but very critically—the basic power shifts that would tend to promote self-sustaining black development lagged behind more specific improvements in the areas of education and health. Indeed, compared to the money and effort that went into income maintenance, in-kind aid, and human resource development efforts, institution-building has received a relatively low priority. The Model Cities program—designed to improve urban living conditions—was invariably under the wing of the local power structure, even though its rhetoric fostered community participation. The private sector was enlisted, through a variety of financial "carrots," to encourage minority-owned business, but this approach had only a marginal impact and often had the effect of excluding blacks and community groups from the decision-making process. Community development corporations, once widely touted as effective instruments of local empowerment, were difficult to place on self-supporting bases and now face an uncertain future because of the demise of the Office of Economic Opportunity which supported them.[13] Cooperatives for low-income, rural blacks have occasionally proven effective in raising income, "but the government has been reluctant to work toward large-scale organizations which could compete on equal terms with agri-business."[14]

The reason for the lesser success of these participation and institution-building efforts is essentially that they are both technically and politically much harder to implement, their immediate payoff is limited, and their achievements are difficult to measure over the long run. The effects of an

---

[12] Ibid., p. 307.

[13] The OEO was succeeded by the Community Services Administration in 1973, but much of the momentum for the integrated antipoverty attacks was lost in the early 1970s as many programs were cut and others transferred to other federal departments and to state and local jurisdictions. Whether and how they will be substantially revived under President Jimmy Carter's domestic antipoverty program is yet to be seen.

[14] Levitan, Taggart, and Johnston, *Still a Dream*, p. 308.

equal dollar amount devoted to welfare, medical care, or vocational training are much more visible—and politically less threatening—than the benefits of community control. And in allocating funds, relatively risky efforts that can claim no quantifiable benefits tend to lose out. It is partly for this reason that policymakers are not often interested in supporting institution-building programs.

Policymakers are also subject to fads: community action agencies in 1964, community demonstration agencies in 1966, community development corporations in 1968, and revenue sharing in the 1970s. Yet, as the George Washington University study points out, "lasting institutions cannot be built by panacea hopping, and organization rearrangements are no substitute for certain and substantial funding."[15] A clear example of the need for long-term commitment can be drawn from the logic of the educational process itself:

> An adequate program reaching the 20 per cent of American children who are disadvantaged and are distributed among thousands of local schools requires a long-term commitment to furnish funds and to develop programs and the professional competence needed to guide them. An entire generation of children is involved, which means a 20-year effort. The experience of the 1960's suggests that the cost will be two or three times that of educating children of middle-class background. The development of programs and materials and the acquisition of professional competence to guide new programs is likely to take five to eight years. *Americans are not accustomed to long-term commitments of this magnitude. It is a real challenge.*[16]

If belief in the quick solution is typically American, so is the notion that lies at the heart of such programs, namely, that one can *use* the system to *change* the system. While some would see a central contradiction in the idea that one can alter power distribution through machinery responsive to existing power forces, examples can be cited where this has indeed been achieved in the United States. For example, industrial workers were able to gain more influence over their own affairs by pressing for labor legislation over a period of years and then by organizing themselves under the sanction of the resulting National Labor Relations Act. Women, by purposefully increasing their enrollments in the male-oriented higher education system, have recently begun to gain equal economic and political rights. Southern blacks gained influence over their own political processes through fighting successfully for the removal of obstacles such as poll taxes under the guarantees of the Voting Rights Act, which more than doubled the number of black registered voters.[17] And people previously without access to the

---

[15]Ibid.

[16]Ralph W. Tyler, "The Federal Role in Education," *The Public Interest*, No. 34, special issue entitled *The Great Society: Lessons for the Future* (winter 1974), p. 174. Italics added.

[17]Levitan and Taggart, *The Promise of Greatness,* pp. 155–56.

courts achieved that access through the OEO legal services program and its promotion of relevant changes in statutory laws and administrative practices.

The U.S. experience with black Americans tends to confirm that political power is at the root of any significant social change. During the 1950s, key judicial decisions were made, helped along in their implementation by both the civil rights movement and by the more militant black power struggle and street riots of the 1960s. Collectively, these events led to the initiation and then intensification of a rash of programs to aid poor blacks, as well as other U.S. poverty groups; they also led to setting the scene for considerably increased black and other minority political prominence in federal, state, and local government hierarchies. What was earlier a vicious circle became a more actively beneficent circle.

Yet success also bred failure. The demise of the OEO and the relative emasculation of Volunteers in Service to America (VISTA), of individual rural cooperatives, and of a variety of community action agencies is generally considered to be due to their challenge to the political status quo. The initial activism generated by the war on poverty led to quick reprisals. The powers of community-based organizations were constrained, and control by the local establishment increased. The private sector and the government bureaucracy assumed an ever increasing role in minority entrepreneurship efforts, swallowing the black community's meager "piece of the action." Progress beyond certain bounds posed threats. One could reduce the total number of poor (thanks to America's unique wealth) but not so easily *relative* poverty. One could espouse participation in local decision making but not so easily in controlling sources of wealth.

Government assistance, for all its advantages as a unique source of large-scale resources, is perhaps not the most feasible source for institution-building efforts that either threaten vested interests or require long-range nurturing. Education, health, and housing efforts could perhaps succeed only because they did not threaten any vested interest groups. Besides this, the culture of poverty—even when it is only the poverty of a minority rather than a majority—is inherently very difficult to overcome. Whether the striking increase in black political prominence visible in the United States by 1977 will ultimately bring with it increasing control over *sources* of wealth—and thus foster self-sustaining development progress—has yet to be seen.

What are the major lessons of the American antipoverty experience that are relevant to Third World development? *First*, it is possible to provide for the minimum human needs of large numbers of poverty-stricken people, but only with considerable political will, institutional and manpower resources, and, not least, tremendous sums of money. While all these elements are scarce in Third World countries, some parts of the substantive experience may be replicable. *Second*, narrowing the development gap means changing social and economic structures; it thus requires primarily political solutions. This lesson is a difficult one to transplant, especially since Third World elites are understandably opposed to structural change as well as to outside intervention; yet an appreciation of the politics of development in the more familiar U.S. context should make it easier for Americans engaged in Third World development to understand the larger political issues overseas.

Indeed, the reverse is also true. As the experience of returned Peace Corps volunteers has suggested, many efforts and ideas from the Third World can be usefully applied to the "Third World" in the United States—to domestic antipoverty programs. In a broader attitudinal sense as well, Peace Corps returnees and others with similar overseas experiences can have, and have had, a significant impact on raising American consciousness—not only consciousness of poverty problems in the United States but also of alternative life-styles and thought-styles for Americans.

All this suggests a larger point about the new relationships evolving in an increasingly interdependent world. The problems of poverty, of the gap between rich and poor, and thus also of affluence, are global problems that are as evident in America as in the Third World. The astonishing worldwide success of E.F. Schumacher's book, *Small is Beautiful—Economics as if People Mattered*, shows that development concepts concerning technology, people, and the "good life" are in flux everywhere. Thus Americans who consider the problems of inequities between the elites and the poor overseas would do well to reflect further on their own attitudes, roles, and responsibilities vis-à-vis their own life-styles and the poor in America. The result might be not only improved job performance for those engaged in the more traditional types of development efforts but also raised individual consciousnesses, leading to new approaches to development and interdependence in the future.

Chapter 4

How Humane Is Relief?

American private and voluntary organizations exist for humanitarian—or, in legal terms, "charitable"—purposes. Humanitarianism, according to Webster's dictionary, is "regard for the interests of mankind; benevolence." Just as the definition of this term opens up a broad range of interpretations as to what is in the best interests of mankind, so too do private and voluntary organizations vary in their individual activities as expressions of those interests. Some set as their goal the immediate alleviation of human suffering. Others choose to concentrate on the root causes of this suffering, focusing on the amelioration of poverty over the long run. Most combine elements of both approaches in their programs. Because it is with the organizations that combine both that confusion often arises, it is to this group that the current chapter applies.

Part of the confusion lies in the very broadness of declared organizational objectives; they range from the Ford Foundation's general "dedication to the public well-being" to Heifer Project's relatively specialized "provision of livestock and poultry to meet the needs of developing countries." Because these objectives provide an important backdrop for analyzing their consequently varying action approaches, it is relevant to note a few representative examples here:[1]

> To help the less fortunate peoples of the world in their struggle against hunger, ill health, ignorance and low productivity by converting as effectively as possible the voluntary, people-to-people contributions of Americans and Canadians and the support of host governments into various forms of relief and development assistance.
> *CARE*

> To undertake activities in the field of development, sponsor nutrition education programs, distribute relief supplies (food, medicine, cloth-

---

[1]These objectives are quoted from *U.S. Non-Profit Organizations in Development Assistance Abroad* (New York: Technical Assistance Information Clearing House of the American Council of Voluntary Agencies for Foreign Service, Inc., 1971), and were updated from individual agency formulations of goals as available from agencies.

ing, etc.), and meet emergency needs due to natural and manmade disasters (earthquakes, floods, civil strife, etc.).
Catholic Relief Services

To serve the common interest of U.S. Protestant and Orthodox churches in works of Christian mercy, relief, technical assistance, rehabilitation and interchurch aid.
Church World Service

To give assistance to desperately needy families, with the emphasis on aid to the children in these families; to equip [their] children with the intellectual and physical tools necessary for the development of full and productive lives in their own countries; to help parents make the most of their individual talents and abilities, so they can support their families without the aid of any welfare organization.
Foster Parents Plan

To bring financial assistance and expertise to bear on the problems of population and hunger, the quality of the environment and the development of universities in Asia, Africa and Latin America.
Rockefeller Foundation

To assist low-income people in developing countries to initiate or expand locally-owned, viable, self-help enterprises and cooperatives which directly benefit the communities in which they are located, selecting projects on the basis of maximum social and economic impact.
Technoserve

To adapt and transmit technical information and to provide solutions to technical problems for individuals and organizations who do not have access to appropriate technical resources; to assist people with technical assistance appropriate to their needs, resources, and local conditions.
Volunteers in Technical Assistance

To share resources in the name of Christ and proclaim Jesus as Lord; to establish and preserve an identity as free as possible from those nationalistic, cultural and ideological interests which are contrary to our understanding of faithfulness to Christ, and to seek to meet human need in any nation regardless of political identity or affiliation; to participate in a development process based on local capacity and self-reliance, by which persons and societies come to realize the full potential of their human, natural and spiritual resources; to follow the example of Christ in striving for justice, in identifying with the weak and oppressed and in reconciling the oppressor and oppressed; to provide relief for victims of disasters in ways which encourage their maximum initiative, dignity and participation.
Mennonite Central Committee

These are representative of the articulated objectives of private and voluntary organizations. In addition, most of these groups have at least two unarticulated objectives—first, to achieve a certain sense of psychic satisfaction, and second, to see that the givers gain the educational benefits inherent in international experiences. The absence of these two from the list of objectives may be a matter of oversight, of a failure to recognize them as objectives, or even of an intentional lack of candor based on a feeling that neither the constituent donors nor the aid recipients would appreciate their inclusion. Discussion elsewhere in this volume focuses on these donor-related objectives. The focus of the current chapter will be on the manifestations and effects of U.S. private and voluntary assistance in the Third World.

Private and voluntary activities in the Third World can be classified for present purposes under two main headings: relief and development. While not all agency representatives observe a sharp distinction between the two types of activities, it is critical to draw one, since they focus on two fundamentally different problems. Indeed, the failure to observe the distinction has resulted in much of the frustration over aid in the past. Relief, after all, attempts to fill stop-gap needs for human survival. Development efforts, on the other hand, have—or should have—as their goal the achievement of improved standards of living, defined on a variety of planes and capable of being self-sustaining into the future. This is not to say that there are no borderline cases where short-term relief efforts may pave the way for longer-term developmental efforts. The problem is that too often the transition has not been made to broader and longer-term development.

Relief Aid: Pros and Cons

Of all the forms of U.S. assistance abroad, whether public or private, relief has the longest history. It is also, from a conceptual standpoint, relatively straightforward: essentials of life must be made available to those temporarily deprived of them due to events beyond their control. U.S. relief aid began, as noted earlier, with ad hoc aid shipments for victims of political upheavals in Santo Domingo and earthquakes in Venezuela soon after the founding of the United States. Comprising virtually all of American aid during the first historical period and most of it during the second period that began around 1900, relief still comprises a large percentage of American private assistance overseas. (Because of the way programs are defined and statistics kept, it is impossible to know just what percentage.) It is sent to victims of recurring famines in South Asia and the Sahel, to those made homeless by floods and earthquakes in Honduras and Guatemala, and to people whose lives have been made intolerable through changes in political systems, as in Indochina. Millions of tons of emergency food, clothing, and housing materials have been shipped over the years to people in legitimate need, people who in many cases would have died without that help. American responses to disasters abroad, as at home, have been magnanimous, even overwhelming, and a profound testimony to mankind's basic humanity and solidarity.

This solidarity has a way of knocking down all obstacles. Where transportation is a problem, helicopters and airdrops are mobilized. Where bureaucracies are slow-moving, the quick movement of papers and people in a crisis makes a farce of the inertial norm. The American enthusiasm for helping people in sudden need is exemplified not only by the blankets and dollars they donate but also by the mountains of high-heeled shoes, girdles and bras, gourmet foods, and other paraphernalia of Western affluence that would lend an air of the ridiculous to the relief effort were it not for the goodwill behind them.

One of the obstacles many voluntary agencies tend to brush aside is that of internal politics. Catholic Relief Services, which provided food for South Vietnamese militia families during the vicious Vietnam war, found it difficult to understand why they drew criticism for simply "helping people in need." Another example is the civil war in Nigeria in the late 1960s. In spite of the protests of the Nigerian government and the World Council of Churches' secretary for Africa—and even the stoppage of emergency airlifts by the Red Cross—Church World Service and Catholic Relief Services continued their help to the secessionist Biafrans into the final days of the war. As the CWS executive director at the time wrote later,

> We in Church World Service, commissioned to alleviate acute human need and starvation wherever we could reach, were to be agonized throughout the Nigerian civil war. The deciding factor in my own heart, which I shared with the CWS Board of Directors, was the conviction that if the starving children in Biafra had in fact been starving children of any nation of Europe or North America, they would have been fed. We begged, quite literally, governments and the United Nations to feed the children. They either could not or would not for pressing and valid political reasons. . . . Many have sincerely felt that the relief air effort prolonged unnecessarily the plight of people in Nigeria. This is probably so; I don't have the data on this. At the end of the conflict one thing was clear; the children of Biafra were alive.[2]

The political effects of the Biafran aid role have been likened by missionaries—in this case missionaries from Denmark—to the role of a doctor:

> Was our assistance political interference? The answer must be that our role was equivalent to that of a doctor. Does a doctor perform a political act if he is called upon to treat a patient who is seriously ill, manages to cure him, and later learns that the patient is a politician?

---

[2]James MacCracken, unpublished personal memoirs. CWS also fed equal numbers of people in Federal Nigeria.

Perhaps, but as a doctor he had no choice. . . . It has also been said that the church aid organizations . . . have blood on their hands. We do—in the same way as the doctor does after an operation.[3]

One can argue against this aid-at-any-cost position on a number of grounds. Among the political grounds is the possible effect of prolonging the war and the suffering by nurturing any remaining South Vietnamese or Biafran capability for holding out. Another is the risking of any future ability to be of perhaps greater help through having engendered the hostility of the ultimately winning side; indeed, most American voluntary organizations were subsequently ordered out of both Vietnam and Nigeria because of their support for the "wrong side." "Although relief organizations consistently and sincerely stress their nonpolitical motives one or both of the parties to a civil war usually sees in their work serious political consequences. Nor is that interpretation unreasonable. Any treatment advantaging (for example) the secessionist or minority side changes either the power weightings in the struggle or, what amounts to much the same thing, how the competitors evaluate their own and their opponent's rankings."[4]

In other settings, such as that of drought relief to Ethiopia in 1974–75, one can argue that outside aid tended to prop up an unresponsive, corrupt, and unpopular government which not only was insufficiently responsive to the emergency to commit enough of its own resources and priorities to helping, but which also used the very relief aid for its own corrupt purposes. In Bangladesh and India it has been argued that the easy availability of outside relief food has encouraged those governments to devote less than the necessary political priority to agricultural production. And in many situations it has lulled the people themselves into overdependence on aid and into insufficient self-help motivation.[5] This latter point is exemplified by the observation of an American priest long resident in Bangladesh. Before the mammoth relief supplies started pouring into the country after the 1970 cyclone, he pointed out, the Bengalis were quick to rebuild their own houses and communities after disasters; since then, however, they have become accustomed to waiting for handouts.

Part of the problem lies in how the aid is handled. Relief aid can, with some imagination, be supplied in ways that are less dependency-creating than in the past. In Guatemala in 1976, where about 23,000 people were killed and one quarter of the population made homeless by an earthquake, a debate ensued among the scores of private and government relief groups that

---

[3]Viggo Mollerup, "Kirkeligt hjälpearbejde og politick," interview in "Hjälp over alle gräser?—Kirkernes internationale hjälpearbejde," Synspunkt nr. 12, Danish Missionary Society, Hellerup 1971, p. 40. Translation from the Danish quoted in Jørgen Lissner, The Politics of Altruism (Geneva: Lutheran World Federation, 1977), p. 233.
[4]Morris Davis, ed., Civil Wars and the Politics of International Relief (New York: Praeger Publishers, Inc., 1975), p. 8.
[5]The same criticism, justified or not, has been leveled against the U.S. welfare system.

came to the aid of the survivors. Reduced to its simplest terms, the debate was between advocates of free aid administered by experienced foreign organizations in full control of funds and projects and, on the other hand, advocates of reconstruction efforts based on ideas offered and largely financed by the disaster victims themselves. CARE, in this case, acted on the basis of the first argument, completing a large number of houses quickly. Oxfam-America and World Neighbors, meanwhile, worked with local groups along the lines of the second approach; they completed fewer houses but felt they were contributing importantly to the development of longer-term community institutions for coping with future disasters.[6]

Beyond the question of methodologies lies the more fundamental question of ethnocentricity in one's definition of a crisis and in assessing at what stage, if any, essentials of life must be provided from outside. Studies have shown that in parts of the world where weather patterns are uncertain, social systems tend to respond to crop fluctuations with various mechanisms to insure against the consequences of that uncertainty.[7] Consumption patterns may not fluctuate to the same extent as production. In good crop years, considerable compensatory saving may occur, whether in the form of grain, gold bracelets, or other objects of wealth; this serves as a safety valve for the bad years. Thus what might be seen by some outsiders as a disaster requiring external assistance may not be seen as a "crisis" at all by the local people. Furthermore, there is no worldwide consensus on what constitutes adequate caloric intake for people of varying genetic compositions. The 2250 daily calorie minimum that is assumed for people in the United States may be higher, or lower, than that required for people of different sizes and body structures living in warmer or colder climates.[8] The result, though still little researched, may be that relief programs respond too quickly and excessively for the good of the particular society over the long run. If this is so, it is partly explained by the mixed motivations of the donors described earlier. As one commentator has critically suggested, "disasters tend to attract and engross certain kinds of persons: romantic idealists fixated on reducing obvious suffering; persons interested in an intense professional challenge where one can plunge in and work out solutions without interference; and of course various adventurers."[9]

There is a final argument that suggests more discrimination in the sending of relief—nature's argument. In a world of exponentially increasing population, disasters and disease have been the natural means for preserving a balance between people and land. With medical help and disaster relief now saving so many lives, the ecological balance and thus the life of the

---

[6]Gerry Nadel, "Guatemala After the Terremoto," *Atlantic* (July 1976), pp. 14–21.
[7]See Morris D. Morris, "Diet and Some Nutritional Problems in Contemporary India," mimeographed (Washington, D.C.: Overseas Development Council, 1976).
[8]Davidson R. Gwatkin, "Health and Nutrition in India," mimeographed (New Delhi: The Ford Foundation, 1974), p. 7.
[9]Davis, *Civil Wars*, p. 70.

planet itself soon may be in danger of extinction. On the individual level, the cruelty of death by starvation may be exceeded by the debilitating effects of its frequent alternative, lifelong malnutrition.

None of these arguments cuts much ice with the practitioners of relief, or even with those of the more development-focused programs. To espouse these arguments, they say, is to play God with human life. The point that intervening on the other side can also be construed as playing God may be accepted by them as a counterargument, but by the rules of the Judeo-Christian tradition, arguments in favor of saving the lives of people on earth today generally win. Given, therefore, the inexorable call for relief, the question becomes one of maximizing its effectiveness and, most important of all, its ultimate humanity. For it is crucial to recognize that good motives alone do not ensure good and humanitarian outcomes.

Relief Means to Development Ends? The Example of Food Aid

Much U.S. voluntary aid is given in the form of food. Some of this food comes from private in-kind contributions, some is purchased by voluntary agencies with private contributions of cash, and by far the largest amount is channeled through voluntary agencies by the U.S. government under Title II of Public Law 480 for the disposal of U.S. excess food supplies. Food is given in large part for historical reasons, since it has always been a key need in emergency relief situations. Whether food is as useful for today's increasing emphasis on ameliorating the root causes of poverty is another question, however. Indeed, it is an especially critical question because more than one quarter of voluntary agency income in 1975-76 was in the form of food and its related transportation value.[10] Furthermore, some of the largest voluntary organizations believe that, through food aid, relief and development needs can be met simultaneously. Thus they attempt to use food not only for emergency relief but also for ongoing welfare programs and for developmental purposes.

With careful planning, food can have a favorable long-range economic development impact as well as immediate life-saving effects. This was demonstrated in a 1975 study of food aid by a University of Sussex team.[11]

---

[10]Some 35 per cent of the total income reported by the 94 agencies registered with the Advisory Committee on Voluntary Foreign Aid was in the form of government-provided food, government-paid overseas freight costs, and private donations of general supplies and equipment. While the last two categories include nonfood items as well as food, it is estimated that 25 per cent of total income is a conservative estimate for food-related costs alone.

[11]Paul J. Isenman and H.W. Singer, *Food Aid: Disincentive Effects and Their Policy Implications* (Washington, D.C.: Agency for International Development, 1975). Although the efforts cited in the study pertain primarily to the large-scale Title I food aid offered by the U.S. government on concessional terms rather than to the smaller amounts of free food provided by the government through U.S. voluntary agencies under Title II, the principle remains relevant.

The study shows that food aid—mainly by alleviating strains on the overall economy and by lowering food prices—can have a dynamic effect on growth in output and employment and also can raise demand for food grains in subsequent periods. "Food aid appears to have played a major supply and 'insurance' role in the investment and output boom of the first half of the 1960s, which was important in itself and which generated substantial increases in food grain demand."[12]

Experience has shown, however, that in many other cases, relief and development needs cannot be met simultaneously. Indeed, the blurring of goals may negate developmental effectiveness. To be effective for development, food must be combined with strategically focused financial inputs in the context of carefully synchronized local government policies. This is difficult to ensure, as is illustrated by the case of Colombia, where food aid during the 1960s was widely felt to have had disincentive effects on production. In Brazil, too, "there is no question that the government was able to give low priority to the agricultural sector for many years in part because of the facility with which food commodities could be imported." Indeed, "food programs in Northeastern Brazil have had a marginal impact at best. . . . No doubt some people are alive and healthier today in the Northeast because of the U.S. food aid programs, but the general level of poverty and the resulting malnutrition have not diminished and, in fact, have probably worsened in the past ten years."[13]

In emergency relief situations, it is especially difficult to synchronize policies. Among the problems of food aid are the inherent organizational constraints to guaranteeing a stable and predictable supply. These are not the fault of the voluntary agencies alone. Rather, there is a systemic problem deriving from fluctuations in food policies based on causes as varied as the weather, commercial purchases, congressional whims, bureaucratic processes of the U.S. Agency for International Development (AID), and vagaries of the shipping business. As a result, voluntary agency field people note that frequently they receive only a few days' notice that a ship is on the high seas with food that they must then program for distribution by the time it arrives in port. This inevitably means that the primary objective is to get the food distributed before it rots, rather than to supplement relief needs by promoting development through the use of food.

Other problems arise when unpopular or unnecessarily costly foods are provided. Such commodities often find their way into local markets so that the initial recipients can earn cash to buy preferred foods or larger quantities of less expensive items.[14] Yet the main difficulty here appears to be a legal

---

[12] Ibid., p. 6.
[13] Fred B. Morris, *U.S. Food Policy in Latin America, Northeast Brazil: A Case Study*, (Washington, D.C.: Congressional Research Service, Library of Congress, 1975), p. 59.
[14] See "Poor and Hungry Haitians Sell Food Provided by an American Church," *New York Times*, December 12, 1976.

one, in that the selling of free commodities is against U.S. regulations governing their export. These regulations are said to derive from fears of malfeasance should the funds derived from selling the food wind up in the wrong hands. However, malfeasance is a potential problem with any form of aid and should not be irresolvable with proper administrative safeguards. In economic terms and also in terms of meeting individual recipients' preferences, local sales of P.L.-480 foods should, in fact, be permitted.

One of the major vehicles for distributing food is through food-for-work programs, a concept, in fact, invented by the voluntary organizations out of concern for the problems of dependency creation and recipient humiliation implied in free handouts.[15] Following basically the principle of the U.S. Work Progress Administration during the American Depression of the 1930s, food-for-work operates by bringing disaster-stricken farmers food-earning employment during a period when they otherwise might be starving; they are employed for developmentally useful activities such as digging irrigation channels and wells, and creating other infrastructural works, some of which might prevent the recurrence of natural calamities in the future. In this kind of infrastructure creation, food-for-work has a mixed record. Countless examples can be cited of new water reservoirs that have enabled cultivation of new lands, while countless other examples can be cited of roads built five times over due to lack of proper planning for maintenance.

Another major use of food aid is in nutrition programs, either through school, preschool, or other institutional feeding networks. Proponents of these programs, which comprise a high percentage of the activities of the largest agencies such as Catholic Relief Services and CARE, usually describe them not in relief or welfare terms but essentially as development programs. While acknowledging the difficulty of assessing such programs due to the lack of relevant economic indicators, a 1969 CARE position paper noted a generally "positive gain. The indicators that exist are largely social. There is general agreement that among school age children benefitting from CARE school feeding programs . . . a contribution has been made to general improvement in health and vigor, there has been increased ability to concentrate, that attendance has been increased and made more regular."[16] The assumption—no doubt correct—is that the impact of better nutrition on the mental development of the child will further the child's ability to contribute to its own development, to that of the larger community, and ultimately to that of the country.

---

[15]Voluntary agency experiments with food-for-work were first carried out in the late 1950s. Initially, the U.S. government was opposed to the imposition of work conditions for food aid, but by the 1960s the regulations were modified to permit tying the release of food to work performed.

[16]Ralph Montee and William Langdon, "The Importance of Feeding Programs to Economic and Social Development," Program Department Position Paper, mimeographed (New York: CARE, 1970), p. 21.

One of the livelier battles in recent years has, in fact, revolved around the optimum age for best affecting this type of child development, with the majority consensus being that maternal and infant feeding (ages 0–5) is more effective than school-age feeding. A study conducted at the Harvard Institute of Economic Research concluded that infant malnutrition is significant in explaining variations in children's IQs, with a 10 per cent gain in a particular relative weight leading to an IQ increase of 5 to 6.5 points.[17] It was then calculated that the cost of a milk feeding program that would thus raise IQs would be less than the total increase in earnings likely to be generated by the affected person over his lifetime. Indeed, the study concluded, the rate of return of investment for feeding programs was found to be higher than the rate of return from investments in either physical capital or schooling (to cite two examples). Although preschool feeding is logistically more difficult than school feeding (because the children are not so readily organized in one place on a more-or-less regular basis), this kind of scientific evidence—plus strong encouragement from AID and other donors—has led to a significant shift from school to preschool feeding around the world.

The results of the Harvard study notwithstanding, even preschool feeding has about it as much an air of relief as one of development. The mental enrichment argument is not only a very long-term and uncertain one, but it is also invariably limited to the small number of infants actually reachable by a voluntary agency or, for that matter, by any outside program. Indeed, the question hardly seems to be asked as to what will happen to the same children, or succeeding generations, when this free outside food supply does stop, as it almost inevitably will. If one forces the question, the voluntary agency answer is either an insistence that the supplies must be continued if people are not to starve or suffer severe malnutrition, or that one should hope that nutritional and agricultural education will be raised to sufficient levels so that continuity can become self-sustaining on the basis of local production increases and improved practices. Yet virtually no evidence has been brought forward of any program that convincingly combines these necessary ingredients or that shows where the benefits of initial feeding efforts have become self-sustaining after the phasing out of external assistance. Nor do feeding programs appear to have been planned in such a way as to suggest what time phasing is required for self-sufficiency.

Many argue that the fundamental problem in malnutrition is that of income constraints. One study conducted in India, for example, suggests that hunger is more likely to be a function of an individual family's inability to grow or buy sufficient food than of the overall availability of that food in the country or particular area. While special feeding programs aimed at "target groups" may occasionally be justified in making available minor

---

[17]Marcello Selowsky, cited in C. Capone, Catholic Relief Services Field Bulletin 21, Nairobi, Kenya (August 15, 1974).

nutrients not always present in the normal diet (such as vitamin A), "all too often the target groups do not benefit much; children fed at school often receive correspondingly less to eat at home, or take the food home where it is divided among the family. And where basic calories are deficient, many of the artificial protein-enriched foods that are distributed are simply an expensive means of providing calories. . . . Such programs have not been very successful in India, not at least in terms of their specific goals (they probably have had some small redistributive effect)."[18] The same study points to a larger economic question that is too rarely confronted in either relief or development planning: the most productive allocation of resources.

> People work out feeding programs at a cost of $x per recipient per year, with y recipients; they then tell us that for only $xy we can solve a large share of the country's nutritional problems. But $xy in India usually comes to a figure of hundreds of millions. An important question is whether India can afford simply to give away $200 million or $400 million in a feeding program; whether, if such sums are available, they should not be used as the wages of useful employment that creates durable assets. For this and other reasons, we believe that—with minor exceptions—the nutrition problem in India must fundamentally be seen as a problem of income generation.[19]

Ideally, one can envision situations in which a complementarity exists between nutrition and income benefits, rather than an either/or dichotomy. For example, for many years the government of Sri Lanka has had a policy of regular free food distribution to every resident of the country. This constitutes part of a larger welfare package, an equivalent, in a sense, to a guaranteed minimum income. Yet this kind of program creates its own problems and is generally least feasible in the poorest settings where it is most needed. In Sri Lanka, for example, the government's policy has been considered reckless by many economists who despair that the economy's GNP is too low to support it.

Some types of institutionalized feeding programs—such as aid to day-care centers, orphanages, old age homes, and hospitals—could be justified as "developmental." They are concerned with long-term relief (more properly described as welfare) in the sense that people confined to such institutions would not have the necessary sustenance of life without such aid, and that in most cases the institutions are unlikely to ever become self-supporting. At the same time they include development goals insofar as day-care centers permit mothers to work and thus supplement family income, and insofar as local governments are being made aware, perhaps for the first time, of their own responsibilities for the inevitable welfare sectors of their

---

[18]Robert Cassen, "Welfare and Population: Notes on Rural India Since 1960," *Population and Development Review*, Vol. I, No. 1 (September 1975), p. 47.
[19]Ibid.

societies. If simultaneously with the running of such programs local people are being trained to fill leadership roles in them, and if local food production is being encouraged to replace the imports from outside, then the effect may indeed be developmental.

Needed: A Developmental Approach

None but the harshest critics dispute the need for relief assistance as long as it is well-timed, targeted, and administered.[20] If it is also planned to serve some of the longer-range needs noted above, so much the better. In the absence of such developmental components, however, one can rightly dispute the manner in which such efforts sometimes perpetuate themselves to the point of becoming counterproductive. To avoid undue dependency creation, some voluntary agency executives have suggested limiting relief programs to a particular time period—perhaps 60 or 90 days after an emergency need has arisen—in order to ensure that thereafter the longer-term perspective will not be lost. No one arbitrary time frame can be established to meet all conditions, of course, and to some extent the dependency problem can be eased only by building into local governments and private organizations a continuing capacity for coping with relief needs, with or without the broader development component. Indeed, one of the positive outgrowths of the unfortunate congruence of unanticipated natural disasters in the 1972–1974 period has been an emerging movement toward institutionalizing disaster-planning capabilities for Third World countries so they can take the primary responsibility for their own future emergency relief needs. On the international side, there has been discussion in favor of centralizing disaster responses under either the U.N. Disaster Relief Office or the International Committee of the Red Cross. This type of centralization would not only offer potential efficiency of operation; it would also offer a forum that would be expected to serve as an objective countervailing force in cases where local governments might be inclined, for domestic political reasons, to risk endangering their citizens' lives in the interests of national self-sufficiency and pride (for example, in the Ethiopian case cited above).[21] If any such initiatives—including a proposed world food reserve—are actually implemented, there are likely to be significant consequences for

---

[20]For accounts of poorly managed relief assistance, see Roger Morris and Hal Sheets, *Disaster in the Desert* (Washington, D.C.: Carnegie Endowment for International Peace, 1974); and Jack Shepherd, *The Politics of Starvation* (Washington, D.C.: Carnegie Endowment for International Peace, 1975). These books document in dismal detail the Sahel drought of the 1970s; in the Sahel, official recognition of need was unconscionably slow in forming, and relief was thus late in coming.

[21]For fuller discussion of these issues, see Stephen Green, "Disasters and Disaster Relief in the 1980s," mimeographed (New York: Council on Foreign Relations, Inc., 1976); and *Need for an International Relief Agency*, Report to the Congress by the Comptroller General of the U.S. (Washington, D.C.: U.S. Government Printing Office, 1976).

voluntary agency food and relief programs. It is difficult to predict at this stage, however, the precise nature of these long-range consequences.

The voluntary agency trend to emphasize development as much as relief is based on a growing recognition that if solutions can be found for the root causes of poverty, then ultimately one can break out of its "bottomless pit" and, among other things, be better able to cope with disasters as well. Yet there is still a certain ambivalence in agency programming, an ambivalence that derives partly from pragmatic perceptions of diverse needs and partly from the conflicting signals given by different types of donors. Human nature being what it is, the movement toward "development" is inevitably influenced by the lure of the dollar. Among some outside funding agencies, most notably the U.S. Agency for International Development, there is currently a clear emphasis on supporting programs aiming for long-term development results. The American public, on the other hand, has barely begun to make the transition to understanding the longer-range complexities of development; it responds most generously to emotional relief appeals. Agencies must understandably maximize income, and this encourages them to be as ambiguous as possible about their goals and ideologies. "Ambiguity increases the number of contributors to whom agencies may appeal; it is therefore rational strategy for fund-raising agencies to 'becloud their policies in a fog of ambiguity.'"[22] It is this dichotomy that may partially explain the curious mix of programs that emphasize both visible short-term and less visible long-term goals to please both types of supporters. On the other hand, the tendency to blur relief and development may lie in a failure within the organizations themselves—their boards and executive ranks—to comprehend fully what in fact is meant by "development." It is to more clearly developmental approaches that the next chapter thus turns.

---

[22]Jørgen Lissner, *The Politics of Altruism* (Geneva: Lutheran World Federation, 1977), p. 85.

Chapter 5

The Many Faces of Development Assistance

"Development" is defined in so many ways that a common understanding is needed before any meaningful discussion can ensue. As defined here, "development" is not merely an end goal but rather a historical process in which all people and their communities are engaged socially, psychologically, culturally, politically, and economically. It is a process that involves the mind and heart as well as the bare physical needs of the body. It must be characterized, therefore, by participation, self-reliance, and social justice.[1] The ultimate goal of development is not simply higher incomes, longer life expectancies, or higher literacy rates, but rather the capability for people and communities to realize their full responsible and creative potential. The community emphasis is especially significant in many Third World settings, where Western brands of individualism are alien and often considered antisocial.

Development, furthermore, must be a self-determining and self-sustaining process, internally motivated and directed. Outside forces—including aid—should influence development only insofar as in chemistry a catalyst indirectly, rather than directly, influences the functioning of life processes. In a major departure from the chemical analogy, however, the catalyst should not itself remain unchanged; in the larger context, indeed, the only way to escape the perpetuation of inevitably unequal aid relationships is to hope that the donor too will undergo a major change in terms of a more equitable interdependence. What is critical here is the recognition that the outside aid infusion is temporary, relatively minor, and useful only insofar as it abets the overall development process. It should preferably be under a significant degree of control by the recipients. The yardsticks for evaluating the success of developmental programs are therefore exactly the

---

[1]For more comprehensive insights into development as a process, see Denis Goulet, *The Cruel Choice* (New York: Atheneum Publishers, 1971); and Goulet, *World Interdependence: Verbal Smokescreen or New Ethic?*, Development Paper No. 21 (Washington, D.C.: Overseas Development Council, 1976).

opposite of those for relief, where immediate short-term sustenance of life, which is dependency-creating by definition, is the essential goal.

Because in one sense development is another term for life itself, attempts to significantly influence its course must inevitably aim at basic changes, indeed, at the very structures of human society. Yet many programs of the past have been described as developmental without substantially affecting these basic structures. Like relief aid, they have been more palliatives for superficial problems than efforts to make a more fundamental and lasting impact. This chapter will explore the range of private and voluntary agency activities and the sometimes fine dividing line between these palliatives, on the one hand, and more basic changes leading to equality of opportunity for the poor, on the other.

For purposes of discussion, and notwithstanding considerable overlapping, one can group most efforts of private and voluntary organizations in development under the following three headings: *development of physical and income-generating infrastructure; development of institutions*; and *development of human resources*. The first type of effort refers to the development of both physical infrastructure such as roads, irrigation works, and industrial installations, and other types of production-oriented inputs such as seeds, pumps, and fertilizers that directly or indirectly give people their livelihood and physical sustenance. The second refers to the administrative entities, whether at national or local levels, that provide channels for organizing solutions to problems. The third hearkens to the awareness and ability of individuals to responsibly fulfill their needs for survival, to contribute to the larger community, and to enable more creative individual and community self-realization. While all this may sound like exalted terminology for private and voluntary organizations that are relatively minor players on the world scene, it directly reflects the grass-roots needs of the world's poorest people and the various U.S. and other international responses to them.

Physical and Income-Generating Infrastructure

People, to survive, need at a minimum water to drink, food to eat, shelter and clothing for protection from the elements, and both preventive and curative health care. To some extent, these minimum needs are more difficult to ensure today than they were in the distant past, when most people lived in rural areas, when population pressures had not placed such constraints on the availability of new land, when relative lack of mobility limited diseases to a few against which people tended to have built up some modicum of resistance, and when the stresses of modernization had not yet set in with their disruptive effects on family and community life and traditional patterns of organization. To say this is not to suggest that the days of the "primitive savage" were inherently better, nor is it to wish a return to them, even in remote areas where that might be feasible. For the vast majority of people, after all, these were also periods of drudgery, lack of alternatives for significant self-development and creativity, and limited life expectancy; and while the values implied in such a statement may suggest attributes of the good society only by modern Western standards, they have by now been adopted as virtually global norms.

The point is that development as it has occurred over the past years and decades has carried along with it a series of additional needs for new development adaptations and innovations at an ever increasing pace. Thus because in many areas of the world there is no new cultivable land available, means must be found to exploit hitherto untapped water and soil resources through wells, irrigation facilities, fertilizers, and better crop varieties and cropping patterns. Where whole forests have been cut down to fulfill the fuel and construction needs of expanding populations, new means for providing energy and building houses have to be developed. Where migrations have brought new diseases in their wake (for example, venereal disease introduced by the West to the Third World and cholera from the Third World to the West), new methods for health protection must be evolved. All this needs to be done simply to meet minimum human needs.

The ramifications, however, extend to higher levels of human fulfillment as well. In resource-scarce societies, there are invariably discrepancies between those who through birth and whatever fortuitous combination of other happenstances have *more* and those who have *less*. Such social and economic inequities—even where minimum needs are met—retard development as it is more broadly defined. It is thus clear that physical and income-generating infrastructure must be created in such a way that it helps to meet not only minimum human needs for survival but equity as well. This is not easy.

Many private and voluntary organizations have contributed, and continue to contribute, to physical infrastructure development in the Third World. A study of aid to Brazil noted that "more than half of the aid of private bodies goes for schools and hospitals . . . [and] that construction and equipment absorb almost half of the aid . . . . This could well be an indication that the criteria are often *palliative* or [reflect] the desire to achieve visible results that can give satisfaction to the contributor."[2] The question, indeed, is whether these efforts to create physical infrastructure are both income-generating and equity-promoting over the long run. Not surprisingly, the largest contributions on the physical side have come from the largest agencies, such as CARE. These efforts have made extensive use of U.S. government food resources to build up physical infrastructure, not so much because food is a better instrument for such programs (though it sometimes is), but because U.S. domestic politics have made it more readily available than cash for foreign aid purposes.

---

[2]Michel Rousseau, "External Aid and Projects in Brazil," mimeographed (Rio de Janeiro: 1975), p. 34. (Translated from the Portuguese.)

Physical infrastructure tends to be popular with private organizations, as it is with government and multilateral organizations, for three reasons. First, as suggested by the Brazilian example, the end product is highly visible, thus demonstrating to those who have contributed the resources what they have accomplished (and making them happy to contribute and build more). Second, physical infrastructure is relatively easy and straightforward; one has only to design what is needed and hire people to build it. "Self-help" programs are a more imaginative variation here, involving as they do the local population to help in construction in a less dependency-generating fashion, thus helping to ensure their continuing interest, maintenance support, and (theoretically) further participation in improving their own lives thereafter. On the other hand, the local initiative involved in such programs is sometimes exaggerated, with the effect occasionally being one of outside government or voluntary groups simply getting a job done with cheap labor. There is also a third and more culture-bound reason for the popularity of physical infrastructure projects, namely that because communities in the West have developed infrastructures, there is assumed to be an obvious need for physical facilities everywhere. The danger lies in the Western assumption—often misleading—that a village without a school or a hospital automatically needs a school or hospital. Ivan Illich is one commentator who has testified convincingly (if with some exaggeration) on the societal deformities wrought by modern Western assumptions about education[3] and on the inefficiencies and inequities of promoting hospitals and clinics with overqualified medical professionals, rather than relying on auxiliaries or Chinese-style barefoot doctors, for example.[4] Some efforts that contribute through physical infrastructure may thus be counterproductive to more favorable development goals. They tend to be palliatives more than contributors to real change.

Health. A case in point in the field of health is exemplified by a young and talented Bengali doctor who, unlike the majority of his more profit-oriented peers, was committed to improving health care for the people of a rural area not far from Dacca, the capital of Bangladesh. Realizing that any program, to be viable over the long term, would require its own self-financing mechanism, he devised a medical insurance scheme inexpensive enough for the villagers to afford yet sufficient to cover at least part of the recurrent costs of the medical services offered. Realizing, too, that local involvement was necessary in order not only for this particular scheme to succeed but also for the people to begin to enjoy some of the fruits of broader developmental processes, he engaged some thirty-five committed auxiliary health workers to interact intensively with the villagers. Their main task was not only to intervene in cases where curative medical treatment was required but also to convey to the people information and guidance on

---

[3] Ivan Illich, *Deschooling Society* (New York: Harper & Row, Publishers, 1971).
[4] Ivan Illich, *Medical Nemesis* (New York: Pantheon Books, Inc., 1976).

preventive medicine—for example, the need for sanitary drinking water and food handling and for optimizing the nutritional value of their diets—as well as on family planning.[5] Because gastrointestinal maladies accounted for a major share of the illnesses in that area, the need for scarce capital-intensive hospital facilities could be reduced by following such labor-intensive paramedical practices in the villages themselves. Indeed, the doctor's initial mistake, as he himself observed in a candid moment, was to allow his own ego, and that of the foreign voluntary agency supporting him, to permit the construction of a relatively large central hospital building, the grand design of which was in obvious contrast to the simpler local setting and overall approach. As the building was going up, he observed for a time a decreasing sense of motivation among his staff members to mingle with the poor; in the early months they had been enthused by the challenge of their rural development role, but they then became increasingly spoiled, he felt, by the rich impression created by the new hospital building.

This situation and others similar to it indicate that, although poor working conditions can also discourage staff and lower morale, one of the key problems of overfinanced infrastructure is that its ostentatious image (not to mention its subsequent maintenance costs) may conflict directly with the values one wants to encourage—or that are otherwise more realistic—in very poor settings.

Education. In the case of schools, one does not have to be as radical as Ivan Illich, who advocates a deschooling of society, to express mixed feelings about the result of school-building programs undertaken by a number of large private and voluntary organizations. The common development doctrine has always been that education, and especially literacy, is critical to development because it enables people to gain access to knowledge through the printed word—knowledge on improving their farming practices, their sanitation and nutrition, and thus their health and their lives as a whole. Because education is assumed to be transmitted through schools, schools must therefore be built. The logic is irresistible, and some voluntary organizations have contributed in a major way, in significant part through a "self-help" strategy, to the goal of more schools, more teachers, more pupils, and ultimately more graduates. Much of this help has been constructive, since, for right or for wrong, diplomas are passports to jobs and to enhanced opportunities in the future.

Yet as anyone who has lived in the Third World (indeed, in the First World) can testify, the learning that goes on in schools is frequently irrelevant to the current or prospective daily lives of the pupils. In some cultures,

---

[5]This particular project, the *Gonoshasthya Kendro* [People's Health Center] in Savar, Bangladesh, has subsequently broadened its program to one of more nearly integrated rural development. For a valuable and balanced case study, see Manzoor Ahmed, "The Savar Project: Meeting the Rural Health Crisis in Bangladesh," mimeographed (Essex, Conn.: International Council for Educational Development, 1977).

for this and other reasons, girls are actively discouraged from attending schools in the first place; given women's special roles as home managers, food preparers, and child raisers, their absence from school has far-reaching implications for future generations as well as for the present one. In other settings, the dropout rates are high for both girls and boys. In some countries, simultaneously, one of the key development problems is that of "overeducated" and unemployed—indeed unemployable—youth. This fact is illustrated most sharply in Sri Lanka, a nation which has an astonishingly high literacy rate of 76 per cent and which is thus one of the best educated Third World countries. In 1971, large numbers of frustrated, unemployed, rural Sri Lankan youth staged a rebellion against the government. Their problem, in part, was that their schooling had educated them out of their village cultures but was not good enough to qualify them for the scarce urban jobs to which they aspired.

In measuring, therefore, the cost-benefit ratios of school construction programs, one must consider far more than the number of pupils enrolled; one must consider—imponderable as this may be—the overall socio-economic composition of the students, the educational content offered to them, and the larger societal effects of varying educational investment policies. The point here is not to criticize only the voluntary agencies engaged in school construction, for the problem is a far broader one extending to the entire worldwide aid establishment and to the Third World governments themselves, whose policymakers have been trained in the Western classical education mold. Solutions are difficult. Rather, the point is to suggest increased emphasis on thoroughgoing reforms in the education system on the one hand, and, on the other hand, on experiments now under way in many parts of the world in what is called "nonformal education." These latter efforts are conducted today too much at the fringe of the system, accounting for only a miniscule percentage of the funds expended, while the traditional system, with some occasional job-oriented tinkering at best, continues on its inexorable way to distort whole societies, economies, and values. The problem is that because a societal value has been placed on a traditional product—the type of classical education that has Indian untouchables struggling through *David Copperfield* to learn English (to cite one example)—few are willing to risk trying any alternative approach to get ahead in the world. What is needed instead is a fundamentally new approach to learning, one that may be better conducted in the fields, community centers, and homes of the Third World than in the traditional four-walled classrooms. In the absence of such a new approach, social change is unlikely.

Agriculture. Because there are only a few voluntary organizations that have sufficient resources to build many schools, hospitals, feeder roads, bridges, or irrigation facilities, their major contributions to physical and income-generating infrastructure tend to be in the area of small- to medium-scale agricultural development. The classic example is the introduction of what has become popularly—and misleadingly—known as the Green Revolution. In the 1960s, new high-yielding varieties of wheat and rice were introduced that have the potential for multiplying crop yields but that require intermediaries to bridge the gap between the originators and the millions of potential poor farmer users of the technology. Because the new seed varieties require more fertilizer and more careful regulation of other inputs, especially water, they have been criticized for being more helpful to rich farmers than to poor farmers because the latter are less able to afford these inputs; also, poor farmers tend to lack both the knowledge base required to utilize the new technology and the risk-taking capability to try it out.[6]

On the other hand, however, many observers feel that the poor, with their small plots, can profit more from Green Revolution technology than can the rich, with their large plots, because of the former's increased proclivities for the more intensive cultivation required by higher-yielding varieties. It is here, in fact, that the voluntary organizations have made particular contributions in spanning the information, technology, and input gaps to the otherwise ignored poor farmers. International Voluntary Services and the Mennonite Central Committee with their agricultural technicians; Oxfam-America through its small but strategic grants of seeds and well equipment, and its institutional support; and World Neighbors and a whole host of church and secular organizations assist in promoting the new technologies. They assist in the production not only of wheat and rice, but also of soybeans, vegetables, and other nutritious dietary supplements previously either unknown in particular settings or infeasible until faster-growing wheat and rice varieties permitted multiple cropping patterns and thus more efficient use of land. World Neighbors, for example, reported in 1970 that in one cooperative project with a Gandhian group in South India, "the output of vegetable foods . . . gave an increase of 6,050,000 pounds or an average per capita *increased* availability of vegetable foods of 60.5 pounds. There was also an increase of 650 grams per person in animal foodstuff, largely from eggs and poultry."[7] For every dollar invested by World Neighbors, this amounted to an annual food value of $43 for local consumption.

If incentives were ever needed to expand efforts in agricultural infrastructure, the widespread droughts of the mid-1960s in India and of the 1970s in all of South Asia and Sahelian Africa served to furnish them. Although there have been cycles of fat and lean years throughout history, only in these recent periods did it somehow "register" that the vulnerability of whole populations to climatic shifts could be eased by invoking the new

---

[6]See E.G. Vallianatos, *Fear in the Countryside: The Control of Agricultural Resources in the Poor Countries by Non-Peasant Elites* (Cambridge, Mass.: Ballinger Publishing Company, 1976).

[7]John L. Peters, *Cry Dignity* (Oklahoma City: World Neighbors, Inc., 1976), pp. 26–27.

technologies and the affluence of the West to deal with the root problems of food scarcity and poverty itself. This is not to suggest that irrigation and water storage efforts had not been undertaken during all the previous years; rather, the recent congruence of events lent added urgency and poignancy to the cause. It thus became a logical extension of relief feeding efforts to dig wells, construct water channels, contribute pumps, and train local people in the potential of agricultural advance. Church World Service, Lutheran World Relief, Catholic Relief Services, Africare, CARE, Community Development Foundation, their local counterpart organizations (particularly among the churches), and many others—including European and Canadian voluntary organizations—found themselves contributing.

The problem, again, is how to make sure that this assistance really helps the poor majorities in the Third World. Poor farmers lacking risk capital to attempt new cropping methods or livestock breeds will almost always be bypassed in the introduction of new technology. The geography of irrigation and drainage flows does not necessarily coincide with equity considerations in the sense that a dam needed to control the flow of water to both rich and poor farmers may have to be placed, for reasons of nature, in the rich farmer's field; this tends to give him control through easier access. Organizations attempting to introduce improved breeds of animals will naturally have more confidence in the most reliable farmers with a reputation for being able to care for them well; this is understandable since everyone loses if the animals fall into the hands of untrained farmers unable to ensure their survival and reproduction. Poor farmers have no proven track record. This is why Heifer Project schemes, for example, insist that the initial, better-off beneficiaries repay their original animal grants to poorer, higher-risk farmers by giving them the offspring as they are born. Otherwise the poor will be left still further behind.

Handicrafts and Light Industry. When sufficient productive land is lacking, as in many areas, some private and voluntary efforts encourage employment-generating small enterprises for handicrafts and light industries, as well as various commercial and service trades. In Kenya, the U.S. and European church-supported National Christian Council trains and sponsors handicraft artisans; their products find a ready outlet through the tourist trade. Partnership for Productivity is helping with the managerial training required in introducing people to small business ventures in western Kenya. In Honduras, Technoserve has assisted in the establishment of carpentry shops in which the country's timber-growing advantages are exploited to make wooden caskets for export. The Community Development Foundation assisted a group of Honduran women in purchasing a corn-grinding mill to enable increases in their production of biscuits. And in Bangladesh, the Christian Organization for Relief and Rehabilitation, the Mennonite Central Committee, and Oxfam cooperated to establish the Jute Works, an organization committed to enabling women—initially widows of the Bangladesh liberation war—to achieve self-sufficiency through the fabrication of jute handicrafts; by 1976 the Jute Works had an annual turnover of $500,000.[8]

While all these physical and income-generating efforts may help to some extent, the testimony of both voluntary agency people and other observers suggests that while needy people *do* benefit from the efforts of the private and voluntary organizations, it is not always the poorest who benefit. Indeed, some say that the only way to help the very poorest is through welfare rather than through development programs. They say this on the assumption that development presumes total participation, including the commitment of one's own resources in an uplift process, and they question how people without financial resources or basic knowledge can have anything to commit to their self-generating improvement. The problem, in short, is that of the familiar vicious circle where poverty breeds poverty unless aggressive intervention points are found and exploited. What is needed is a combination of appropriate education, new societal incentive systems, new institutional structures to provide equality of access to such basic economic goods as land and credit, and a new definition of the very concept of resource commitment whereby investments of labor and risk are assessed on a par with investments of cash. In the absence of this kind of approach, the efforts of private and voluntary organizations are more likely to constitute mere palliatives rather than provide a basis for larger structural change enhancing the prospects for equitable development for all groups of people.

Development of Institutions

Less tangible than physical infrastructure, but at least as important to development, is the institutional context of planning, decision-making, and implementation of change-oriented policies. Irrigation channels are not generally dug as a result of unique and sudden inspiration but rather through some process of needs assessment, solution formulation, and then action. Needs and solutions, of course, are assessed and formulated at a variety of levels, whether within an individual family framework, a village council structure, or a district, state, or national government hierarchy. With increasing Western influence, modernization, and "development," decisions traditionally made at lower levels have tended to be made at higher levels. People's—especially poor people's—access to centers of influence has simultaneously diminished. This process began in much of the Third World with colonial rule and continued when national elites, well-schooled in Western colonial bureaucratic principles, took over with independence.

---

[8]Although some Dacca observers felt this was the most effective voluntary agency effort in Bangladesh in really helping the very poorest of the poor, a sad epilogue to the case is that macroeconomic considerations intruded subsequently. When the first handicrafts landed in New York, U.S. Customs clamped a 20 per cent import duty on the widows' handiwork. However, efforts have since been made to obtain duty exemption under the generalized scheme of preferences.

Centralized bureaucracies, in fact, constitute one of the most entrenched Western legacies in the Third World, a legacy that served well the needs of colonial masters and their elitist successors, but less well the needs of development emphasizing local initiative and participation by the poor.

U.S. private and voluntary organizations—along with the international aid establishment generally—have been active at several levels in both building and opening up institutions to give the poor greater access to resources. The foundations and university groups frequently help at the higher, or "apex levels" of the government or the private sector, and the smaller voluntary organizations tend to help closer to the grass-roots level.

Planning Institutions. A major "apex level" activity of the foundations and universities has been the assistance given to national planning commissions in a number of Third World countries, notably in Asia. For newly independent nations with a dearth of both material and managerial resources, the need for careful planning and allocation of those limited resources is crucial. Colonial administrations, more concerned with political control and commerce than with improved livelihoods and development for the countries' poor majorities, were not organized for this kind of planning. Thus, for example, the Ford Foundation financed advisory teams from Harvard University to help Indonesia and Pakistan, while other American universities, particularly the land-grant institutions, became involved in these countries at different levels of national agricultural, educational, and management planning under either foundation or U.S. government funding. While generalizations are usually risky, it can safely be said that these efforts succeeded in their goals of institution building to the extent that 1) they were able to recruit competent and culturally sensitive American or European advisors, and 2) the setting afforded minimal local political and bureaucratic impediments.

Still, events often take unexpected turns, and the Indonesian and Pakistani cases are instructive on this point. In Indonesia, highly intensive foundation-funded and university-conducted efforts to train entire economics faculties failed in a sense when the Sukarno regime was overthrown in 1966-67 and replaced by General Suharto's more technocratically oriented government. With economic revival an immediate priority, the U.S.-assisted economics faculties were quickly depleted of their best talent as Suharto drafted the U.S.-trained economists to high government-planning posts. While the universities suffered, however, Indonesia's national economy improved dramatically under the tutelage of these economists. Less happily, corruption also increased, and because equity was sacrificed for growth, Indonesia's poor suffered at least as much as before.

In Pakistan, the Ford Foundation funded high-level and competent U.S. academic assistance to the government's planning group. Political and bureaucratic priority was attached to many of the group's recommendations, and the country's gross national product rose encouragingly. Yet there, too, events took an unforeseen and unhappy course. First, in 1969, the Ayub government toppled due to discontent over the unevenness of economic and political progress, and then in 1971 Bangladesh went its separate way, in large part because it had been an especially neglected (if not exploited) region. The Harvard advisory team, though perhaps more concerned than the Pakistani government with equity considerations, was charged in its planning with a lack of sufficient sensitivity to either Bengali or poverty-group needs; and the Ford Foundation was jolted into undertaking in 1969 an introspective postmortem of its role in assisting those planning efforts.

While the evidence from Indonesia and Pakistan is clearly an insufficient basis for a broad generalization, it would seem that equity is ultimately good politics. And any foreign organization, particularly one engaged in institution building as opposed to physical construction, risks seeing its aid prosper or suffer according to local political pressures and events.

Research Institutions. If policymaking is partially based on political judgments and realities, it must also draw on knowledge derived from research. U.S. private assistance groups have made major contributions here too. They have supported academic institutions and field-oriented institutions on the principle that Third World decision making should be based, at least in the long run, on Third World research.

Agriculture is a good case in point. While voluntary organizations have been instrumental in spreading Green Revolution technology among the poor farmers, the foundations—principally Rockefeller and Ford—are responsible for establishing and funding the centralized research institutes that developed the new technology initially. In fact, there are now nearly a dozen such institutes linked together for support through the Consultative Group on International Agricultural Research, which operates under the auspices of the World Bank, Food and Agriculture Organization, and U.N. Development Programme and deals with crops such as wheat, rice, various tropical agricultural products, coarse grains (millet and sorghum, for example), and potatoes. If one adds in the various institutes' country-level affiliates in a number of Third World nations and considers the amount of new food production resulting from the new technology, the network has proven to be an immensely significant one that represents perhaps the greatest single contribution of the private nonprofit sector to world agricultural development.

Broad-Based Community Development Institutions. Community development theorists and practitioners have long held that broad-based participation on the part of all segments of a local community is necessary if equitable development is to occur. One form of institution building in the Third World that is directed to these goals is represented by U.S. cooperatives. The zeal that has gone into spreading cooperative structures for housing, rural electrification, small enterprises, credit unions, and so on often appears at least as intense as the zeal that infuses religious missionaries. Because cooperatives have been successful and influential forms of social and economic organization in parts of Europe and the United States—the

Cooperative League of the USA (CLUSA) states that 50 million Americans belong to cooperatives broadly defined—they have considerable political support in the U.S. Congress and thus in U.S. AID, and are seen, like physical infrastructure, to be essential to development in the Third World. At times one has the impression that co-ops are seen more as an end in themselves than as a means toward the end of a self-sustaining process of development.[9] Indeed, co-ops have succeeded in a number of Third World settings, particularly in parts of Latin America where the bulk of U.S. attention has been focused and, perhaps more importantly, where the levels of education and development are relatively higher, enabling more informed membership participation and shared responsibilities. Some other societies, particularly in their more traditional and rural sectors, are culturally less receptive to the U.S. style of cooperatives. An example is India, where industrial-level cooperatives—most notably a CLUSA-assisted fertilizer complex in Gujarat State—have succeeded, while primary-level agricultural co-ops (with a few major exceptions) have not worked well at all. The failure of the latter may be largely due to the social inequities of the caste system and the ability of politicians and other elites to exploit those differences for personal or party gain. Village-level co-ops, not surprisingly, work best where social and cultural homogeneity is greatest. The fact that inequity rather than homogeneity is characteristic of most Third World societies makes the co-ops, like other forms of organization, susceptible to manipulation of the poor and impotent by the rich and empowered.

There is considerable controversy over the extent to which cooperatives, by their very philosophy and methodology, can by definition be capable of responding to the levels of poverty that are typical of the Third World. In order to join a co-op, one must pool some portion of one's wealth to subsidize the organization and its activities. The poorest are usually not in a position to do this. Some co-op leaders argue that the capacity to work or to contribute work units should serve as sufficient contribution for these people, and indeed there are random examples of this being done. Experience suggests, however, that these types of cooperatives are not common. In fact, sometimes the co-ops hire laborers from among the poorest groups, with the result that the co-ops—however well-meaning their employment-generating rationalizations—perpetuate income gaps rather than narrow them.

Among the most interesting models for promoting development is that of some of the Latin American credit unions. Because the credit gap is one of the major constraints to development in a number of Latin American settings, a variety of outside assistance agencies, both governmental and private, have attempted to help in that area. Yet worldwide experience has

---

[9]On this point, see Judith Tendler, "Inter-Country Evaluation of Small Farmer Organizations—Ecuador, Honduras," Office of Development Programs, Latin America Bureau (Washington, D.C.: Agency for International Development, 1976), pp. 8 and 10.

shown that credit in the absence of necessary technical assistance and overall supervision is either insufficient or, where it profits the wrong people, counterproductive. Thus both the U.S. Credit Union National Association and the Pan American Development Foundation have assisted in the formation of associations throughout the continent that dispense not only credit but also technical and supervisory support to local cooperatives and other groups. As a result, no doubt, of this inherently more integrated approach, their loan repayment rates are very high, in sharp contrast to the repayment rates of governmental and other lending institutions offering fewer support functions. In Honduras, for example, the private co-op repayment rate was about 88 to 90 per cent in 1975, and the government co-op rate was about 65 per cent.[10] The Honduras case is illustrative in another sense in that at least one major private credit organization has been a member of a larger institutional grouping called CONCORDE, the other members of which are engaged in education (including the influential radio schools), technical assistance, and various types of community development activity. Through the cooperative programming that is thus possible, the impact of the credit—as of other individual component inputs—is magnified.[11]

Another attempt to institutionalize participatory development at local levels is reflected in the methodology of the Community Development Foundation (CDF), also known (mainly for fund-raising purposes) as the Save the Children Federation. CDF insists that the inputs it provides and the activities it supports must be governed by a committee on which all local groups are represented—rich and poor, powerful and powerless, men and women, and whatever variety of castes and religious groups may be present in the particular area. Theoretically, this could have a significant impact in many situations, for traditional societies are not usually known either for their democratic "one person, one vote" modes of governance or for representation of all groups in the governing process. In practice, therefore, such efforts are fraught with difficulties. For example, it is not clear that if an issue arises in which the committee and CDF representatives have differing views, the committee will always prevail; nor is it clear that broad-based decision making would be applied more generally to non-CDF funded activities that would continue into the future. The point is that local traditions and patterns of organization tend to be strong and that transitory outside projectizing, no matter how well funded, is usually unable to force permanent change of this basic nature.

A further example of efforts to institutionalize increased broad-based participation can be seen in the growing number of programs currently being

---

[10] Information provided by the Instituto de Formacion e Investigacion Cooperativa, Tegucigalpa, Honduras.

[11] See Kathy Desmond, "Three Examples of Self-Reliant Community Action in Latin America," mimeographed (Washington, D.C.: Overseas Development Council, 1976).

promoted by some private and voluntary organizations, including CDF, to enhance women's roles in development.[12] Development planners have not always taken this new concern seriously, considering it to be an export of a Western movement that has little application to traditional societies. Yet the women's movement has its own manifestations in the Third World, and increasingly, groups of Third World women are exerting pressure on their own governments to respond to their needs and action priorities.

Moreover, there are valid reasons why Western assistance programs should reassess their impact on women in the Third World. Past Western development efforts frequently have had negative effects on women which must now be corrected. There have been errors of omission, by failing to utilize or recognize the roles that women have played and are today playing in these societies. It is estimated that, due to migration, abandonment, or polygamy, one out of every three households in developing countries is headed by a woman.[13] Furthermore, in many Third World countries women have been the principal food producers. There have also been errors of addition, by superimposing Western values of what is appropriate women's work onto other societies, and errors of reinforcement, whereby outside assistance has supported those values existing in Third World societies that restrict women's activities to household, childbearing, and child-rearing tasks.[14]

Yet both voluntary organizations and other aid-giving agencies—operating on Western assumptions about male and female roles—have frequently overlooked these factors and have thus excluded women from programs of training and technical assistance (including training in the use of farm and other machinery). In some cases the training has been wasted, for example, where agricultural extension workers call only on men when in fact it is women who perform a major part of the agricultural labor.

> [Women] comprise a large part of the agricultural labor force in many developing countries. In parts of Asia, for example, women often do most of the rice planting and also help with the harvesting. In many parts of Africa women do as much farming as men and sometimes more. In some areas, family-subsistence crops are customarily grown in the "women's fields" and cash crops in the "men's fields." Women often handle the marketing of crops, keep records and exercise important farm management functions. It follows, therefore, that the educational needs of girls and women for knowledge of improved

---

[12] See Subcommittee on Women in Development/Committee on Development Assistance, *Criteria for Evaluation of Development Projects Involving Women* (New York: Technical Assistance Information Clearing House of the American Council of Voluntary Agencies for Foreign Service, Inc., 1975); and Christine Fry, "Private Voluntary Organizations and Women," mimeographed (Washington, D.C.: Overseas Development Council, 1976).

[13] Judith Bruce, "Women and Basic Needs," mimeographed (1976).

[14] See Irene Tinker and Michèle Bo Bramsen, eds., *Women and World Development* (Washington, D.C.: Overseas Development Council, 1976), p. 5.

agricultural practices may often be at least as great as the needs of boys and men. So-called women's programs are typically on a token scale and are designed with the implicit assumption that the place of rural women is solely in the home.[15]

The overall result is that in increasingly monetized economies, the gap in both skills and income between men and women has widened, and often women have been ignored in the planning and institution-building process. Thus there is now a concern, through activities such as the Bangladesh Jute Works and the Honduras corn-grinding mill cited above, to explicitly address women's special needs in the development process. Also required are efforts to take women's potential contributions into account in integrated community development programs aimed at men and women alike.

Churches. Among the major institution builders overseas are the churches. Indeed, they were the original institution builders, responsible for establishing the schools and colleges that trained many of today's most prominent Third World leaders. Now the major Catholic and Protestant denominations are increasingly channeling their support to the Third World through their local sister institutions, partly in recognition of the substantive desirability and long-term efficiency of such an effort, and partly in view of the political sensitivities toward outside religious groups on the part of many Third World governments. Thus Catholic Relief Services, like the worldwide Catholic hierarchy, has given priority to building up the capabilities of the Caritas or other local Catholic assistance organizations in countries where CRS works; and Church World Service, like the World Council of Churches network as a whole, has assisted the various national Christian councils of Asian, African, and Latin American countries. CWS, at the same time, has moved increasingly from an emphasis on programs to an emphasis on the quality of interpersonal and interinstitutional relationships, simultaneously increasing the size of its own international (as opposed to U.S.) staff and of its multilateral approaches. Much the same has been true of the smaller Quaker and Mennonite bodies.

In stressing this kind of institutional development, while also aspiring to promote development in the poor villages and slums of the Third World countries, the churches are essentially doubling the complexity of their task. In many countries, the churches were originally a key force in the extension of Western dominance that accompanied colonialism; church leaders were favored by the colonial powers and achieved their elite status as a result of colonial rule. Today church leaders find themselves in a highly ambiguous position. With the growth of nationalism, they are on the one hand forced to confront the tainted aspects of this past and on the other hand are invited to share in the fruits of national independence, enjoying increased power as nationals of their own countries. At the same time, their traditional elite

---

[15]Philip Coombs and Manzoor Ahmed, *Attacking Rural Poverty: How Nonformal Education Can Help* (Baltimore: Johns Hopkins University Press, 1974), p. 20.

status often gives them difficulty in understanding and communicating on a basis of relative equality with their poorer countrymen even as that status hangs in an uneasy balance with respect to the new groups of postindependence elites. In short, many Third World church leaders are redefining their identities. This multi-directional orientation affects the nature and intensity of their commitment to some of the goals espoused by their U.S. and European church funders—the equity goal being a prime example.

A further problem is that of trained and committed second-level manpower. If it is true that voluntary agencies are largely creations of entrenched middle-class societies, then, by virtue of history, many Third World societies are too new, too poor, and too lacking in a broad-based middle-class constituency from which to recruit very many capable people committed to voluntary action for equality of opportunity.[16] This manpower gap places limitations on the ability of U.S. and European churches (and of other groups, too) to promote institutional development among their Third World counterparts.

Besides all this, the varying range of domestic constituencies which the umbrella church groups must attempt to represent poses a problem. For those familiar with the stresses and strains in the U.S. Catholic and ecumenical Protestant hierarchies, it will come as no surprise to realize that an analogous situation exists in Third World settings. Finally, there is a psychological problem that exists in any donor-donee relationship. Third World churches, having been founded and nurtured by their parent bodies in Europe and North America, are naturally anxious to spread their wings and enjoy their freedom; to this extent, the demand for independence may demonstrate the very effectiveness of the nurturing role. On the other hand, if, out of their freedom, they use outside church assistance for purposes that are potentially counterproductive to development for the poorest people of the society, they are hardly reflecting a desirable institution-building process.

In the preceding pages, examples of some of the major institution-building modes have been described. But there are also dozens more that could be cited: the various Third World national volunteer corps for student and youth involvement, which were given a significant impetus by the U.S. Peace Corps; the Peace Corps itself, which was substantially modeled after the volunteer-sending programs of the International Voluntary Services and the American Friends Service Committee; the YMCA and YWCA movements, which involve young people in group activities, sports, and training programs; the 4-H Clubs for rural youth leadership development; the Salvation Army; the Red Cross, which began in Europe in the nineteenth century and soon became an important international movement, institution-

---

[16]The U.S. Peace Corps has faced a similar problem in the United States in recruiting members of minority and disadvantaged groups. See *The Peace Corps: Perspectives for the Future*, Report of the Ad Hoc Committee on Development Assistance Opportunities in the Next Decade for the Peace Corps (Washington, D.C.: National Academy of Sciences, 1974), p. 22.

alized in the form of national organizations in nearly every country of the world; the Boy Scouts and Girl Scouts, which began in the United Kingdom with Lord Baden Powell and which, with both colonial European and U.S. encouragement, extended throughout the Third World; a variety of U.S. and European child adoption and other welfare agencies; and CARE and Catholic Relief Services (cited earlier), which played both initiating and exemplary roles in the institutionalization of social welfare functions both in governments and in the voluntary sectors of Third World countries.

Notwithstanding the widespread existence of some kind of welfare mechanism in most traditional societies, U.S. and European private and voluntary organizations have probably done at least as much to encourage appropriate adaptations of such institutions for current realities as they have contributed to other forms of development infrastructure. The institutions they have supported have sometimes had only palliative effects but other times have contributed to broader changes in favor of greater equality of opportunity for the poor. The analytical problem is that the positive and negative results of institution building—particularly insofar as they abet access and equality of opportunity for the poor—are far harder to assess than those of physical infrastructure. Still harder to assess are the results of human resource development, as will become quickly evident in the pages that follow.

Development of Human Resources

People are both the subject and the object of development, a point which sounds obvious but which has tremendous implications for developmental activities. Generally speaking, people have been considered more the *object* of development. Raise children's nutritional levels, and their enhanced mental capacities should enable them to contribute ultimately to national GNP. Dig wells and build roads, and people can use them for improving agricultural production and marketing and thus for increasing their incomes. Create institutional infrastructure for better policymaking and improved technology, and scarce resources will be more effectively allocated to increase physical facilities, social services, and thus standards of living. While there are always variations of degree and shading, these types of activities tend to aim at doing something *for* people. Even self-help programs have tended to be seen primarily as a better methodology for aid that leads to creation of infrastructure—in the sense of motivating recipients for continuing the required maintenance—while lesser priority has been directed toward the inherent values attached to the act of participation itself. While these values may not be critical at the minimum physical human needs level, they are critical at another important level of need—that of dignity.

While virtually any developmental activity somehow affects human resources, those that place primary emphasis on their improvement are considered here. The gamut is broad, ranging from social welfare and child adoption schemes at one extreme to consciousness raising leading to the possibility of more radical change at the other. In between lie people-to-people volunteer efforts, scholarship programs, skill-training efforts, "technical assistance," and, of course, the religious efforts of the missionaries.

Social Welfare. The most straightforward way to affect the level of human resources is through direct gifts and provision of services to poor people. The child sponsorship agencies, such as Christian Children's Fund and Foster Parents Plan, are typical here in that they raise money from U.S. "foster parents" and convey it (after covering administrative expenses) to a particular child in the Third World. The voluntary organization is thus providing a brokerage service between two individuals who then exchange letters periodically to enliven this mutual involvement. Partly because the notion of pure handouts and their implied paternalism have come under increasing attack both in the West and in the Third World, the child sponsorship agencies are increasingly applying portions of the donor gifts to service programs benefiting not only the child but the larger family and community as well. Foster Parents Plan in Colombia, for example, divides the $16 contributed monthly by each parent by giving $5 directly to the child, applying $6 to community services such as education and health, and leaving approximately $5 for administrative expenses. In this way the organization is better able to ensure that at least some of the funds are utilized for the general well-being of the child and family, perhaps in ways that improve their long-term development outlooks. On the other hand, the child sponsorship agencies still justify their direct handouts—the monthly grants plus special holiday gifts frequently sent by the foster parents—as increasing the participation of recipient families in their own development. Indeed, they argue, it is in some ways *better* to give cash, for it can be spent according to the families' own priorities rather than in accordance with some cultural arrogance which decides from outside what is best for them.[17] Economists might add that however frivolously the poor spend their money, the leakage effect that multiplies local economic activity should also work to the advantage of the poor. Yet a certain degree of societal paternalism can be justified to the extent of exercising an enlightened channeling of assistance toward such essentials as nutrition, health care, and education. Indeed, welfare experience in many settings has demonstrated the purely short-term value, largely palliative effects, and thus the wastefulness of indiscriminant handouts.[18]

Another example of the social welfare approach to human resource development is that of the Salvation Army and the variety of schools, daycare centers, and programs for the aged and handicapped conducted by them and by a number of other religious groups. In Kenya, for example, the

---

[17] See Melvin Burke, *A Socio-Economic Study of the Foster Parents Plan Program in Bolivia* (Orono, Maine: University of Maine, 1973).

[18] A.H. Okun, *Equality and Efficiency: The Big Tradeoff* (Washington, D.C.: Brookings Institution, 1975), p. 112.

Salvation Army has established literacy and homemaking centers for teenaged girls, training in farming and bee-keeping, and vocational workshops in schools for the crippled and blind (the Salvation Army being the first in Kenya to assist in the latter area). Many other religious and non-religious groups have assisted in similar efforts in some of the most remote parts of the world. Of course, some observers would say that these are not developmental activities, because most are dependent on continuing foreign funding, generally on the foreigners' terms. At a different level, however, these activities are encouraging the development of a generation of people who could, in turn, affect general community advancement in the long run. This suggests, therefore, that one should judge the developmental effects of such efforts as much by their impact on *people* as by their impact on *institutions,* as long as dependencies on unsustainable outside funding sources are avoided.

The hallmark of the private and voluntary organizations has been their ability to concentrate on the more human aspects of development. Founded on the notion of people-to-people assistance—for it is this element that primarily distinguishes their efforts from governmental ones—their typically small size, humanitarian motivations, and overall ethos combine to reinforce the personal approach. If a reaction to the too-fuzzy humanity of the past has begun to lead some organizations to more technocratic and bureaucratized approaches today, such organizations still tend to have advantages over large bilateral and multilateral efforts.

Training and Technical Assistance. One of the most useful contributions of private organizations has been the provision of fellowships for study abroad, enabling thousands of Third World nationals to learn the skills necessary for managing modern economies and technologies. The endowed foundations have been particularly active in this arena, not only in funding students but also in sponsoring joint research efforts, conferences, and other forums where Third World people can come together with each other and with their peers from the West. Of course, not all aspects of this coming together are positive for development as defined here; many people have criticized the Western exportation of the jet-set scholar phenomenon. In an interdependent world, however, sharing must be presumed better than not sharing, the vital point being the need to ensure equitable sharing of opportunities for knowledge *within* societies as well as across national boundaries. While private scholarship programs are not by definition superior to governmental programs, experience suggests, even in the absence of hard data, that the more personalized attention possible in smaller-scale programs permits people to be selected more carefully for training and then to be assisted with greater substantive support during and after the training period.

On the other side of the coin, training in the West has increasingly come under fire for tending to alienate the trainees from the realities of their own less affluent situations when they return. Scientists, for example, become accustomed to more advanced laboratory conditions and are then reluctant to return to the rudimentary labs of their own countries. An Indian ambassador once described the emigration of scientists to the United States as "technical assistance in reverse."[19] For example, there are now many thousands of Indian doctors practicing in the United States, when the vital need for their services at home is well known. Furthermore, the investment in early education lost to Third World countries when their citizens choose to stay abroad is sizable. The brain-drain problem is of course a complicated one in the sense that it is the poverty syndrome itself that makes it difficult for Third World countries to create the satisfactory conditions that their highly trained—or overtrained—professionals demand. The problem is not only a financial one; it also reflects the broader context of overall working conditions and the need for social satisfaction and a feeling of accomplishing something for a larger, progressing community and nation. While various counter-brain-drain devices have been tried, the solution to the problem is frustratingly the same as that for the vicious circle of development as a whole: amelioration will come only when other indicators of development improve as well.

Not only because of the brain-drain problem but also because much of the overseas training has proven less than relevant to location-specific Third World needs, private assistance efforts are increasingly focusing on training conducted either within the individual country itself, or at least in analogous Third World settings. The Ford Foundation, for example, has moved very substantially in the direction of funding Asians to study in Asia, Latin Americans in Latin America, and so on. This permits grappling with local problems in "field" situations and with peers who have had experience in solving them. In a period of tighter funding for such programs, it also means that each dollar spent will go farther, given the lower transportation and living costs involved. The transition is not an easy one; Sri Lankans accustomed to the glamour of a British university experience find that studying in neighboring Indian institutions provides a less prestigious credential upon their return home. Some, of course, see the logic, especially as certain Third World institutions have gained sufficiently in competence and prestige to serve as regional resources. An extension of this trend is for short-term training to be conducted by Western technical specialists in the particular Third World country itself. While numerous trade-offs are involved in deciding whether to provide training by exporting students or by importing experts, increasingly the preference is for local training, which can have a broader impact by exposing more people to foreign specialists while at the same time ensuring relevance to a specific Third World country's conditions.

---

[19]T.N. Kaul, quoted in "Kaul Dubs Immigration 'Reverse Aid' to U.S.," *India Abroad* (October 8, 1976).

"Technical assistance" is the term that has been used over the past years virtually interchangeably with "development assistance" on the assumption that technology was the primary requirement for economic advancement. Technical assistance, in fact, is perhaps the most common rubric for voluntary agency efforts (and also for organizations like the Peace Corps). It describes much of the rationale behind several volunteer-sending organizations: International Voluntary Services and the Mennonite Central Committee, with their agriculture and public health specialists; some of the cooperative organizations, with their specialists in credit and co-op management; some of the member organizations of PACT, with their small enterprise backgrounds; and VITA, which serves as a source of information on increasingly popular appropriate technologies for Third World development organizations.[20] The point of technical assistance, of course, is to transfer improved techniques of agriculture, public health, education, nutrition, and management to people in the Third World. In recent years, increasing attention has been given to structuring these transfers to increase the certainty that those trained—usually recipient-country "counterparts"—will fill critical roles in their countries' development efforts, thus multiplying the initial contribution of the foreign volunteer. While this has happened to an impressive extent in many places, the fact remains that because technical assistance is not being transferred in a vacuum, political, administrative, and larger economic imperatives still play the largest roles in affecting the fates of individual technical assistance efforts.

The more sensitive technical assistance organizations of course recognize these constraints on their activities. In isolated cases these same factors can even be turned to their advantage if, for example, a particularly successful project is seen at the right time by a policymaker in a position to spur its replication on a broader plane. It is here, in fact, that the person-to-person element of the approach is critical. Many of these programs, after all, see their goal to be not only that of spreading technology but also that of spreading an attitude toward development—especially the Western notion (to return to an earlier theme) that change is possible and that individuals can effect change to improve their livelihoods and those of others. Third World counterparts of U.S. volunteers, frequently caught in their larger bureaucratic webs, often remark upon the "can-do" attitude of the Americans who automatically assume there are solutions for problems and have the energy to find them. Unfortunately, while this attitude from abroad may produce extraordinary results in specific settings, it too often happens that after a foreigner's departure, the local attitudes revert again to those of the

---

[20]For a both extensive and intensive view of how voluntary organizations promote appropriate technology in the Third World, see the case studies prepared for the Lilly Endowment, Inc., Intermediate Technology Development Group Conference on the Effective Use of Appropriate Technologies, Indianapolis, Indiana, April 24-27, 1977.

bureaucratic web and the larger context that had stifled significant development in the first place. Unless the context itself can be made to adapt—unless structural change occurs and offers the poor equal access to resources—the effect of U.S. voluntary organizations is limited to one of mere palliatives.

Consciousness Raising. Contexts cannot be made to change unless they are first understood. What lies at the center of so many criticisms of voluntary organizations is the feeling that theirs are "bleeding heart" activities conducted by do-gooders—and thus by implication nonthinking people who are unaware of the future ramifications of their efforts, who have not taken a hard enough look at the intricacies of the development process, and who do not realize that acts of social service may perpetuate elite class dominance over the poor rather than provide the poor with the wherewithal to liberate themselves. Voluntary organizations are confronted with the old choice between providing palliatives within an unjust system or completely changing the unjust system.

It is here that the concept of consciousness raising, which finds its most articulate expression in the writings of the Brazilian educator, Paulo Freire, comes to the fore. Freire's experience with people in northeast Brazil led him to the not uncommon observation that people are exploited or otherwise fail to realize their full human potential because they are not aware of their situations, of the factors that cause them to be as they are, and of their potential options for self-improvement and self-actualization. Thus he advocates an educational method that would enable people to change such structures through a "critical consciousness raising" process that leads to "appropriate actions." Traditional forms of learning are of no use, after all, unless people can apply what is being taught to their daily lives and to ways of improving them. Traditional extension programs and other developmental activities may be similarly useless, even if they are focused on helping the poor, *if* the poor do not know how to internalize their meaning in order to take optimum advantage of them.[21] More commonly, as it happens, the poorest groups have been bypassed by development assistance—much less have they been allowed to shape and control it—because they have been largely voiceless, an inevitable cause and effect of their poverty syndrome.

Consciousness raising has found its most fertile response in Latin America because landholding and broader social patterns there have made the gap between rich and poor especially glaring. In many areas the gap is now widening further. In northeast Brazil, for example, government policies emphasizing GNP growth and export expansion have led to increasing amounts of land being devoted to large sugar plantations and cattle ranches, with the poor either being forced off the land altogether (in which case they generally swell the numbers of urban unemployed) or being forced into sharecropper roles or into paying higher prices for the use of land. Efforts at

---

[21] See Paulo Freire, "Extension or Communication," *Education for Critical Consciousness* (New York: Seabury Press, Inc., 1973).

consciousness raising would help these people understand what is happening to them and what is behind these changes, rather than blindly accepting them as fate. Because Freire insisted on a methodology that would not explicitly incite rebellion—after all, this would be tantamount to using poor people as fodder for someone else's revolution—his notion of consciousness raising calls for a subtle self-questioning process by which alternative courses of society and action can be explored. It is essential to his methodology that the search for solutions be initiated from within the group so that the group determines its own actions with all the dignity that such internalized responsibility implies. Indeed, it is this element that distinguishes the consciousness raising approach from the more traditional forms of community development in which many voluntary organizations have been involved over the years. Traditional community development too often aims at local participation, while in reality outsiders make decisions for subsequent local acquiescence. Similarly, outsiders frequently initiate self-help activities, often using a "carrot" of substantial outside aid. Ironically, in one instance involving a Latin American housing project that really *was* a self-help effort, a new term had to be coined: "unaided self-help."

Perhaps because the notion of consciousness raising is so difficult to "implement," one tends to find few pure examples of it in practice. Particularly for Americans, accustomed both to efficiency and to seeing direct results of their efforts, it is highly frustrating to be unable to insist on implementing what they "know" to be needed in a particular local community. It is difficult to be relegated to a subsidiary role, seemingly wasting time while waiting for the local group to decide to come together to discuss a situation, only to perhaps conclude by doing nothing, delaying weeks, months, or even years before making anything "happen." By definition, any outside support for such efforts must be subtle and sensitive. The perspectives of outsiders and local people, after all, are very different. The outsider, often impatient, sees needs and wants action to justify his or her own involvement and time, both to himself and to superiors and outside funders. Yet, the local group, which has existed in the given circumstances for generations, often has other full-time employment or commitments and almost certainly has none of the same pressures to act; if anything, such groups feel pressures in the opposite direction.

Yet studies have shown that only participatory and locally directed developmental action is successful and durable over the long run. The classic example cited in this connection is that of China. Mao Tse-tung described his philosophy of participatory action as follows:

> All work done for the masses must start from their needs and not from the desire of any individual, however well-intentioned. It often happens that objectively the masses need a certain change, but subjectively they are not yet conscious of the need, not yet willing or determined to make the change. In such cases, we should wait

patiently. We should not make the change until, through our work, most of the masses have become conscious of the need and are willing and determined to carry it out. Otherwise, we shall isolate ourselves from the masses. . . . There are two principles here: one is the actual needs of the masses rather than what we fancy they need, and the other is the wishes of the masses, who must make up their own minds, instead of our making up their minds for them.[22]

For these reasons, it may be that consciousness-raising activities cannot be conducted by traditional U.S. private and voluntary organizations. Where these activities do exist, it is largely local voluntary agencies—*funded,* perhaps, but not *led* by foreign groups—that are involved; or else it is the missionaries who live in given settings for their lifetimes, or at least for very long periods, with different types of standards applied to judging their effectiveness.

The consciousness-raising approach is now very much at the forefront of development strategies discussions, and practical applications are being attempted in Tanzania, Guinea-Bissau, Thailand, Bangladesh, and India, as well as in Latin America and no doubt in other places. While the theoretical virtues of the approach seem clear, its relatively recent application—as well as the difficulties inherent in its implementation—has meant a paucity of current evidence as to its effectiveness in actually enhancing the possibilities for improving people's lives. Part of the difficulty is that consciousness raising is subject to so many definitions. Like "development," the term is frequently appropriated by those wishing to sound in vogue but who are still practicing the same approaches they have always practiced. The term consciousness raising is frequently used, for example, to describe traditional education programs. This is not totally without reason, for education, no matter how irrelevant, presumably does make people aware of some things of which they were not earlier aware; yet education usually deals more with facts than with basic thought processes. At the other extreme, consciousness raising has also been used to describe direct political activity, which, again, it is not. While political action could be one of the logical outgrowths of self-analysis (if it were concluded that no other means would bring about improvements for the local community), other logical outgrowths—for example, decisions to dig wells—are equally likely. What *can* be said is that the consciousness-raising approach is *potentially* more threatening to many entrenched power wielders. This is hardly surprising unless one believes that equality of opportunity for all can never constitute a threat to anyone.

Many consciousness-raising efforts in Latin America—indeed, most nonunion, nonparty development activities of any kind—have been initiated by the Catholic church. This is hardly coincidental, given the strong influence of the church on the continent, its perceived sense of social

---

[22]"The United Front on Cultural Work," *Selected Works of Mao Tse-tung.*

mission—at least on the part of some of its component entities and members—and the relative lack (compared with a number of Asian and African countries) of governmental commitment to genuine social change. Because the church, by its very mission, is concerned not only with economic growth but with the development of the whole person, it is not surprising that the more spiritual approaches to development find favor there; consciousness raising, after all, is nothing more, nothing less, than an appeal to the moral and ethical spirit of the whole person. This concern for the more spiritual aspects of development lost importance during the 1950s and 1960s, when economic goals dominated development thinking and the missionary approach fell from favor among nationalistic Third World leaders and Western "pragmatists." While sectarian religious proselytizing is not particularly relevant to sound development and, as practiced in some cases, may even be antithetical to it, it is regrettable that the strengths of the missionary approach have been lost sight of in the rush for economic advancement. If religious proselytizing has conveyed undertones of paternalism, Western values, and ethnocentricity, so too has the concentration on economic growth fallen into disrepute for some of the same reasons.

A case in point is that of a U.S. medical missionary in Honduras who was criticized for providing assistance only to those who followed the teachings of his own particular sect. This form of restricted humanitarianism was understandably criticized by other voluntary agency representatives who felt it was callous in its parochialism. The missionary's reply to the criticism? There was no point, he said, in passing out help to everyone, because his experience had been that many recipients, however needy, failed to use the assistance responsibly. Many squandered their resources on drinking, and unless such people could be inspired to a path of development in a spiritual sense, there would be no hope. It was not so much a matter of whether the person followed the teachings of the particular sect, he explained, as of whether there was some relationship between the assistance and the whole person. Even if one discounts the possible element of rationalization in this argument, the need for an involvement of the larger consciousness is a significant one, one that is very related to the development of overall human resources.

Like most people engaged in development efforts, the missionaries often find themselves in highly problematic situations. An example is that faced by a Summer Institute of Linguistics group in eastern Ecuador at a time when foreign oil companies were prospecting for new supplies in extremely remote jungle areas populated by members of the xenophobic Auca Indian tribe. The SIL missionaries were the only outsiders who had contact with the Aucas. Believing it immoral not to give people choices about how to lead their lives—choices that could help them escape from bad health or from the spirit world—they were providing both educational opportunities and encouragement for the establishment of legalized Auca protection zones. Some argued that the missionary brand of education amounted to an intrusion of foreign values, and that "protection zones" would be as bad as the system of reservations to which American Indians were effectively confined. But the SIL members argued that this was a good way to help the Aucas actually strengthen their local culture in preparation for more equitably defending themselves against the inevitable new cultural and political interventions of the future. When the oil companies entered the scene, the SIL faced the question of whether to collaborate with them and help in pacifying the Indians for commercial purposes or whether to shun such a controversial role. The SIL's decision was to accept financial support from the oil companies and to collaborate with them "in order to save lives"; this decision was based on the assumption that if the oil explorers went in on their own, carrying guns as they certainly would for self-defense, many Aucas (as well as some explorers) would be killed. To pacify the Aucas, they devised a plan to air-drop baskets containing gifts and, most critically, radio transmitters; the Auca conversations thus transmitted would reveal the names of individual Aucas. It would then be possible for previously pacified members of the tribe to broadcast personal appeals from airborne loudspeakers urging Auca cooperation with the oil company personnel. Was the SIL decision in the best long-run interests of Auca development?

As in most real-world situations, there are no clear-cut guidelines as to what decisions and actions will best foster desirable development. Consciousness raising occurs in many ways and from many directions—by oil company personnel no less than by exploitative landlords, equity-oriented volunteers, or missionaries. Development itself is defined in many different ways. In beginning the discussion of the variety of goals and operating patterns found among private and voluntary organizations, it was noted that most of these groups would describe *development* as an objective to be pursued. But it was also noted that development is best defined as a never-ending process in which achieving basic physical needs is only the first step. It is, of course, the most obvious step, particularly for Americans appalled at the sight of poverty. By Western standards, attention to what appear as higher-level demands often seems inappropriate as long as the scourge of physical poverty remains. Yet in the Third World, one often hears of a willingness to remain in poverty rather than lose one's social values; it is clear that self-respect and dignity are important goals in the minds of Third World people. It is in fostering self-respect and dignity that the people-to-people programs have an impact, if for no other reason than that through such programs, those in the Third World may be taken seriously and respectfully by representatives of the so-called "superior Western races." The programs that concentrate explicitly on genuine personal interchange are appreciated—after initial skepticism—by most Third World people for just this reason. Indeed, the poorer the setting, the greater, perhaps, the satisfaction when an outsider shows interest in local cultural practices and in people for their inherent human qualities rather than for what they have or do not have.

Cultural awareness is an intrinsic part of consciousness raising in the sense that an image of one's individual and community identity is a necessary prelude to sound development. Private organizations such as the JDR III Fund, the Asia Foundation, the Ford Foundation, and Obor have recognized the importance of local cultural expression as a concomitant of development, each pursuing articulated needs in its own individual way. John D. Rockefeller's JDR III Fund was a pioneer in offering support for the cultural preservation and development of Asian arts. The Asia Foundation, which funds a variety of training activities, has been especially innovative in its support for training Buddhist monks in Thailand to become involved in local development activities in ways culturally relevant to the strongly Buddhist traditions of that country and its people. The Ford Foundation's overseas cultural involvement has been recent; although its support of archeological and arts activities constitutes only a small share of its overall budget, that support is significant in symbolizing the recognition that there is more to development than economic indicators alone. Obor, a small organization run on a shoestring budget, is dedicated to the publishing of books in the Indonesian language in order to encourage indigenous discussion of development topics that were earlier the exclusive province of the foreign-language-speaking elite.

Increasingly, Third World groups are themselves placing emphasis on development strategies that are more consistent with their own cultural values than with those of the West. In part, this is a result of their increasing self-confidence in the face of the spiritual malaise found in the Western countries; it is also due to the lack of success experienced with Western development models in the Third World. Just as black Americans have taken up the "black is beautiful" banner, many Asian, African, and Latin American groups are seeking a better understanding and appreciation of their own cultural roots as a prerequisite to defining their desired development directions. Some groups are engaged in studies and analyses of their local folklore. Others are more action oriented. In Sri Lanka, for example, thousands of adherents of the Sarvodaya Shramadana movement are seeking a spiritual reawakening of individuals, families, and communities to their full potential. Inspired by both Buddhist and Gandhian traditions, they place primary emphasis on attitudes and only secondary (though important) weight on economic and social development. Combining these two qualities, the movement has become a significant force in Sri Lanka, particularly in the rural areas. Within many countries of the Third World similar efforts are under way, including a large number of neo-Gandhian organizations spread throughout India, a variety of church-inspired groups in Latin America, and other types of groups throughout Asia and Africa.[23] They are frequently unknown beyond a small circle of people and are particularly unknown to

---

[23]See John Sommer, Pratima Kale, and Ranjit Gupta, eds., *Rural Development at the Grassroots—The Catalyst Role* (New Delhi: The Ford Foundation, 1974).

foreigners, but their very existence is significant. Just as de Tocqueville was impressed to find such a profusion of voluntary associations in America, so modern-day Americans are often surprised at the increasing—if still insufficient and fledgling—efforts to form development-oriented voluntary associations in the Third World. Increasingly, it is these indigenous voluntary organizations, with their local roots and local expertise, that will have the most influence—besides that of local governments—over the course of development in the Third World in the future.

Some U.S. and other international voluntary organizations are already working with such groups. They recognize that a concern for human dignity is important at every level of development, in one's perception of ends as well as of means to promote those ends. Minimum physical needs cannot be achieved except in ways that are largely self-determined and that bear at least some spiritual relationship to local values and cultures—to the whole person. Nor can they be achieved unless the poor majority gains and maintains a measure of access to resources. For this, structural change is often necessary. Physical and income-generating infrastructure must be made available to the poor in ways that encourage their further development. Institutions must follow not the path of least resistance but what is usually the path of most resistance; they must find ways to break into the vicious circle of poverty and ensure equality of opportunity for all. In the development of human resources, high priority must be accorded to the broadened consciousness and dignity of the individual, not merely to technological expertise. Indeed, there can be no creative development without an affirmation of dignity. Development without dignity for all is not development.

Chapter 6

Measuring Success and Failure

Were development an end product rather than a process, it might be relatively easy to evaluate programs aimed at its achievement. One could decide on certain attributes—cash income, literacy, caloric intake, mortality rate, days lost to work through illness, or whatever—and conclude whether one's "development" efforts had succeeded in measurable statistical terms. The measuring could be done on national, provincial, district, community, and even individual family levels; in fact, this would represent a significant improvement over the relatively exclusive traditional reliance on GNP indicators. There would always be a problem of separating the foreign aid influence from all the other influences on any given situation, but one could presumably cope with this problem through subjective analysis and common sense.

The fact, of course, is that development is not so much an end product as it is a process of history. Grappling with far more than the amelioration of poverty, it involves the very essence of the whole person with his self-reliance, sense of dignity, and culturally defined spiritual attributes. It is nearly impossible to evaluate success on these exalted planes other than through highly subjective, sensitive interactions with the local group that is being aided. Before tackling the hardest aspects of the evaluation problem, however, it is useful to survey how various types of private and voluntary organizations have grappled with the effectiveness question—a question of concern not only to individuals involved in the development process, but also, increasingly, to the funding agencies that choose whether or not to support the voluntary organizations.

Until the past few years, Mark Twain's observation about the weather applied to evaluating voluntary agency development programs: everyone talked about evaluation, but few did anything about it. It was widely felt that the private humanitarian agencies, many of church origin, were effective simply because they were "doing good"; missionaries were acting as witnesses to God's works on earth, and they interacted with the poor; these were good ends in themselves. Their relief and rehabilitation programs distributed goods from the rich to the poor; this could hardly be anything but laudable. Their motivations, too, seemed pure. What more was there, then, to evaluate? As times and standards changed, doubts increased—doubts fostered by widening poverty gaps between rich and poor; by disillusionment within the United States that aid to the Third World was not having the same effect as earlier aid to Europe; by a growing recognition of the existence of poverty and injustice at home as illustrated by the civil rights movement, the Vietnam involvement, and the controversy surrounding multinational corporations; by the decline in overt cold war competition; and by all the basic reassessments of American values, identity, and interests that these developments helped spawn. Simultaneously, increasing concern was being expressed within the Third World countries themselves—concern that having shed their colonial chains, they still found themselves affected by new manifestations of Western paternalism, including those inherent in the classical aid relationships. This considerable flux in the self-perceptions and "other perceptions" of both sides is inevitably leading both to new ways of assessing successes and failures and to new modes of joint action in the future.

All this is not to say that a number of organizations had not, in their own ways, already been giving attention to assessing grant and activity performance. Yet it is fair to state that for the majority of organizations, especially those receiving U.S. government funds, it was the 1973 Foreign Assistance Act that spurred what has now become a real trend toward more regular evaluation. On the one hand, the 1973 foreign aid bill provided a clear mandate to the U.S. Agency for International Development to channel more of its funds through private and voluntary organizations, thus increasing the amount of monies available to more organizations for overseas programs. This mandate was itself largely grounded in a belief that private agencies tended to be more effective than government agencies in reaching the poorest segments of Third World populations; to this extent, it represented one manifestation of the growing disillusionment with official overseas aid. On the other hand, AID felt enjoined to prove its worth in reaching the hitherto neglected poor majority; to do so, it became increasingly seized with the importance of project evaluation, both internally and for its voluntary agency grantees. The congressional debate made it clear that support for official aid, having already significantly declined, would decline further, or even disappear, unless it could be shown that poor people rather than rich elites and military causes were benefiting from it. By 1974, therefore, AID was propagating the virtues of the "logical framework matrix" (the logframe) as a methodology for impelling proper planning and evaluation of foreign assistance projects.

With its one-page, sixteen-box format, the logframe requires concise statements about 1) broader program goals, 2) specific project objectives intended to meet those goals, 3) project outputs, and 4) inputs for achieving the desired results. It then calls for 5) objectively verifiable indicators by which one could demonstrate whether the above four objectives were being achieved, and 6) a listing of the means of verification as to how one would measure the achievements. Finally, the logframe requires 7) listings of important assumptions behind each heading of goals, purposes, outputs, and inputs, requiring the organizations to reflect on the minimum necessary conditions without which their purposes could not be achieved.

At the time it was introduced, the logframe appeared to represent everything the majority of voluntary agencies did not: scientific exactitude in a world of amorphous human imponderables, and the triumph of statistics and computers over what were seen as fuzzy-headed do-gooder mentalities. Many voluntary organization staff members, resentful of their dependency on U.S. government financing in the first place, were further offended by the U.S. government's apparent condescension in making that financing dependent on their adoption of the logframe methodology. Many felt that this overly quantitative approach failed to recognize the human elements in their programming. Thus they either resented the apparent attempt to fit them into AID's mold or found themselves filling in the boxes in order to satisfy AID requirements without significantly changing their program approaches in practice. On the other hand, some appreciated the logframe as a device to focus their thinking about projects in a more orderly way; for these groups the device proved useful. Whatever their reaction to it, the logframe did challenge the voluntary agencies to think of their programs in a different light than before.

Performance Versus Significance

The difficulty with much program planning and evaluation—that of bilateral and multilateral agencies as well as of private organizations—is their virtually exclusive concentration on *operational performance* rather than *larger significance*. Too often projects are seen as entities unto themselves. In reality, however, a project is an intervention into a continuing social process from which it cannot be isolated. There is thus an important need for evaluation of the political, social, and economic structure as a whole and of each project link with it.[1] It is this kind of distinction between a project and the larger context that the logframe, used properly, helps to clarify. Some of the large organizations, for example, conduct first-level inquiries to see whether x amount of food reached y number of people, or whether y number of people reflected z rate of nutritional improvement; or they may ascertain whether a amount of money resulted in b number of classrooms constructed and c number of new pupils in school; they may even ask how much new agricultural production, how many additional jobs, or how much more income has resulted from new inputs of knowledge or technology. But more

---

[1] See "The Quality of Aid," Commission on the Churches' Participation in Development, Document 8 (Geneva: World Council of Churches, 1976).

ultimate types of questions are not often asked. What difference does it really make if nutritional improvements are z and school-going populations increase by c? What does all this mean for the development process and for improved lives? What are the degree and quality of local participation in program formulation? Who is benefiting? And how? What are the costs and possibilities of maintaining the benefits without continuing outside help? How long will any program benefits last? Have the poorest groups increased their sense of dignity, self-reliance, and overall capacity to deal with the world around them? Did the program represent the best and most effective use of the particular inputs?

One should not be too critical in pointing out the dearth of evaluations that include these ultimate kinds of questions, since they are exceedingly difficult to accomplish. It is difficult to design them—for governmental and international agency programs as well as for private ones—and difficult to measure their results.[2] This is true for both domestic and overseas antipoverty programs. To a significant degree, the difficulties are rooted in the frequent failure to formulate clear and assessable goals and objectives in the first place.[3] In a relief situation, this is much easier: one confronts an immediate nutritional requirement, usually measurable in pounds of food or in calories, and judges success by the number of pounds or calories distributed to—or consumed by—each designated recipient. The formulation of goals was easier in the colonial period, too, when the missionary hospitals and schools were the very first types of development assistance of any kind to Third World people; one could then assume that any introduction of services could not help but do some good. The same was true of the first roads and irrigation systems. But with the independence of Third World countries, higher goals were set—specifically, to promote equality for *all* people—and the development context is now more complicated. In part this is because the trickle-down assumptions of the past have not had the desired effect of helping a large majority of the poor; in part it is for the related reason that social and political programs are at least as critical to development as the more narrowly defined economic programs. The question now is

---

[2] For an excellent overview of the issues involved in the whole area of evaluation, see *Evaluating Development Assistance: Problems of Method and Organisation* (Paris: Organisation for Economic Co-operation and Development, 1972). Another overview, focusing on the evaluation of functional education programs, is presented in James A. Farmer, Jr., and George Papagiannis, *Program Evaluation: Functional Education for Family Life Planning, III* (New York: World Education, 1975). For a striking example of varying approaches to a specific project evaluation, see Richard M. Hunt and Nancy S. Truitt, "The PODER Project in Colombia"; and Csanad Toth, "A Comment on the PODER Project"; both in *International Development Review* (1971/4), pp. 14–20. An excellent and thoughtful set of case studies is offered in Wahidul Haque, Niranjan Mehta, Anisur Rahman, and Ponna Wignaraja, *An Approach to Micro-Level Development: Designing and Evaluation of Rural Development Projects* (Bombay: U.N. Asian Development Institute, 1977).

[3] For a discussion of the special problems of evaluating the achievement of voluntary agency goals, see W. Keith Warner, "Problems in Measuring the Goal Attainment of Voluntary Organizations," *Journal of Adult Education*, Vol. XIX, No. 1, 1967, pp. 3–14.

not only how much food was distributed, or even how much more was grown through a crop improvement program; rather it extends to the issue of who is benefiting in a self-sustaining way from the project and how these benefits improve the individual's or family's sense of dignity and relative position within the larger community. The poor person made richer may not *feel* richer if others within his purview are gaining at a still faster pace. The problem is that while income gaps can be measured, feelings of dignity and well-being cannot be, not with a logframe or indeed in any way other than through sensitive, subjective observation and discussion over a period of time.

The time factor, indeed, is a critical element here. While it is theoretically desirable to have the benefit of years of local experience to decide most sensitively how to assist in the development process, and years after assisting to be able to assess the results over time, this is realistically an impossibility for all but the missionaries who reside on the spot and devote their lifetimes to the local setting and its people. Theoretically, assistance given through Third World voluntary organizations might be seen as the answer; after all, they should know their own people and problems. Yet the local elites who generally head these organizations may be as divorced from the mentality of the rural and urban poor as are the foreigners. A further problem is that the institutional memories of voluntary agencies—indeed of most types of agencies—are notoriously limited, so experience is not readily transferred from one "generation" to another. As a result, most development projects are selected in a relatively ad hoc fashion without any hard and fast rules. If project requests are not submitted by would-be recipients, then the agencies themselves may shop around for potential takers, seeking to fill in with their own program inputs whatever program gaps may exist in various local government ministries or private bodies. Third World absorptive capacities being low, it is very difficult, in practice, to find good projects, and interagency competition for them is keen. If a sudden need for aid becomes apparent, there will be an impulse to go ahead with assistance, even if the implementation scheme is not articulated as well as it could be. After all, the flexible, pragmatic approach is the hallmark of the voluntary agency, as is the charitable rather than the banker's approach to work.

In planning stages, therefore, the luxury of time does not always exist—or at least it is not perceived to exist. Action is preferable to its perceived opposite—bureaucratic reflection—if for no reason other than that it satisfies the souls of the donors. To the extent that hasty action results in imprecise goals, it understandably affects the ability to assess progress during the implementation phases, when relevant feedback could usefully lead to improvement in problem areas. It also makes ex post facto evaluation both difficult and relatively less useful. In any case, ex post facto evaluations have not been particularly favored in the past for several reasons. First, most people are too busy focusing on present and future activities; second, given the institutional memory gap, the role of such evaluations is considered largely archival; third, evaluations are believed to require impossibly large amounts of time, expertise, and money; and fourth —and most serious of all—if the results are anything short of positive, such evaluations may jeopardize future fund-raising success.

Criteria for Dignity and Self-Reliance

In 1975, a group of voluntary organization executives, including several agency heads, convened under the auspices of the Overseas Development Council to define the most critical issues they foresaw for their programs over the coming years and decades. One of the critical issues they agreed on was the need for some framework within which they would be willing to be judged by themselves and by others, and they thus attempted to evolve a set of relevant program criteria. The criteria they agreed on, while expressed in generalized terms, address the issues of dignity and self-reliance, and could have extremely far-reaching and constructive program implications if really implemented.[4] For example, recognizing the problem of lack of continuity in their efforts, the participants noted that a local group must be able to sustain and improve on any progress after an outside agency's help is withdrawn. Hearing their efforts criticized for having the effect of fostering the status quo, in which the rich dominate the poor, they stated that their programs should result in increasing—or at the very least not diminishing—the power of a poverty group within its own local or national system. Furthermore, "the local group must be as aware as the PVO [private and voluntary organization] of the political, cultural, and economic implications" and risks of embarking on any given program. In response to the frequent complaints of paternalism, the participants agreed that "the power of the local group vis-à-vis the PVO should grow during the course of the program," and that "the PVO should make itself actively accountable to the local group, sharing power over the program with that group." Besides, "the local group must participate fully and increasingly throughout the implementation of the program, both in decision making and in contributions of materials and personnel." Indeed, they agreed, it must be the local group that defines its own needs in the first place and that then has the major responsibility to decide with the PVO the terms and conditions of the program. To minimize the dangers of overly ethnocentric Western approaches, "the PVO should work

---

[4]For the full text of the criteria, see Annex B. The voluntary agency executives participating in their formulation came from such agencies as CARE, International Voluntary Services, Volunteers in Technical Assistance, Church World Service, CODEL, Catholic Relief Services, Lutheran World Relief, Save the Children Federation/Community Development Foundation, PACT, Oxfam-America, Africare, Cooperative League of the USA, and the American Council of Voluntary Agencies for Foreign Service. While few of the representatives were in a position to commit themselves corporately to these criteria prior to consulting their respective boards, only one organization's higher authority subsequently disavowed any official identification with the criteria.

in a manner that respects the primacy of local cultural values, while at the same time not violating its own cultural standards.... The PVO must openly state to the local group its own motivation, goals, and evaluation criteria for the program ... [and] evaluations should be made, or at the least shared, with local groups."

This emphasis on the critical primacy of the local group over the foreign voluntary organization raises the related question—answered by the voluntary agency executives only in general terms—of *who* evaluates the programs. To date, the issue has been primarily one of agency insiders versus outsiders. Africare, for example, in order to ensure objectivity of results, insists that only outsiders should assess its programs. Other organizations insist that only insiders conduct evaluations. They fear that outsiders may be biased by their own preconceived notions or by unfamiliarity with all the elements that went into the program's history; or they feel that if evaluation is to be useful for future programming decisions, it should be an internal process to ensure that the lessons are learned and internalized by those with a proprietary interest in the process for the future. Still other organizations set up assessment teams comprised of both insiders and outsiders, this being theoretically, and usually in practice, too, the best model of all.

The above criteria notwithstanding, surprisingly little attention has yet been given to the need to include Third World participants in the evaluation process, in large part, no doubt, because their active participation in the program-formulation stages has also been rare. It is this broader lack of involvement that constitutes the more critical problem. Because the cultural and social aspects of development are as important as the more traditional economic aspects, the unique insights of local participants, quite apart from the justice of their participation, are critical to a meaningful understanding of what has happened and what should happen in any given situation. Indeed, it would appear that one of the multiplier contributions U.S. voluntary organizations could make would be to share not only the best of their assessment methods, but also their broader program-planning expertise with their overseas colleagues. After all, this type of management input is at least as important a part of the development process as the new crops, wells, schools, and clinics themselves.[5]

The need for local participation in the project planning, implementation, and assessment stages has been demonstrated most conclusively so far in a sophisticated computerized study of thirty-six rural development projects in Africa and Latin America by Development Alternatives, Inc.

---

[5]The importance of care in choosing only the most appropriate planning and assessment methods to share with Third World countries is worth emphasizing. See Denis A. Rondinelli, "International Requirements for Project Preparation: Aids or Obstacles to Development Planning?" *Journal of the American Institute of Planners*, Vol. 42, No. 3 (July 1976), pp. 314–25. Rondinelli points out that unnecessarily complex foreign standards and procedures are often imposed on Third World settings without sensitivity to local needs and constraints.

(DAI), a private consulting firm.[6] The primary finding of the study was that to maximize the chances for project success, the small farmer should be involved in the decision-making process—particularly in the implementation stages—and should also be persuaded to make a resource commitment to the project. While relatively few of the thirty-six projects examined were sponsored by voluntary organizations (most were conducted by local governments with bilateral or multilateral aid), those that were sponsored by voluntary organizations tended to be more successful simply because they usually involved more participation at the grass-roots level. Some of the larger, more bureaucratic, government-sponsored programs came in for considerable criticism, in fact, because of their distance from understanding the local economic and social/cultural factors that can impede project success, and because of their consequent relative inflexibility toward changing the methods of project implementation when altered circumstances required such changes.

DAI reached these conclusions by scoring the projects numerically on the basis of four distinct components of success: increase in the small farmer's income; increase in agricultural knowledge; increase in self-help capability; and the degree of probability that the project benefits would become self-sustaining. The DAI researchers discovered that most of the baseline information required for planning a good project was available from the local people themselves. The ideal data-collection system consisted of small sample surveys and open-ended interviews conducted by Western and Third World professionals who were both involved in the project planning (to ensure the subsequent use of the data) and able, during the collection process, to establish good personal relationships and thus ensure cooperation for continuing data flows during implementation. In analyzing data, DAI found that special attention needed to be paid to the influence of landholding patterns and income and power distribution in order to target project benefits at the intended participants among the poor majority. While thorough data-collection processes were preferred, the study showed that large sample surveys and highly detailed statistical studies were not necessary; indeed, many of the most successful projects were also the most simply designed ones.

The DAI approach has been criticized for attaching too much significance to computer and statistical approaches and for attempting to "score" such elusive qualities as knowledge, self-help capability, and potential for becoming self-sustaining. Like the logframe, it has appeared too technocratically impersonal to judge the more human aspects of development. On the other hand, proponents of the methodology argue that the statistical approach is not a substitute for the sensitive human assessments required,

---

[6]Elliott R. Morss, John K. Hatch, Donald R. Mickelwait, and Charles F. Sweet, *Strategies for Small Farmer Development: An Empirical Study of Rural Development Projects*, 2 vols. (Boulder, Colo.: Westview Press, Inc., 1976).

but rather is based on those assessments; project scores are assigned by subjective judgments and are computerized primarily for purposes of aggregation and regression analysis of different factors relating to project success. Like the logframe, this methodology is to be used as a tool—with the important caveat that it not be seen as sacrosanct.

Another criticism is the cost of the approach. The DAI study itself cost some $350,000 for thirty-six projects. While the methodological innovation is always more expensive than subsequent replication, incorporating this degree of professional input into the average voluntary organization would certainly not be cheap. On the other hand, there are varying levels at which the same approach could be applied, and it is possible that "proxies" that accurately reflected the more elusive data might sometimes be substituted.[7] Also, it is usually not necessary to send large, specially-hired data-collection teams to gather information for planning and assessment; one can rely equally well on local contacts—including affected members of the aided communities—and then double-check information for objectivity and cross-sectional validity. Indeed, many voluntary organizations that rely on local people and extension agents during the implementation phases would be well advised to rely more heavily on their knowledge and sensitivity in the prior planning stages too, rather than limiting this process, as frequently occurs, to top-level staff alone.

Evaluation, in short, will never be cost-free. Yet even at high cost it still can be worthwhile if it saves more than would be spent on costly mistakes that might otherwise be made. It can certainly be done effectively for less cost than is commonly believed necessary (the high-cost belief being partly perpetuated by profit-oriented consulting firms) if one takes great care in formulating overall program goals, individual project objectives, and accomplishment indicators expected along the way. Sound evaluation, after all, primarily requires wise and sensitive people asking the right questions at the right times. It also requires a demythologizing of the very term "evaluation"—away from the notion of a dangerous process that threatens funding flows, and toward a notion of constructive process aimed at improving effectiveness and making intelligent replication possible. Indeed, for those understandably concerned about fund-raising implications, evaluation should lead to more rather than less funding in the long-range future—if the programs are, in fact, as effective as they should be.

If the impact of programs and funds is difficult to measure, still harder to assess is the impact of the *individual* American or other expatriate "change agent." Many organizations have struggled with this problem, feeling that individuals can help to promote progress through either their catalytic or direct involvements, but being unsure of how to ascertain the nature or magnitude of the impact. There is also a perennial question of

---

[7]See "Information Systems to Support Rural Development Projects," mimeographed (Washington, D.C.: Development Alternatives, Inc., February 1976).

whether there is still a role in the Third World for the generalist as opposed to the technician. The U.S. Peace Corps, which has gone through several shifts in evaluation methodologies, at one stage sent special evaluators to conduct general interviews among volunteers and counterparts in recipient countries and at another stage developed a cost-effectiveness measurement system. The latter, being simultaneously too simplistic and too complex, demonstrates the potential pitfalls of evaluation; wisely, it was never fully implemented. The method would have involved taking Department of Labor average salary figures in the various fields in which Peace Corps volunteers were serving, adding administrative overhead at 100 per cent of salaries, and then dividing by the actual cost to Peace Corps of one volunteer in order to determine the cost-effectiveness ratio! Because the Peace Corps was paying only subsistence and modest readjustment allowances, its average cost-effectiveness ratio of 1:1.7 was not surprising. However, this said nothing about the impact of individual volunteers on their communities. To measure this, the proposed plan was to multiply the number of host-country nationals with whom the volunteer was working by the net dollar increase attributed to this contact, and then divide the result by the average cost per volunteer. For agriculturalists the net dollar increase was to be determined by the increase in crop productivity over five years, for management experts by the overall profit increase, for educators by the estimate of the volume of information transferred, for health specialists by the cost of providing the same service through other means, and so forth. The attempt to assess the impact of individual volunteers was laudable, but it proved only one point—that rigid data-based modes of evaluation are inadequate and that sensitive interaction with people in the local setting is likely to be much more revealing of what has happened as a result of the presence of individual volunteers.

The Predictable, the Unpredictable, and the Role of Evaluation

One of the most exemplary evaluations of a voluntary organization program—remarkable both for its thorough methodology and its revealing conclusions—is that of the American Friends Service Committee's Barpali multipurpose village development project in the State of Orissa in India.[8] The AFSC had sponsored this project from 1952 to 1962, and in 1971 one of the American participants returned to the scene to study what results were evident nearly ten years later. No other organization is known to have taken this detailed a retrospective look at its earlier village efforts. The results, while not necessarily representative, were instructive. Through interviews with several local project staff members, as well as with local government

---

[8]LaVonne Platt, *Barpali After Ten Years: Observations Made in Revisiting Barpali* (Philadelphia: American Friends Service Committee, 1973).

and other officials, it became clear that lasting changes in agriculture and health had come to Barpali through the AFSC involvement. But the feature of the program that seemed most remembered was the AFSC confidence in the local people's ability to help themselves. "They did not give gratis or charity. Instead of doling out, BVS [Barpali Village Service] extended a helping hand. . . . The most important feature of BVS was a sincerity of purpose which was lacking in Government programs whose only purpose was to spend money allocated for a project. . . . Mixing with the people was the most important feature of BVS. . . . The project helped people to become self-sufficient."[9] Significantly, the main criticism seemed to be that the AFSC project should have continued longer: ten years was long enough to teach about the need for new agricultural and sanitary practices, for example, but not long enough to bring about all the changes required. The self-help approach was foreign to local customs, which had been shaped by caste hierarchies and colonial structures. Since the new approach was not subsequently emphasized by government development programs, villagers gradually reverted to their old roles after the AFSC departure. This negative turn of events was countered only to the extent that former project associates who later went to work for the local government were considered more effective workers because of their earlier experience. Still, the evidence hardly leads one to conclude that an extended AFSC involvement would have made much difference in the long run.

> Generally, those programs continued which were direct responses to "felt needs" of villagers (e.g., medical care) or were responses to awareness that had developed because of BVS work in the *thana* [district] (e.g., more schools). On the other hand, programs begun because of a need recognized by BVS but not felt by the villagers (e.g., use of audio-visual training by village teachers) were not continued . . . . Changes of practice which had already taken place while BVS was working in Barpali Thana and which had resulted in individuals' acceptance of BVS teaching programs had generally continued in 1971, except where intervening factors, such as drought, had interfered . . . . When BVS's original aims and goals were changed by the institution to which the programs were transferred, acceptance of the programs by the villagers declined or changed in focus. . . . When the institution that had accepted responsibility for a particular aspect of [the] BVS program failed to continue the service, acceptance was not continued through other channels. . . . When greater emphasis was placed on programs by the institutions that took over the programs, greater success in acceptance generally resulted.[10]

---

[9]Ibid., pp. 84 and 86.
[10]Ibid., pp. 93–94.

The Barpali case study provides a most informative vignette of the development process in a particular setting over a period of time. More importantly, it demonstrates the usefulness of sensitive evaluation in better understanding the influence of the larger context on voluntary programs. Only on the basis of such an evaluation can one begin to understand which types of outside assistance are most successful under given local conditions and which types are likely to have the longest-term development impact.

It may be helpful to take one more case—that of World Education—to illustrate the benefits of evaluation and particularly of examining development programs in their larger environmental contexts over time. World Education, like many of the more creative U.S. voluntary organizations, grew out of the vision of an extraordinary person—in this case an American dowager, Mrs. Welthy Fisher, who decided at an advanced age to take up the cause of increasing literacy in India. Throwing herself wholeheartedly into the cause, Dr. Fisher raised enough money to create in Lucknow, on the banks of the Ganges River, an institution called Literacy House. Literacy House grew and thrived and soon became India's principal center for developing innovative educational curricula and instructional materials for teaching functional literacy outside the constraints of the traditional classrooms of the formal school system. While the formal system was placing emphasis on literacy for literacy's sake, the new voluntary institution saw literacy primarily as a tool for people to improve their everyday lives through access to written materials on better hygiene, nutrition, agriculture, animal husbandry, and family planning. While the formal system relied primarily on rote teaching, Literacy House developed methods of teaching through the use of puppets; this attracted village audiences and held them spellbound, thus increasing the likelihood of the multiple educational messages sinking in. The curricular and instructional materials developed by Literacy House, with assistance from Dr. Fisher's U.S.-based World Education organization, were soon being used for ad hoc nonformal education efforts in many parts of India, and were translated into languages besides the Hindi of the Gangetic plain. To be sure, there has been no institutional way to propagate the instructional methodologies pioneered by Literacy House other than through these local adoptions on the part of interested but scattered groups; the overall education systems of India's states are far too entrenched and tradition-bound for reforms to be instituted more broadly. Yet this is not to say the attempt should not have been made; in the long run, ad hoc successes can add up to a significant whole.

More problematic—at least for a time—was the question of continuity. Dr. Fisher, for all her extraordinary energy and vision, had incorporated into the Literacy House effort one tragic flaw: an over-reliance on her charismatic leadership and personal ability to draw and provide sufficient funding to keep the effort going. When she retired from the scene in her mid-nineties, and when AID funding faded away with the deterioration of diplomatic relations between the United States and India in the early 1970s, there was no one to pick up the bulk of the Literacy House bill. The talented local staff was plunged into a mood of gloom, and several lost their jobs. Subsequently, the national and state governments picked up enough of the bill so that work could continue. But whether the lost momentum and resulting bureaucratization can still be reversed is one of those questions that crops up repeatedly in the annals of short-term histories of development efforts.

If the need to plan ahead for local funding was one lesson that emerged from World Education's India experience, another lesson relating to unpredictable environmental influences emerged from that organization's "functional literacy and family life education program" in Thailand. In the Thai program, and in contrast to the Literacy House experience in India, World Education made sure that its effort was well plugged into the Thai government structure for the sake of proper support and continuity. As its title suggests, the program encompassed much more than literacy alone. Its goal, indeed, was nothing less than to create critical-thinking and problem-solving people: people who recognize their own potential in producing changes in their lives; who identify problems and relate them to their causes; who are capable of gathering information on alternatives; who select the alternative most acceptable to their own values in relation to their political and social environments; who agree, at least temporarily, to a lesser solution while making way for the solution of their choice; who are able to justify their decisions, at least to themselves; and who accept the consequences of their actions. In short, its goal was consciousness raising.[11] The methodology for achieving this state of consciousness was a series of group discussions in which the teacher was to relate village concerns first to symbols on charts, then to language and literacy, and, in the process, to problem solving. When most overseas assistance programs were still struggling to find ways to evaluate their impact on local rural communities, World Education cosponsored, with its Thai hosts and leading experts from several countries, an intensive international workshop with the goal of establishing valid and workable criteria and procedures for determining the results of their efforts.[12] Everything seemed to be going very well indeed. Gradually, however, it became evident that the Thais who were responsible for the effort were unwilling to run the risk of negative impact results and all that this might imply for their individual careers in a strongly hierarchical government civil-service structure. The program seemed destined for an early demise. Then, in another of those quirks of the larger context, the World Bank stepped in and made a loan to the Thai government for educational development. One of the stipulations of the loan, relatively sure

---

[11]Kowit Vorapipatana, "The 'Khit-Pen' Man," *World Education Reports*, No. 8 (January 1975), p. 5.

[12]See workshop report, "International Workshop for Evaluation Specialists on Nonformal Education for Family Life Planning," Ministry of Education of the Government of Thailand, and World Education, Chiengmai, Thailand, 1974.

to be followed because of the quantum of resources at stake, was that an evaluation system be continued—with World Education support.

In the World Education Thailand case, there is relatively little that better planning and evaluation could have done to reduce the intermittent outside impediments to program success. The nature of development is such that what is predictable is unpredictability. Thus one can never be sure if lessons learned in one program will prove relevant to another program in another setting. Development, in this sense, is unique and particularistic. Private and voluntary organizations that wish to be truly innovative and effective over the long run should not be overly concerned with temporary setbacks, or even with more permanent setbacks and failures. Indeed, it is often—and correctly—argued that risk-free programs cannot be expected to lead to the kind of fundamental social and economic change that is needed, particularly given the structural problems of poverty. If anything, *more* calculated risks need to be taken than in the past, as long as their implications are well understood in advance by both the outside agencies and the concerned local people. Voluntary organizations—because they are relatively small, flexible, and low visibility entities—are especially well suited to taking such risks for progress.

Chapter 7

Uncle Sam and the Voluntary Ethos

Cynics are fond of pointing out that the private and voluntary organizations are neither private nor voluntary nor indeed organizations. Not private because an average of one third of the sector's support comes from U.S. government sources, with percentages ranging closer to 80 per cent in the case of many organizations, including the largest ones—CARE and Catholic Relief Services. Not voluntary because many employ people at professional or nearly professional salary scales, and these people often live overseas at higher standards than they would in the United States itself. And finally, not organizations because the charitable and voluntary ethos has not always been perceived as congruent with the kinds of sound management principles implicit in modern organizational structures. One does not have to agree either with the word play of these cynics or with the overall thrust of their thesis to admit to a small kernel of truth in what they say. This chapter is concerned with the first of the cynics' points—the relationship between the voluntary organizations and the U.S. government—and how it can be improved.[1]

How Private Are Private Organizations?

Many of the organizations funded by the U.S. government exhibit an anxiety that borders on the neurotic about how to maintain a reasonable measure of independence from the government and at the same time be able to draw on the government's funding and commodity supplies. Ironically, this concern has blossomed at a time when government funding—though not changing substantially in total dollar amount—has dropped as a proportion of overall agency income from 60 per cent in 1964 and 1965 to an

---

[1]Because foundations have their own endowments and therefore do not confront the funding problem in the same way, the primary emphasis here is on the voluntary organizations that must regularly raise monies from extra-institutional sources.

average of 33 per cent between 1973 and 1976.[2] AID support has also become more flexible with the initiation of additional cash grants and contracts as a result of the 1973 and 1975 congressional mandates, which favor channeling more assistance through American private groups. AID grants have become available for the agencies' internal organizational development purposes as well as for operational programs overseas, thus adding further flexibility of utilization. AID's increasingly forthcoming attitude has come partly as a result of its own impressions of voluntary agency contributions and partly as a result of the congressional mandates. In a 1975 report, the U.S. Senate Committee on Appropriations expressed its enthusiasm in this way:

> As in the past, the Committee again applauds the outstanding contribution to development made by the numerous groups of dedicated people known collectively as Private and Voluntary Organizations. We have been impressed by the ability of these select organizations to address basic human needs on a person-to-person level. They exhibit the finest qualities which may be inspired by a tradition of voluntarism and a sense of mission. Their Spartan-like expenses, and their ability to get things done stand in marked contrast to other, larger national and multinational organizations.[3]

Why, then, the concern on the part of the voluntary organizations about their relationships with AID? The fact is that AID commodity and ocean freight support is relatively simple and straightforward—even businesslike—and both AID and the private agencies know more or less what to expect of each other with respect to it. "Development," however, is anything but simple and straightforward. Philosophies and approaches vary considerably, the more so when one is grappling with problems at the grass-roots level, where the voluntary organizations tend to have considerable experience that, for right or for wrong, is not always appreciated by the bureaucrats. Whereas a bureaucracy by its very nature is set up to handle commodity shipment types of programs, it is less well set up to comprehend and manage the human factors of local development efforts. In a sense, the nub of the problem lies simply in the bureaucratic ethos, which is directly opposite that of either the rural setting or self-help participation. Development efforts, to be successful, must be timely, sensitive, and always flexible. These are not traits characteristic of bureaucracies, no matter how well-meaning the individuals therein may be.

---

[2]These figures apply to the ninety-four largest agencies listed in "Voluntary Foreign Aid Programs," Reports of American Voluntary Agencies Engaged in Overseas Relief and Development Registered with the Advisory Committee on Voluntary Foreign Aid (Washington, D.C.: Department of State, AID, 1964, 1965, 1973, 1974, and 1975).

[3]U.S. Congress, Senate Committee on Appropriations, *Foreign Assistance and Related Programs Appropriation Bill, 1975: Report to Accompany H.R. 4592*, 94th Cong., 1st sess., 1975, S. Rept. 94-39, p. 70.

Another aspect of the problem is that of the voluntary agencies' own "revolution of rising expectations"—a phenomenon that can only lead to disappointments along with successes. When the congressional mandate prompted AID to lay more stress on collaboration with them—a collaboration widely heralded through meetings and workshops that brought together AID and voluntary agency people—the voluntary agencies understandably had their hopes raised. Add to this the fact that organizations previously outside the AID orbit also stood a good chance of receiving grants, and it is clear that the scale of any potential problems (and also potential benefits) increases.

Besides the structural and ethos differences that have come more to the fore with the shift from relief to development programs, and besides the ramifications of increasing congressional interest, there has been a significant change in the world's overall mood during the past decade. In the Third World, nationalist sensitivity to extensions of U.S. power has become increasingly articulated. In the United States there has been a growing tendency, engendered in large part by the Indochina experience, for private organizations and individuals to be suspicious of and even outraged at their government rather than uncritically supportive of it. Revelations about Central Intelligence Agency involvements overseas have justifiably served to add fuel to these feelings, particularly among voluntary organizations that have always taken pride in their independent and nonpolitical roles. Such feelings are not universal, of course, and they are in any case subject to cyclical change. Although in the mid-1970s Americans tended to regard their government with memories fresh from the Vietnam War and Watergate, a National Academy of Sciences group noted in 1974 that "moods of enthusiasm for, and disenchantment with, government service have come and gone in the past and undoubtedly will do so in the future. The difficulties caused by these fluctuations should not lead to drastic and unrealistic prescriptions."[4] By mid-1977, with a post-Vietnam and post-Watergate administration having assumed office in Washington, the mood did, indeed, appear to be changing.

Yet sensitivity to U.S. power is constant and reflects the ambiguous role in which the agencies so easily find themselves. Whether supported by the U.S. government or not, they have willy-nilly been seen in many parts of the world as fitting the pattern of U.S. global domination. Third World people do not always draw the distinction between public and private sectors that some Americans draw, in part because in many of their countries the two are blurred.

Even where they do draw distinctions, they see common psychological forces at work among all Americans as people, whether they are Americans serving in public or private capacities. The missionary zeal to spread U.S.

---

[4] *The Peace Corps: Perspectives for the Future,* Report of the Ad Hoc Committee on Development Assistance Opportunities in the Next Decade for the Peace Corps (Washington, D.C.: National Academy of Sciences, 1974), p. 48.

values and notions of modernity is at work in a subconscious way, even among the most sensitive development professionals. To many, it is this force as much as the more overt and obvious foreign policies of the government that carries political connotations. In the same way, many Third World people see U.S. corporate extensions overseas as part and parcel of the spreading tentacles of American power. They view corporations not necessarily as extensions in a foreign policy sense (though policies often accompany and support them), and not necessarily with any conscious intent of exploitation or malevolence (though instances of this are hardly unknown), but in the sense that this outward extension is simply a part of America's manifest destiny which is often found threatening by newly independent and still-consolidating nations.

Because the Vietnam experience is so illustrative of the larger issue of U.S. government/private agency relations, and because it has been so influential on public opinion at home and abroad, it is worth discussing at least briefly in this connection. Of course some people say that Vietnam was a special case and that voluntary organizations function quite differently vis-à-vis U.S. foreign policy in other places. Yet the difference seems to be more one of degree than of substance. Whereas in Vietnam, and subsequently Cambodia, U.S. voluntary agencies were at least implicitly part of the larger war effort, in other parts of the Third World they may be seen as part of a more subtle effort to propagate American values and the climate for American business and foreign policy.

As a high-level delegation to Saigon from the American Council of Voluntary Agencies for Foreign Service pointed out in 1965, "The role [in Vietnam] of the voluntary agencies, whose programs vary considerably from one to another, is supplemental to that of the government. . . .There should be no slackening of support for both types of activity, governmental and private, especially since they are working in increasingly close and effective collaboration."[5] This closeness was illustrated by the fact that 94 per cent of the Catholic Relief Services' 1972 Vietnam budget of $3.9 million came from U.S. government sources.[6] The collaboration included controversial efforts by CRS in contributing large amounts of food and clothing to Saigon military personnel and dependents. In Cambodia, the presence and assistance of CRS in handling refugee relief helped give the U.S. embassy the appearance of staying within the tight personnel restrictions imposed by the U.S. Congress.

CRS was not alone in its support of U.S. government policies in Vietnam. Vietnam Christian Service—founded by Church World Service, Lutheran World Relief, and Mennonite Central Committee (until MCC

---

[5]David Marr, "The Politics of Charity," *Indochina Chronicle* (October/November, 1974), p. 3. See also Richard Rashke, "GVN/CRS/USAID," *National Catholic Reporter* (December 17, 1976), p. 1; "Catholic Charity Allegedly Aided U.S. War Effort," *Washington Post,* December 13, 1976, p. 1; and "Priest Denies Mishandling Viet Aid," *Washington Post,* December 14, 1976, p. 3.

[6]"Priest Denies Mishandling Viet Aid," p. 6.

later withdrew from the consortium)—became involved in a principal part of the Saigon administration's psychological warfare operations: the *Chieu Hoi* camps for National Liberation Front defectors to the Saigon side. CARE, World Vision, the Red Cross, International Voluntary Services—indeed, most of the U.S. agencies in Indochina during the wartime period—were in some way involved in the Saigon government's cause, whether through contributions to the strategic hamlet program or to refugee relief. This was the case regardless of how much they may sincerely have felt they were eschewing politics. The many agencies concerned with refugee relief, for example, were in effect helping the military enjoy a freer hand in burning villages and in creating free bomb zones. Not atypical was the case of an International Voluntary Services volunteer who heard American soldiers radioing in from an operation to ask their military headquarters whether there was anyone who could take care of fifty "Viet Cong suspects." "When headquarters told them that La Hai had a refugee man who could handle the problem, the soldiers announced that they would then go ahead and burn the whole hamlet and bring in 350 people."[7]

For the most part, these programs were not developed out of political concerns; rather, they were born out of a sense of responsibility to stand for Christian or human witness amidst suffering. Yet the question must be raised of where this sort of witness ends and where psychological self-gratification begins. Some Americans became psychologically dependent on the agony of the Vietnamese. For them, and for others, Christian witness seemed to imply that well-meaning volunteers could atone for the collective sins of their fellow countrymen by their individual presence and actions in Vietnam. Yet, as one Saigon University professor said, "What these humanitarian agencies may not realize is that the real effect of their presence here is to make the destructive nature of the total American intervention in VietNam less evident."[8] The existence of the volunteers helped keep alive the legend at home of a uniquely altruistic and pluralistic America, an America that does things abroad because it is its historic mission to assist and defend the underprivileged, not because, like all other nation-states, America perceives certain selfish foreign political, economic, and military interests to be promoted and defended.[9] In other words, as Washington journalist I.F. Stone once put it, the voluntary agency role was "to place a corn plaster on an amputation."

As the brutality and futility of the war became more glaringly obvious, many voluntary agency people began to protest against U.S. government policies. First they criticized the way the policies were being implemented, under the basic American can-do assumption that by tinkering here and

---

[7] Don Luce and John Sommer, *Viet-Nam: The Unheard Voices* (Ithaca: Cornell University Press, 1969), p. 16.
[8] Marr, "Politics of Charity," p. 12.
[9] Ibid., p. 2.

there the war could still be won. Then it became clear the war could not be won under any circumstances by the Saigon and U.S. government side. In September 1967, the director and key staff of International Voluntary Services—an organization funded in Vietnam entirely by AID—resigned from their positions to the accompaniment of an anguished protest to President Lyndon Johnson. The U. S. embassy in Saigon attempted through modest intimidation to suppress the letter of resignation before it was released (the mission coordinator pointed out that the signers would find it impossible to ever get admitted into the foreign service), but the letter to President Johnson quickly became front-page news in the *New York Times* and in newspapers around the world. After all, its writers were felt to combine grass-roots knowledge of the real situation in Vietnam with a close understanding of U.S. government workings in that country. To U.S. officialdom, theirs was the first significant case of defection from within the ranks. In spite of the fact that many remaining IVS volunteers then began to supply supporting data to the antiwar movement in the United States, the organization as a whole was not expelled from Vietnam until 1971. However, this was largely because earlier dismissal would have created more political problems than it would have solved for the U.S. government.

There are other, less glaring examples of how U.S. foreign policy considerations influence voluntary agency programs. These examples fall under roughly two headings, depending on whether or not the agency accepts U.S. government funds. Under the first heading are the programs actually funded by the U.S. government, particularly those wholly, or nearly wholly, funded by it. It is hardly surprising that these are subject to various limitations and controls since, from the point of view of the government, there would be little reason to support programs that do not enhance U.S. foreign policy interests in some identifiable way. Under the second heading are those privately funded programs that run counter to these interests as perceived by the government. Interference in both types of programs is resented by the voluntary organizations as an improper infringement on their judgment and flexibility of action.

U.S. Government-Funded Programs. Among voluntary organizations that receive U.S. government funding, there is a feeling that while direct project support may understandably be withheld for countries enjoying low U.S. government priority, indirect support should not be so closely tied to political or other policy considerations. The example of Catholic Relief Services in South Asia is a case in point. In 1976, under a development program grant from AID, CRS sent a regional planning and evaluation representative to be based in New Delhi. The representative had no sooner arrived and established himself when AID announced that his posting there was improper because of a cooling in relations between the U.S. government and the government of India. (Substantial food and commodity support, however, was still being shipped by the United States to India.) Somewhat related examples are those of Colombia, Brazil, and Ecuador, where political relations are relatively good but where AID is disengaging because the countries' GNPs are now deemed sufficient to manage their own problems. In Ecuador disputes over corporate nationalizations, fishing rights, and OPEC cartel involvement have furnished additional reasons for a cessation of U.S. official aid. In all these countries voluntary agency representatives argue that neither political relations nor the level of GNP allows one to perceive the true extent of poverty and thus the need for outside assistance. They correctly note that it is the poor who are often left in the lurch if the void created by departing international agencies is not filled by local sources of support.

Many, of course, would argue that withdrawal of foreign aid is the only way to force the rich in such countries to come to grips with the problem of their own poor. But this begs the question of *how* the withdrawal is announced and planned. For example, voluntary agency representatives argue that the cut-off decision in Ecuador was made too abruptly and without consultation with them. Consequently, CARE suddenly found this political act influencing the nutrition outlook for 300,000 children. The one-year lead time before cut-off was insufficient, CARE said, to make alternative arrangements for transferring to local hands its fourteen-year-old feeding programs.

There are other ways in which U.S. government policies may adversely influence private and voluntary organizations funded by AID. It is argued, for example, that the concentration of the recent U.S. congressional legislation on the *rural* poor makes it more difficult to procure government support for assistance for the *urban* poor. The urban poor are an important group in Latin America, where they account for more than half the total population, and in India, where they add up to 20 per cent of the population —indeed, enough people to make urban India alone the sixth largest country in the world. It is also argued that congressional and AID preoccupation with family planning adversely biases development programs in ways that sensitive Third World recipients may find unacceptable. Indeed, Congress has considered introducing a legislative clause requiring that a family planning component be considered for every aid project. Finally, some U.S. voluntary organizations, and even more Third World critics, bemoan what they see as overly conservative criteria for U.S. government funding of programs generally. This is particularly true of some of the consciousness-raising efforts in Latin America, through which political sensitivities may be raised. Because so many poverty problems are rooted in political inequalities perpetuated by the entrenched "establishment," and because the U.S. government generally is unwilling to risk its relationships with national leaderships, consciousness-raising programs with "destabilizing" connotations cannot generally be funded by AID. Sometimes these groups turn to European donors, as in the case of a highly regarded Colombian organization working in *campesino* consciousness raising. As a priest in Bogotá put it, "That organization is very good—but too radical, of course, to receive U.S. support!" To be sure, some such projects are funded by the Inter-American Foundation, probably the most creative U.S. government aid agency, but the IAF has the virtues of being young, relatively unbureaucratized, and—perhaps most relevant here—removed from an immediately subsidiary role to the U.S. State Department.

In addition to significantly assisting existing voluntary organizations, the U.S. government has in some instances helped to form new U.S. voluntary organizations as explicit instruments of U.S. policy abroad. One of these is the American Institute for Free Labor Development, the official overseas arm of the largest U.S. labor union, the AFL-CIO. Once supported by the U.S. Central Intelligence Agency, it is now financed in large part by AID funds. AIFLD stresses its private role and currently is primarily concerned with training Latin American labor leaders and providing loans and other economic assistance to their unions; indeed, it has made contributions to improving the livelihood of labor on that continent. However, politics rather than economic development is its basic operating rationale. With the establishment of its Latin American program in 1962, during a period of heightened cold war tensions and the early Alliance for Progress, AIFLD hoped that its assistance would help prevent communists from becoming too powerful in Latin American labor movements. It also hoped that improving conditions for labor in those countries would have the effect of protecting U.S. workers from the competition of cheap foreign labor. Thus by urging increases in Latin American labor wages, it was possible to have happier, noncommunist workers there at the same time as more even competition for U.S. workers at home.

A somewhat similar example is that of Partners of the Americas, also founded at the time of the U.S. government-initiated Alliance for Progress and intended as the people-to-people analog of that government-to-government effort. Under the Partners' banner, various U.S. states were linked with Latin American countries, and in some cases with states within countries, for cultural and technical exchanges. Although the program title suggests the notion of partnership and two-way exchange, many of the activities thus far have been in the form of one-way aid—mostly technical assistance—from the United States to Latin America. Partners' linkage with governments is suggested by the fact that the president of the United States has served as the national honorary chairman in the United States, that more than thirty U.S. governors have been honorary chairman of their respective state committees, and that there is a close connection with the Organization of American States. The program is a novel form of aid in that it follows an explicitly governmental mandate yet also involves at least some element of the U.S. public in a way that purely governmental aid programs do not. Indeed, Partners is now hoping to expand its narrow membership base in order to become both more effective and more independent of U.S. government funding.

Quite aside from the political and other policy implications of U.S. government funding for voluntary (or nongovernmental) organizations is the whole issue of administrative controls. Around this issue swirl many emotions and heated exchanges. When voluntary agency executives meet together, it is not uncommon for an agenda of substantive development issues to devolve into discussion of AID bureaucracy and its attendant problems. This is not surprising. Because of the way in which the Washington AID bureaucracy has been structured, the private agencies have had to deal with innumerable branches in the course of their grant or contract negotiations. Some grants are made through the several parts of the Technical Assistance Bureau, and others through the various regional bureaus, the Food-for-Peace office, or the Office of Private and Voluntary Cooperation. Virtually all, at some stage, are processed through the Bureau of Program and Administrative Services, which handles the final administrative details. In addition, most grants go through various processing stages at AID offices in the Third World capitals (still ethnocentrically referred to as "the field"). For example, during the 1975 fiscal year, one voluntary organization had at least twenty-seven contracts or grants in effect that were administered by seven regional and functional bureaus in Washington and one overseas mission. As a 1976 report by the U.S. General Accounting Office (GAO) observed, "Each AID bureau had its own management style, criteria, and priorities to which the PVO was required to conform. . . . The lack of a uniform policy on implementation procedures between bureaus has resulted in considerable confusion and annoyance to PVOs, which contend that their limited staffs must spend an inordinate amount of time complying with AID requests for information and program management requirements."[10]

With all these levels of consideration and consultation, not to mention the sublevels and many different individuals within each level, it is hardly cause for astonishment that decisions take months and even years to reach. In the interim, conflicting signals may be given at different levels suggesting a need to reformulate proposals one way, then another, then still another —all requiring not only valuable staff time but often innumerable and costly trips to Washington and to "the field"—until all the actors are satisfied with the result. Then come the aggravating conditions and regulations, including one that obliges AID-funded voluntary agencies to report all staff travel—even short visits—to the relevant U.S. ambassador or AID mission director; another that requires utilization of U.S. carriers for air transport (except under certain extenuating circumstances); and—most sensitive of all—the audit.

In a world as diverse as that of the voluntary agencies, it is hardly surprising that many different audit methodologies are followed, with some obviously less reliable than others. To many agency people—and one must remember that flexibility is their hallmark—AID's audit rules seem unduly bureaucratic. The problem is even more annoying to Third World organiza-

---

[10]*Channeling Foreign Aid through Private and Voluntary Organizations,* Report of the Comptroller General of the United States (Washington, D.C.: U.S. General Accounting Office, 1976), p. 8.

tions, for many of whom this stringency and the psychological subservience it implies are so unbearable as to persuade them not to accept any U.S. government grants at all.

Of course there are reasons for these various rules and stringencies, as AID is quick to point out. While many individuals within the bureaucracy might prefer fewer regulations, there is invariably resistance to change at other levels. U.S. ambassadors generally insist on being kept informed of movements into and out of their country bailiwicks by individuals funded by the government they represent—for understandable reasons, when looked at from the point of view of their responsibilities. Also, the U.S. economy is better served by policies designed to keep dollars at home instead of letting them flow abroad to non-American airlines. And—as Congress and the GAO make abundantly clear—sound auditing is essential if AID's responsibilities are to be duly exercised over the taxpayers' funds it dispenses. Evidence emerging from 1974 hearings before the U.S. Senate Subcommittee on Children and Youth suggested that some voluntary organizations have, in fact, been remiss in exercising their financial responsibilities, even though exhaustive investigations by the General Accounting Office of five principal children's charities turned up no flagrant abuses and the investigation was ultimately laid to rest.[11] Meanwhile, the Council of Better Business Bureaus has addressed itself to the issue of financial responsibility, and in 1974 it issued a set of standards for charitable solicitations. The National Information Bureau keeps partial evaluations of voluntary agency qualifications in order to respond to queries from the public, but their lack of thoroughness and in some cases their arbitrary standards have been criticized as discriminatory, especially by the newer and smaller voluntary organizations. AID has made available a certain amount of guidance on the subject of auditing procedures and is considering allowing agencies, in the future, to furnish simply their own audited accounts within certain guidelines, rather than insisting on burdensome additional AID audits.[12] Overall, the problem is one of defining the line beyond which acceptable monitoring becomes counterproductive to the larger goals of promoting Third World development through U.S. private and voluntary organizations. Many voluntary organizations feel the line is already being overstepped, while many at AID feel the voluntary agencies require the kind of discipline their audit procedures impose.

---

[11]The Subcommittee's hearings, chaired by then-Senator Walter F. Mondale, considered primarily the children's charities: American-Korean Foundation, Christian Children's Fund, Foster Parents Plan, Holt Adoption Program, and Save the Children Federation. They uncovered some instances of misleading advertising and lack of current information on Third World counterparts' utilization of funds, deficiencies which the concerned agencies note they have since corrected. See U.S. Congress, Senate Committee on Labor and Public Welfare, Subcommittee on Children and Youth, *Children's Charities, 1974: Hearings*, Part 4, 93rd Cong., 2d sess., 10 October 1974.

[12]See *Standards of Accounting and Financial Reporting for Voluntary Health Organizations* (New York: National Health Council, National Assembly of National Voluntary Health and Social Welfare Organizations, and United Way of America, 1975).

Non-Government-Funded Programs. Meanwhile, of course, voluntary organizations have the right not to apply for U.S. government grants for overseas programs, a position taken by such organizations as the American Friends Service Committee, Mennonite Central Committee, Unitarian-Universalist Service Committee, and Oxfam-America. Yet even they are constrained in some cases by American government policies. The most obvious example concerns aid to Vietnam both during and after the war. In a well-known test case in 1965, a Quaker action group sent a ship, the Phoenix, to North Vietnam with medical and relief supplies for victims of U.S. bombing raids. This was an overt violation of U.S. laws prohibiting trade with the enemy (even with an officially undeclared enemy), and the U.S. government retaliated by confiscating the group's bank accounts. Undaunted, the Quakers opened an account in Canada but continued to suffer other forms of harassment until the U.S. government ultimately relented and allowed ad hoc shipping permits. At this point, in 1969, the AFSC itself began to send relief and rehabilitation supplies to North Vietnam. However, they discovered that blankets, for example, were allowed as humanitarian assistance, while wool to *make* blankets—ironically considered a contribution to economic rehabilitation—was disallowed. Ultimately, exceptions to rehabilitation aid bans were also permitted by the U.S. government, but not until 1975, after AFSC collected citizen petitions from forty American cities and towns. This constituency action showed that individual Americans were actively joining in the cause and making themselves equally (and unmanageably) culpable under the law—the law that AFSC was otherwise considering breaking or skirting by making shipments via Canada if the U.S. government did not relent.

A handful of other voluntary organizations also felt that Vietnam's needs were more compelling than the U.S. government's policy. As a result of their desire to aid North Vietnam, Medical Aid for Indochina and the Bach Mai Hospital Fund had difficulties in obtaining and keeping their normal tax-exempt status from the Internal Revenue Service. Medical Aid for Indochina reported that its offices were raided. The Bach Mai group was told that since the Democratic Republic of Vietnam was a socialist country, its hospitals were by definition governmental; thus aid to them was not in the nature of humanitarian assistance but rather was considered aid to a hostile government and therefore had to be prohibited. Church World Service evaded this problem, rather nervously, by funneling modest humanitarian support to North Vietnam via the World Council of Churches in Europe. Then in 1975, CWS joined the Mennonite Central Committee, Lutheran World Relief, Bach Mai, and others to form a consortium called Friendshipment, which has continued sending aid to Vietnam—legally—under case-by-case dispensations of the U.S. government.

Those organizations that by policy do not accept U.S. government funding for overseas programs feel strongly that this position enables them to retain their integrity both at home and in Third World circles critical of the United States. They argue that organizations such as CARE and Catholic Relief Services—the largest general relief and development organizations—serve, in effect, as contract agencies and thus to a large extent as extensions of the U.S. government overseas. Indeed, in 1974 these two organizations together accounted for 93 per cent of all U.S. government commodities and ocean freight payments channeled through the ninety-four voluntary agencies registered with the U.S. Advisory Committee on Voluntary Foreign Aid.[13] Yet CARE and CRS officials are the first to deny that they are any less independent than the others. And to a large extent they are right, for they, too, are free to accept or reject the assistance offered by the government if the terms do not fit with their images of their own organizations.

It is here, however, that the historical perspective is important. After all, these organizations grew out of the post-World War II relief period when the interests of the U.S. government and the U.S. public were perceived as identical. While their size and nature, compared with the government bureaucracies, have enabled them to be more innovative and flexible, their institutional ideologies have always had much in common with those of the governmental aid program. Thus from their point of view they are independent, while from the point of view of some outside observers, the natural congruence of ideologies is seen as reflection of a forced adherence to a "party line."

Governments and the Voluntary Sector in Canada and Europe

The extent to which U.S. voluntary organizations are particularly susceptible to charges of governmental identification is usefully illustrated by examples from other donor countries—for instance, that of Oxfam in the United Kingdom as contrasted to Oxfam-America. In the United Kingdom, where Oxfam originated, its ties are relatively close with the British government and especially with the government's Overseas Development Ministry. In the United States, however, the policy of Oxfam-America has been that funds should not be accepted from AID. The reason, simply, is that in international realpolitik, links with a large-power government like that of the United States have entirely different connotations than U.K. government links. To this extent, U.S. voluntary agencies suffer from having their locus in a nation that is a superpower.

In terms of the quality of relationships between voluntary organizations and their own national governments, distant pastures may indeed be greener. Certainly, to many Americans, they *appear* greener. The relationship in Canada between the official Canadian International Development Agency (CIDA) and local voluntary organizations is a case in point. CIDA

---

[13]*Channeling Foreign Aid*, p. 4.

will fund up to half, or in some cases more, of individual project costs with a relative minimum of inconvenience to the private agencies concerned. Indeed, some U.S. agencies have established Canadian branches in order to qualify for these funds, an issue of some sensitivity for nationalistic Canadians concerned about competition from their "big brother" across the border. CIDA officials, trying to understand their relative popularity with the local voluntary organizations, point to two possible explanations. First, the Canadian government as a whole, especially in recent years, has placed a high priority on Third World assistance and has appreciated the usefulness of Canadian voluntary organizations in building a larger popular consensus in favor of that policy—thus a special reason for encouraging CIDA to support Canadian voluntary organizations with a minimum of inconvenience. Second, CIDA's Nongovernmental Organizations Division—a centralized (and thus simpler) operation—is run almost entirely by people who have themselves come out of voluntary organizations, especially from the Canadian University Service Overseas, and who thus understand the special sensitivities and problems involved. How long the Canadian pasture will continue to appear greener is open to question. Parkinson's Law—work expands to fill the time available for its completion—knows no national boundaries. Some observers feel that creeping bureaucratization and tensions have already begun, with more of it inevitable as government/voluntary agency relationships accrue longer histories of collaboration, as in the United States.

In certain countries of Western Europe, the relationship between the public and private aid sectors is qualitatively different from that in the United States or Canada. In many cases, private organizations exercise significant influence on governmental decision making. In the Netherlands, for example, the Catholic and Protestant churches and their aid agencies make their weight keenly felt, contributing to an overall political consensus as to the desirability of Third World assistance. Governmental and nongovernmental aid cooperation have grown up around four essentially private intermediary panels that fill a peer-group screening function for all individual agency proposals for government support. This decentralized decision-making pattern is said to work with a minimum of political interference.

Sweden and West Germany also seem to enjoy smooth relationships between their governments and private organizations. The tax systems of both countries are structured in such a way that a supplement is charged to the individual income taxes of church members. In Germany, for example, the supplement amounts to 8 per cent of the tax bill. The amount raised is then returned to the appropriate churches for their own program priorities, with a certain proportion recommended for overseas development aid. Channeling private monies into government coffers and then back into private church groups for overseas development may obscure the character of the funding source, but it does not mean that some degree of independence is not possible. Indeed, West German voluntary organizations were allowed to channel aid to Tanzania at a time when that country's relations with East Germany would normally have caused such aid to be considered a violation of the law.

What is behind these apparently better relationships between governments and private organizations in other countries? The basic explanation must be found in the overall histories and social and religious compositions of the various nations. Whereas the United States has assiduously maintained a policy of separation of church and state—indeed, many Europeans came to America specifically in search of freedom of religion—the distinctions in European countries have been less clear-cut. Thus the above-mentioned influence of the Dutch churches on Dutch politics. The fact that churches have enjoyed greater temporal influence in European countries than in the United States, combined with the fact that well over half of all private and voluntary aid in most of these countries is church-related (in Germany about 80 per cent is said to be church aid), suggests the importance of this difference in traditions alone.[14]

Another frequent difference—in Sweden and the Netherlands, for example, if not in West Germany—is in the relative ideologies and influence of the trade union movements and political parties. In the first two countries, the unions espouse a liberal social consciousness on a transnational basis, embracing the unity and solidarity of workers everywhere. While solidarity may not apply any better there than in the United States to specific cases of trade policies—cases in which encouragement to competing workers' industries overseas might result in lost jobs at home—the unions do at least tend to advocate aid. To the extent that they support private and voluntary organizations, the latter gain that much more influence. In some cases, political parties also engage in transnational causes and activities, this being an accepted role for them, given their transnational identities and perceived responsibilities. In West Germany, for example, each of the three main political parties has its own overseas aid-giving foundation, something that would be most unusual for Republicans or Democrats in the United States.

Another difference is rooted in varying systems of government. Some observers have suggested that the parliamentary system provides an easier backdrop to government/voluntary agency collaborations because there is virtual unity between the executive and legislative branches. The government thus speaks with one voice in matters such as support for Third World aid and for giving aid through private agencies. As a result, there is less reason to be apprehensive about legislative criticism or GAO investigations, and thus no need to overaudit and overcontrol.

---

[14]See John D. Lange, Jr., *Private Foreign Aid From Europe and North America*, prepared for the 17th Session, Senior Seminar in Foreign Policy (Washington, D.C.: Department of State, 1975); and Jørgen Lissner, *The Politics of Altruism*, (Geneva: Lutheran World Federation, 1977), p. 89 ff.

Finally, there is a difference in the nature and degree of the past overseas involvements of various countries. Several European governments have had intensive colonial experiences that, for all their negative aspects, have conditioned their people to have at least some sense of understanding of the Third World. The United States, on the other hand, lies geographically self-contained on its own continent; its people, as suggested earlier, have both a reputation for naiveté about other societies and a missionary zeal deeply rooted in the American experience.

Public and Private Cooperation in the United States

By drawing these contrasts in the quality of relationships between funding governments and voluntary organizations, one should not be too critical of the AID role in the United States. Although other governments have channeled more money through voluntary agencies, the U.S. government has also channeled a significant amount of food aid, which—for all its attendant problems—has meant a very large overall U.S. voluntary aid figure.[15] As both the GAO and the U.S. Senate Committee on Appropriations have observed, AID's recent initiatives, in particular, have aimed at making government resources available to private agencies for mutually acceptable purposes and in a meaningful spirit of collaboration. "We wish to lend our support to the spirit of cooperative and complementary association demonstrated by the evolving relationship between AID and the various Private and Voluntary Organizations. AID is to be commended for the initiation of new concepts in this continuing relationship. The Committee is hopeful that the new directions in AID's association with Private and Voluntary Organizations will lead to an even more productive exchange of ideas and programs."[16] It is only natural that this relationship should entail certain costs, namely, "that a relationship which too closely joins the Private and Voluntary Agencies with AID may erode the unique character of these organizations. We are fearful that a relationship which involves joint planning and operations will lead to the bureaucratization of these organizations whose strong point has often been their ability to reduce administrative costs and to avoid administrative entanglements. . . . AID's role should be that of ensuring that sound fiscal policies are followed, and that the objectives of Private and Voluntary Organizations [presumably meaning those actually supported through government resources] are in accord with those of the United States and the recipient countries."[17]

Even with its attendant ambiguities, the advantages of U.S. government support are undeniable in filling critical needs, especially in development activities. Development organizations such as Private Agencies Col-

---

[15]See Annex A, Table 4 for figures on the different components of U.S. government aid given through private and voluntary organizations.
[16]U.S. Congress, "Foreign Assistance," p. 70.
[17]Ibid.

laborating Together, International Voluntary Services, Near East Foundation, and World Education all tend to receive significant percentages of their funding from AID for development programs; without this support, their effectiveness would be severely constrained and their very existence endangered. Also, existing membership organizations such as the National Council of Negro Women, the YMCA, and the Boy Scouts have been encouraged to expand into international development directions in ways that may not have been feasible without AID stimulation and support. The fact is that organizations such as these have yet to tap the public consciousness for the volume of creative development funds they need—all of which raises the separate problem of fund raising that will be dealt with in the next chapter.

Structures for Interface. There are two principal organizations for promoting liaison and understanding and for grappling with the various interface problems between the voluntary agency sector and the U.S. government. The more official one is the U.S. Advisory Committee on Voluntary Foreign Aid, which had its origins before the U.S. entry into World War II. At that time it was felt that, in order to preserve America's neutral status, all voluntary agencies soliciting contributions from the U.S. public for relief activities in warring countries should be listed with the Department of State, presumably in the event that controls might be necessary. The result was the President's War Relief Control Board, established by an executive order in 1942, and in 1946 succeeded by the Advisory Committee, as it is called now. The duties of the Committee (the secretariat of which is situated within AID) have been essentially "to register qualified U.S. private, nonprofit organizations voluntarily seeking and accepting registration . . . to assure their bona fides to the public and to maintain and publish a register of such organizations; to provide information and advice to AID (and other U.S. Government agencies) relating to foreign assistance in which U.S. Government and the private voluntary organizations interact; . . . to provide assistance to the community of private and voluntary organizations working abroad relative to problems and issues in their relations with AID and other Federal agencies; . . . [and] to foster public interest in voluntary foreign aid."[18] By virtue of registration with the Advisory Committee, agencies have been eligible for transportation reimbursement for commodities shipped overseas, for government-owned excess property donations, and for P.L.-480 food grants. Out of an estimated total of some 700 voluntary (including missionary) organizations, 94, including most of the principal ones, were registered with the Committee as of 1976.

Perhaps because the Committee was originally established to coordinate agency relief efforts, it has found itself in an increasingly uncertain position in recent years. Without the staff capability to monitor the

---

[18]*The Role of Voluntary Agencies in International Assistance: A Look to the Future* (Washington, D.C.: Advisory Committee on Voluntary Foreign Aid, Agency for International Development, April 1974), pp. 22-23.

performance of the organizations registered with it, the "good housekeeping seal" of the Advisory Committee has become relatively meaningless. Because AID grants for development programs frequently have been given regardless of registration status, and because these grants are becoming increasingly important, much of the overall purpose of registration has been lost.[19] As a result, the Committee has been left to fill essentially the role of a goodwill forum between the private sector and the government—a moderately useful role but a limited one, particularly given the types of interface problems noted above. For these reasons, a substantial reorganization and strengthening of the Committee is currently under consideration and is, indeed, vital. Such a restructuring and rejuvenation should focus on making the Committee more representative of the diversity of the private sector, on giving it a more substantive registration monitoring capability, and on encouraging it to actively exercise advisory powers over a broader range of relevant issues concerning U.S. government relations with the private sector overseas.

The other principal organization for liaison is the American Council of Voluntary Agencies for Foreign Service (ACVAFS). Incorporated in 1944 and having a current membership of forty-four organizations, the Council is run by its member agencies, though it is dominated by the largest of them. An adjunct to the Council is the Technical Assistance Information Clearing House (TAICH), an AID-supported service center that gathers and propagates information concerning the overseas programs of U.S. nonprofit organizations generally. In practice, the Council serves primarily as a forum and coordinating point for 1) interagency relief efforts, 2) refugee and migration planning, and 3) relating to the U.S. government on issues of collective concern such as tax exemption policies and AID grant relationships. In its first capacity, the Council served a major coordinating role, for example, in the process of settling Vietnamese refugees in the United States in 1975 and in coordinating disaster aid in the aftermath of Central American floods and earthquakes in 1975 and 1976. Because the Council has been more active and because it directly represents the concerned agencies rather than the more amorphous public represented by the Advisory Committee, it has tended to have a larger influence on government policies that relate to its constituency. Yet it, too, is under fire, particularly from the newer, smaller, and primarily development-oriented agencies, which feel the need for a more universal membership organization (with more affordable membership fees) that is concerned not only with the ACVAFS range of issues but also with the substance of improved development assistance. Indeed, no continuing institutional forum currently exists for meeting the more substantive need for research and analysis into the workings and impacts of private and voluntary organizations in the Third

---

[19]See Bartlett Harvey, *Registration and Approval of Voluntary Foreign Aid Agencies by the Advisory Committee on Voluntary Foreign Aid of the Agency for International Development*, report to the Committee and the Agency (Washington, D.C.: Department of State, 1975).

World. This gap is of increasing concern to many in the field and needs to be addressed if the organizations are to keep up with the challenges before them.

Cooperation with Multilateral Institutions. To supplement the voluntary agency reliance on U.S. government assistance, voluntary organizations are increasingly seeking collaborative relationships with multilateral institutions, especially with the U.N. family of agencies and the World Bank. They are having some success at this because, just as they and the bilateral donors have discovered the failure of the trickle-down approach to development and the virtues of growth from below, so too are the multilaterals making the same discovery. While the relationship between the two sectors is probably still best characterized as a hesitant early courtship, the potential is great. For the U.N. Development Programme (UNDP), as for AID, the lesson is clear that efforts to combat poverty must begin at the grass-roots level where, it is recognized, the nongovernmental organizations are most active. Some UNDP resident representatives are open to collaboration, and official memoranda have gone to the field urging more of it. UNDP headquarters has envisioned three roles for nongovernmental organizations (NGOs) in this kind of collaboration: "(a) as innovators of change, and initiators of new approaches and project activities at community and grass-roots levels; (b) as sources of funds and their own expertise for economic and social development in the LDCs [less developed countries]; and (c) as promoters of public support for development activities and as interpreters of change to local peoples."[20]

Some U.N. organizations, of course, have been working at this level already. Most notably, the Food and Agriculture Organization has worked in various member countries through its affiliated Freedom from Hunger Campaigns. The U.N. International Children's Emergency Fund (UNICEF), unique in the U.N. family for enjoying the benefits of a mass popular constituency in addition to the benefits of government aid, has also supported a large number of grass-roots initiatives throughout the Third World, increasingly with a developmental rather than a relief bias. The U.N. Institute for Training and Research (UNITAR) is engaged in a research effort to make known the potential of voluntary agencies within U.N. and member-nation bureaucracies.

At present, the extent of UNDP-NGO collaboration is limited to periodic meetings to discuss the possibilities of "combining resources." However, there are several impediments to doing so, and to the UNDP actually providing grants for voluntary agency efforts. The one most often cited by UNDP officials is the severe financial crisis faced by the United Nations during the past few years. A more fundamental one, however, is that UNDP grants are made to member governments, which are themselves

---

[20]"Strengthening collaboration with non-government organizations," internal memo, United Nations Development Programme, New York, January 21, 1975.

largely responsible for determining how their country allotments are to be used. Other impeding factors include indifference or ignorance among UNDP resident representatives concerning voluntary agency potential, and the overall drawbacks of single-government bureaucracy which tend to be multiplied proportionately in a multilateral bureaucracy. For both U.S. and European voluntary organizations, therefore, penetrating the complex U.N. system is bewildering and difficult indeed.

To some extent, the same holds true for the World Bank. Although it too has begun to advocate the grass-roots approach to development—since a 1973 speech in Nairobi by Bank president Robert McNamara—Bank officials have noted that it takes time for such a large institution to change its traditional pattern of operation. Whereas the United Nations at least has a system of "organizations in consultative status" (which roughly corresponds to diplomatic recognition of private agencies), the Bank has not had any experience with the extreme diversity of voluntary organizations and approaches to development. Like the UNDP, it generally deals with governments. As Bank officials have remarked, there is also the impediment of a history of intellectual difficulty in setting up links between those whose approach to development is essentially humanitarian or religious and those who operate as development bankers, even if in pursuit of goals other than profit alone. Yet the intended new types of Bank rural and urban development projects inevitably bring the Bank into contact with village and slum situations where individuals and institutions supported by private aid agencies constitute one of the very few reliable—and cost-acceptable—infrastructures for channeling programs. It is only in recent months that the Bank is beginning to grapple with the implications of these types of situations, but it is likely that increasing opportunities for collaboration with voluntary organizations will gradually emerge.

New Structures for U.S. Government Support to the Voluntary Sector

Notwithstanding these new forms of collaboration and the resulting financial infusions they are likely to represent for U.S. (and other) private and voluntary organizations, there is still a need for new structures for the U.S. government/voluntary agency relationship. This is not to say that AID has failed in its mandate to channel assistance through the private organizations; indeed, AID's initiatives since the 1973 congressional legislation have contributed significantly to both the quantity and quality of voluntary agency contributions to the Third World. A relatively new series of "development program grants," for example, has enabled more than thirty organizations to receive assistance for upgrading their planning and assessment capabilities and their overall organizational infrastructures in ways that hopefully will endure long beyond the periods of the individual grants. By the testimony of many voluntary agencies themselves, the process of interacting with AID—and also increasingly with each other—during this period has sharpened development consciousness and insights. That little of this kind of influence is readily quantifiable should not be taken to mean it has not occurred.

Ironically, it is partly because of this recent development "consciousness raising" that the voluntary organizations should now be in a position to be more independent of the constricting aspects of the AID relationship. Although the price of extensive AID supervision may have been justifiable in the past, there are now fewer benefits to its continuation; indeed, the time and money costs of dealing with the bureaucracy are potentially counterproductive, both to the agencies concerned and to the intended beneficiaries in the Third World. For the most experienced voluntary organizations, it is thus time to lighten both the bureaucratic and the political burdens of the AID relationship, while still not abnegating the understandable demands for minimum accountability.

There are a number of options available for accomplishing these goals. *First*, AID's own structures and procedures could be streamlined and strengthened. One constructive step in this direction was taken in mid-1977, namely, to decentralize responsibility and authority for policymaking and grant-giving for voluntary agencies by transferring to AID field missions full authority for making grants to individual voluntary agencies working within their countries of concern. Although a potential disadvantage of this policy is that individual AID missions may be unsympathetic or unresponsive to worthwhile voluntary agency activities, the new policy should minimize much bureaucratic red tape and increase the local relevance of grants that are made. Yet other reforms also need to be considered, including the following possibilities:

(a) At AID's Washington headquarters, responsibility and authority for policymaking and grant-giving for voluntary agencies could be centralized in one, preferably upgraded, bureau of AID. This would have the advantage of giving these programs greater prominence and priority and minimizing aggravating intrabureaucratic delays. The disadvantage would be the lack of line authority for specialized geographic area input from AID, as well as the reduced number of "windows" where enterprising voluntary agencies could apply for AID monies.

(b) AID could give significantly more of its assistance in the form of long-term (three- to five-year-long) general support grants to voluntary agencies, especially to consortia that promote interagency cooperation in both programming and management. These grants, for which there is already some precedent,[21] would combine under one umbrella the variety of

---

[21] Aside from the cases of PACT and CODEL—two consortia which have received multipurpose AID grants—a precedent for giving general support grants lies in the $11.2 million AID provided to fifteen agencies in 1975 alone. It should be noted, however, that the bulk of this amount (some 72 per cent) was provided to two unique organizations, to one of which (the Asia Foundation) AID had an obligation dating from its CIA funding period, and from the other of which (the International Executive Service Corps) AID felt political and business pressures that demanded response. These figures are taken from *Channeling Foreign Aid*, pp. 11-12.

small grants covering several country projects, and the expensive negotiations these now require. Such grants would be negotiated with a general understanding regarding the types of activities to be pursued and mutually agreed terms for both evaluation and audit. Their advantage would lie in a decrease in bureaucratic delay and in enabling a broader and thus better framework for voluntary agency planning. Potential disadvantages are the fears sometimes expressed over inadequate accountability (if the initial negotiations were not sufficiently well conducted) and over increased susceptibility to political pressures to give grants on grounds other than those of merit.

(c) The Congress could establish a separate line item and appropriation for AID grants to private and voluntary organizations, regardless of the way in which AID itself was structured to relate to them. The advantages would be in the greater prominence and priority given to voluntary involvement in international development and in the budgetary incentive thus likely to be evoked among nonenthusiasts within AID to support worthwhile voluntary agency approaches. The possible disadvantages are that additional legislative line items could have the unhealthy effect of reducing AID's overall programming flexibility, and that the voluntary agencies, if they had their own line item, might lose interest in supporting the rest of the AID bill in their public testimony.

A *second* option for easing the bureaucratic and political burdens of the voluntary organization/AID relationship would be to explore structures that do not involve administration by either AID or the State Department. Indeed, it is only this kind of option that would have the much-desired effect of insulating private organizations from U.S. foreign policy involvement. One could envision, for example, the establishment with government funds of a new nongovernmental body, such as the recently incorporated Appropriate Technology International, the purpose of which is to enhance through grants and technical assistance private U.S. scientific and technological contributions to Third World development. ATI grew out of a 1975 congressional mandate calling for more attention by AID to the use of intermediate technology in international development. AID, feeling that creative new talent could be brought to bear on technology problems by Americans from the private sector, assisted in the establishment of ATI as a totally private organization to which it could relate in a liaison rather than a formal control capacity. The long-term hope and expectation is that other funds—from foundations, corporations, and multilateral aid agencies—will ultimately supplement U.S. government support to this new entity. Historically and structurally, ATI thus bears some resemblance to a number of groups mentioned earlier in this volume, which make private use of public funds. The virtue of such arrangements is the removal by one full step of the political and bureaucratic drawbacks of direct government funding.

A *third* option would lie in the creation of one or more government endowments or public corporations that could be modeled after organizations such as the National Endowment for the Humanities or the National

Endowment for the Arts; the National Science Foundation; the Inter-American Foundation; or a possible reorganized version of the Peace Corps that has been discussed by a National Academy of Sciences committee. While none of these precedents guarantees insulation from domestic political pressures—such as calls from congressmen urging support of favored constituents' charities—their relative freedom of action and lack of bureaucracy make associations with them appear more attractive both to U.S. and Third World grantees. The models, of course, differ. The National Endowments for the Humanities and Arts give grants primarily in the United States, although recent legislation permits them to make overseas grants in consultation with the Department of State—a consultation which the Department, at least, feels is mutually constructive and conflict-free. The directorships of both endowments are made up of private citizens, while the staff members are government civil servants. The National Science Foundation, on the other hand, is a federal government agency with board members appointed by the president of the United States; it relies heavily, however, on nongovernmental advisory panels and reviewers to make fair and knowledgeable grant selections.

A more relevant model for this discussion is that of the Inter-American Foundation, a U.S. government corporation that is nevertheless semiprivate in nature.[22] Born as "a child of frustration," it is a frankly experimental organization with a mandate "to locate, define, and assist other experimental organizations."[23] The legislation that established the IAF at the end of 1969 originated in the House Committee on Foreign Affairs Subcommittee on Inter-American Affairs through the efforts of two highly committed congressmen—Dante B. Fascell and F. Bradford Morse. The assumptions behind its establishment were:

> First, that during the past 8 years all too little United States assistance has reached the masses of the Latin American people or made a visible impact on their daily lives; second, that the social development goals of the Act of Bogota, the Charter of Punta del Este and the Declaration of American Presidents, whose objectives of expanding opportunity for the great majority of people form the very cornerstone of the Alliance for Progress, are not being achieved in any substantial, meaningful sense; and third, that while Alliance for Progress programs operating at the government-to-government level have done an impressive job in promoting industrial and economic growth of Latin America, they have proved much less effective in responding to the requirements of social and civic change on that continent.[24]

---

[22]Of the IAF's seven-member board, four are from the private sector and three from the government.
[23]Bennett Schiff, "First Steps: The Inter-American Foundation's First Three Years, 1971-1973" (Rosslyn, Va.: The Inter-American Foundation, undated), pp. 6, 8.
[24]Ibid., pp. 8-9.

The IAF was expected to rectify these shortcomings and to restore "the necessary and proper balance between the economic and social objectives of inter-American cooperation and development." It was to direct its efforts through local organizations dedicated to broader popular participation in development, and generally was to help Latin Americans pave the way for the modernization of their societies. Furthermore, it was seen from the beginning that the organization's effectiveness would be determined not only by the caliber of its directors and staff but also by the institution's insulation from the ebb and flow of political currents that are always present in direct government-to-government relations. To better ensure its independence from day-to-day political considerations, funding on the level of $50 million plus an additional $78 million in local currencies was made available "until expended." This alleviated the normal government bureaucratic need both to hurriedly obligate all annually appropriated funds before the end of the given fiscal year and to expend the considerable amount of energy required to justify and wait for new funds.

The IAF is not without its critics, partly because of its independent operating style and partly because of its highly privileged status of being protected by Congress. Yet its early record, reflected in a 1977 introspective review of its first five years, has been impressive.[25] Its grants—made only to Latin American (rather than U.S.) groups—have focused heavily on local intermediary organizations that have activities in credit and production cooperatives, workers' self-managed enterprises, low-cost housing projects, legal aid clinics, consumer co-ops, peasant associations, cultural awareness programs, health care projects, agricultural extension services, and leadership training programs. As IAF's president, William Dyal, stated before the Subcommittee on Foreign Operations of the Senate Appropriations Committee in 1975, "We attempt to respond to peoples' efforts to solve their own problems by their own methods, recognizing that other societies are different than our own, having different histories, needs, and desires. The focus always remains on *people*—individuals and communities—rather than on macro-economic questions. . . . Once a decision has been made to fund a particular activity we stand aside. While we observe with sympathetic interest, we don't intervene or interfere."[26] Of all the U.S. assistance efforts in Latin America—public or private—the IAF enjoys perhaps the best reputation among Latin Americans for both the relevance of its programs and its open, nonpaternalistic style of operation.

During the period when the IAF legislation was being drawn up, emphasis was placed on the Foundation's experimental role as a possible precedent for equivalent initiatives in other parts of the Third World,

---

[25]Inter-American Foundation, *They Know How . . . , an Experiment in Development Assistance* (Washington, D.C.: U.S. Government Printing Office, 1977).

[26]William M. Dyal, Jr. (President, Inter-American Foundation), testimony before the U.S. Senate Committee on Appropriations, Subcommittee on Foreign Operations, April 30, 1975.

particularly in Africa. The IAF's impressive accomplishments to date suggest that the time has come to replicate the most successful parts of that experiment, particularly the concentration on participation and process and also the organizational structure for channeling U.S. government support for Third World development. Indeed, legislation to create an African Development Foundation was introduced in the U.S. Congress in 1977. One problem with replication is that Latin America offers uniquely favorable conditions that would be difficult to match in Africa and parts of Asia. Latin America, after all, is blessed with a broad range of existing local private organizations—most of them church-inspired or church-related—which are led by highly dedicated, experienced, and competent staff. The equivalent personnel infrastructure on other continents—with notable exceptions, of course—is less in evidence. Also, Latin America is a continent with a special historical relationship to the United States. For that and other reasons, the particular congressional dynamics that led to the creation of the IAF would be more difficult to duplicate for other countries. Yet this difficulty presumably applies more to Asia than to Africa, where the Congressional Black Caucus and other groups are likely to exert their influence. Some people argue further that even an IAF might succumb, in time, to the bureaucratic problems of AID or to more political interference than heretofore. Yet the frustration over existing aid patterns that acted as midwife in the birth of the IAF certainly is present to the same extent with respect to aid to Africa and Asia. In addition, all the difficulties mentioned above should be surmountable. It is in Asia and Africa, indeed, where the vast bulk of the poor majority live and where more effective programs are most urgently needed. The advantages of the IAF model in bureaucratic terms, as well as in terms of being further removed from the short-run foreign policy considerations of the State Department, are as applicable to African and Asian settings as to Latin American ones. Thus the principle of an African Development Foundation should be both supported and extended to an Asian analog.

In so doing, one major change should be considered. The IAF's policy has been to give grants only to Latin American groups and not to U.S. or other expatriate voluntary agencies. However, in view of the relatively less extensive local infrastructures of many African and Asian countries, and also in view of the benefits to both partners involved in a sensitively handled international technical and cultural exchange, some grants under any new African or Asian development foundation should be made available to U.S. voluntary organizations as well as directly to overseas groups. In so doing, the virtues of focusing primarily on indigenous groups should not be forgotten; to preserve their primacy, a specific budget allocation might be considered for cases where channeling assistance through U.S. or other international agency intermediaries would be desirable.

A related aid structure that would maximize the advantages of U.S. voluntary agencies is one that was discussed in 1974 by a National Academy of Sciences committee on the future of the U.S. Peace Corps. According to the NAS model, the Peace Corps—now a part of ACTION, the U.S. government's overall volunteer agency—could be transformed into a public foundation, perhaps somewhat analogous to the IAF model, though with an obviously different mandate and program character. A principal function of such a public foundation would be to cooperate—and share resources—with the private sector. Collaboration between Peace Corps and nongovernmental voluntary programs is now relatively rare and ad hoc. Indeed, as the NAS study pointed out, "The Peace Corps has, in some cases, acted as a competitor rather than a collaborator with the private sector, and has not availed itself of important experience, competence, and complementary resources that, effectively harnessed, could greatly increase its contribution to both American life and overseas development and understanding."[27] By facilitating joint planning and training and perhaps other types of collaboration in certain cases, funding support from such a public foundation to appropriate private organizations could strengthen both development in the Third World and voluntarism in the United States.

From the voluntary agency point of view, an important obstacle to this kind of collaboration has been, since 1970, the submersion of the Peace Corps as a relatively invisible and declining entity (in size and budget) of the U.S. government. While the new leadership of ACTION appointed under the Carter administration has promised to reverse this trend,[28] greater steps may be required "to protect the image of the Peace Corps overseas as a genuine humanitarian enterprise, not an instrument of national foreign policy in the usual sense,"[29] and to encourage closer cooperation with U.S. private and voluntary agencies.

Implicit in each of the third set of options for structural change—all of them U.S. government, but non-AID-related options—is the desirability of separating development aid from U.S. foreign policy (or at least from State Department) constraints. When U.S. aid consisted principally of either military support or emergency relief, motivated in large part by cold war concerns, there may have been some logic to the State Department framework. Indeed, for those types of programs there may still be. While some kinds of overseas assistance are understandably linked to U.S. government political concerns—aid to Israel and Egypt in support of a Middle East peace agreement is one such example—other types of aid for purely developmental purposes should be divorced insofar as possible from day-to-day State Department concerns. This is not to say that in the real world the two criteria are entirely separable. Indeed, even in promoting voluntary organizations, the U.S. government reaps some political benefit by virtue of

---

[27]*The Peace Corps: Perspectives*, p. 50. Much the same suggestion was made in a policy paper prepared for ACTION by Harlan Cleveland, *The Future of the Peace Corps* (Princeton, N.J.: Aspen Institute Program in International Affairs, 1977).

[28]See Sam Brown (Director, ACTION), testimony before the U.S. Senate Committee on Appropriations, Subcommittee on Foreign Operations, March 10, 1977.

[29]Ibid., pp. 50-51.

the influence such organizations have in propagating (however subconsciously) American democratic and pluralistic values abroad. Yet some degree of separation is becoming increasingly imperative. This is partly because of increasing nationalist sensitivities and partly because development must be understood as a long-term effort requiring advance planning, reliability of inputs, and above all, sufficient flexibility to try bold new approaches. Because development programs promote the fulfillment of basic human needs and thus of human rights, they cannot morally be made contingent on extraneous diplomatic considerations or identifications.

How then might one begin to bring together the diversity of institutional forms and structures that currently exist and that seem to be suggested under option three above? U.S. development assistance requires essentially four types of structures: 1) a financial body, already existing in the form of the Overseas Private Investment Corporation, to mobilize and facilitate the participation of U.S. private capital in international development; 2) an international development council, to act as an overall coordinating group for ensuring that international development receives greater emphasis in U.S. trade, investment, financial, agricultural, and export-promotion policies; 3) an international development bank for making capital and related technical assistance loans; and 4) an international development institute (perhaps combined with the bank) for concentrating on research and training in various areas of economic, social, and civic development.

The development institute is of most relevance here, since it could work largely through private organizations from the United States and the concerned countries themselves in people-to-people and institution-to-institution programs, seeking new breakthroughs in the application of relevant Western experience to resources and processes critical to the Third World. Its social and civic development mandate should be to ensure popular participation through organizations such as cooperatives, labor groups, trade associations, and civic associations and through community development programs.[30] This notion of a development institute is sufficiently complementary to that of the IAF, the proposed African Development Foundation, and a reinvigorated Peace Corps that it would make sense for such an institute to evolve into an umbrella organization through which the others would relate to each other. The IAF would effectively become the Latin American division of such a larger body, and its African and Asian equivalents would constitute other divisions. Each would operate with relative autonomy but would share a common board (a combination of individuals from the public and private sectors), a unified appropriation for

---

[30]See *U.S. Foreign Assistance in the 1970s: A New Approach*, Report to the President from the Task Force on International Development (Washington, D.C.: Superintendent of Public Documents, March 4, 1970). For a critique of the report, see Denis Goulet and Michael Hudson, *The Myth of Aid* (New York: Center for the Study of Development and Social Change, 1971).

congressional purposes, and an ability to encourage maximum policy and program interchange.

Of the three general options discussed in the preceding pages, it is the above-mentioned development institute evolving out of option three that appears the most promising. While a narrow concern with the interests of private and voluntary agencies alone might suggest a preference for the fully private (though government-funded) Appropriate Technology International model (option two), a broader concern with both U.S. government and U.S. private-sector interests suggests the desirability of the institute approach. In addition to the attributes suggested above, the institute would need to receive its congressionally appropriated funds in the form of an initial endowment to encourage the kind of forward-looking and consistent development planning that has always eluded the annually funded programs of AID. In order to ensure insulation from short-term political intrusions, the institute would require considerable autonomy; it would not be, like AID, a part of the U.S. State Department. On the other hand, since American taxpayers would rightly insist on its proper supervision, the institute would be expected to submit annual reports to the Congress and to maintain liaison with relevant departments of the executive branch. Various divisions of the institute would be in a position to provide funding for most of the broad range of activities in which AID is now engaged, including both technical assistance and capital loans, plus the more innovative ones suggested. The institute would also include funding for a privatized Peace Corps and would provide partial support for U.S. and Third World private and voluntary organizations. The voluntary organizations, however, would continue to rely primarily on their private constituencies and other sources of private funds.

With an administration in Washington that campaigned on the need for streamlining the bureaucracy and improving the effectiveness of government programs, the opportunity should be seized to modify cumbersome and politically undesirable aid structures. While the new development institute should thus replace AID as currently structured, it is possible, however, that the evolution would be a long one. Thus short-term changes are also needed. It is here that the above-mentioned suggestions for streamlining AID procedures are relevant and necessary (option one). In terms of individual project requests, a good beginning has already been made in devolving more review and approval authority to AID field missions. In addition, AID should make significantly more funds available in the form of general support grants that have relatively fewer strings attached. To ensure that sufficient priority is attached by AID to private and voluntary agency approaches overall, a line item in the congressional appropriation would be useful.

Both the long-term structural changes and the short-term streamlining proposed here should help in better responding to the special needs of voluntary agencies, while being fully consistent with U.S. government interests. Yet the implementation of these changes requires firm and creative leadership in order to avoid equally cumbersome bureaucracies arising in the future. It is commonplace to say, but disastrous to forget, that the quality and outlook of the people who direct and staff these governmental agencies —like the quality and outlook of the voluntary agency people themselves —are critical to success or failure. Furthermore, while the new aid structure of the future must minimize partisan political involvement at home and abroad, it must nevertheless encompass an ideology of development that is in keeping with the needs of the Third World and with principles of equality of opportunity. It must be willing to stand for and promote this equality for the poor majority in the Third World, with an appropriate recognition of the structural changes that this will require in some cases. If it shirks this responsibility, it will be no better able to assist in the development process than are existing structures and institutions. In short, the purpose of new structures is not only to ease political and bureaucratic burdens but also to enable in the broadest sense U.S. private and voluntary organizations to respond sufficiently, efficiently, and sensitively to the new demands for development with dignity.

Chapter 8

Where Do the American People Stand?

The somber-faced child looks up at you with large brown baleful eyes from the magazine you are reading. "You can help save Maria Almanzar for $15 a month," it says, "or you can turn the page." It goes on, in smaller print: "Imagine two tiny rooms. A dirt floor. Mud walls. Straw roof. Put a family of six inside. One that doesn't know what electricity or running water or sanitary facilities are. Hard to believe? For six-year-old Maria, these are the facts of life. Others? Father has deserted. Mother takes in washing. Income, $1 a day. The future for this little girl? Very dim."[1] Just as the reader is plunged into despondency, the prospect of hope is advanced: "But for $15 a month you can sponsor a child like Maria in many countries around the world and here at home. Money for education. And clothing. And medical care. And a portion of your $15, combined with money from other sponsors, can help her whole community. With everything from a hot lunch program to a health center. In simple terms, to help them help themselves." And that is not all, for we can get something out of this ourselves, too. "For you—educated, involved, and in touch with your own heart—there are many rewards. The chance to correspond with a child. Receive a photograph and progress reports. And above all know you are reaching out to another human being. . . . So please: clip this coupon and mail it today. Now you can turn the page."

Rarely has a more skillful advertisement been devised. It evokes the dual emotions of charity and self-gratification. By the insertion of the phrase "to help them help themselves" it also appeals to the basic American instinct for self-reliance and for people who pull themselves up by their own bootstraps. It thus combines the simplicity of the give-away with the Calvinistic work ethic. It appeals to what fund-raising professionals have

---

[1] Save the Children Federation, advertisement quoted in U.S. Congress, Senate Committee on Labor and Public Welfare, Subcommittee on Children and Youth, *Children's Charities, 1974: Hearings*, Part 4, 93rd Cong., 2d sess., 10 October 1974, p. 1183.

defined over years of experience and experimentation as the broad body of church-going, or at least sympathetically motivated, middle Americans who have not had much, if any, experience with the Third World, but who know that basically things are not very good there and that people are suffering. The advertisement is not inaccurate in its description of typical living conditions for many of the Third World's people, nor is it inaccurate in its suggestion as to how $15 a month can help both the beneficiary and the donor, at least in the short term.[2] Furthermore, this kind of appeal brings in the money—more than other kinds tried, say the experts. Yet something appears to be wrong here, something that revolves, essentially, around the perpetuation of a "we/they" dichotomy in what in most other respects is becoming an increasingly interdependent world society. Indeed, at a time when communications advances and intermingling economies are bringing people closer together, these kinds of representations risk having the opposite effect.

American Attitudes Toward the Third World

While numerous attempts have been made over the years to describe and define the American public's views toward overseas involvements, including foreign aid, none have been very exact. The simple reason for this is that the American body politic is so diverse that virtually any statement is accurate for a significant number of people, while none applies to all. Thus it is as simplistic to speak of a new isolationism emerging in the aftermath of the Vietnam War as it is to assume that America is mischievously and consciously engaged in an attempt to make over the world in the American political, corporate, and overall values image. Rather, history is an amalgam of many simultaneous trends and currents of thought. Because all of these affect the roles of Americans overseas, and especially the roles of private and voluntary organizations that directly depend on and respond to the American people, it is important to review some of the most common threads before commenting further on their immediate effects on U.S. private agencies abroad and in the United States itself.

The three major arguments held by those who advocate either limiting or eliminating U.S. involvements overseas are triage, the lifeboat theory, and one that might be summarized as principled anti-interventionism. The advocates of triage would sort the potential recipient countries according to their perceived chances for survival, just as the battlefield surgeons of World War I had to select from among unmanageably large numbers of wounded soldiers those few who could best profit from emergency treatment. According to triage standards, aid decision makers would concentrate available resources on those Third World countries considered most capable of benefiting from foreign assistance. Thus Thailand, as a reasonably successful

---

[2]The $15 amount was subsequently raised to $16 per month.

"developing country," would presumably be eligible for aid; but Bangladesh, a seriously overpopulated "hopeless basket case," would not; nor would Brazil, a sufficiently rich country, albeit with large poverty areas. The question one must raise, however, concerns what it means to say that a country cannot survive—quite aside from the arrogance that such a value judgment presupposes. Countries do not disappear, after all, in the same way that wounded soldiers die. The metaphor is thus a highly misleading one.

To some extent, on the other hand, every agency—public or private—exercises a form of triage in the process of selecting program priorities both among and within countries. After all, it is always necessary to maximize the chances for effectiveness, and few are willing to risk throwing money down the drain. By this standard, one could argue that it is the principle of triage that is responsible for the failure of past assistance efforts to reach the poor majority. The fact is that the trickle-down approach seemed more certain to succeed because resource transfers were channeled through better trained, better off, generally better proven people and institutions. Yet the very virtue of voluntary agencies is that their smaller size and lower profiles should encourage risk-taking; their constituencies ought to understand and support such a policy if in the long run one is to maximize the chances of helping the poorest groups. Triage, therefore, need not be eschewed as an overall principle of selection; rather, only that form of it should be eschewed which unrealistically writes off whole sections of humanity as unsalvageable.

The lifeboat theorists argue more openly from self-interest than do the advocates of triage, though both arguments are based on false assumptions of global resource scarcity (rather than misallocation), and both are given further credence by the sad child advertisements propagated by some voluntary agencies. The lifeboat theorists maintain that the development problem is so overwhelming, and the numbers of the poor so large, that any attempt to "hoist them aboard" the lifeboat earth would cause the entire boat, the rich included, to sink. For them, perhaps the biggest crime of the Third World is its rapidly increasing population, which evokes images of "us" (who happen to be predominantly white) being deluged by "them" (the outside hordes, who happen to be mostly brown, black, and yellow). Yet past experience suggests that there is no inevitability of death for nations and societies; the successes of post-World War II reconstruction and of the remarkable development advances made by a number of Third World countries suggest that history has its ups and downs and that life continues. Like the triage advocates, the lifeboat theorists are also open to charges of arrogance in their implicit assumption that it is they who have the right to control who does or does not get let on board the boat. Since the boat represents the planet earth, it is more logically the poor *majority* (if anyone) who should be in control over the rich *minority*.

The noninterventionists represent a different set of positions and principles, though some of their points are also used to support the two positions cited above. Some of them argue, for example, that the miserable conditions of the world's poor are largely due to unjust ruling structures, which economic aid has tended only to buttress and perpetuate. Elaborating on this, many feel that U.S. aid is taken from poor people in America's "Third World" and given to rich people overseas. Others suggest that assistance to poor countries not only may waste resources that could be more effectively used by others but also that it is cruel to the poor in the sense of prolonging their unavoidable agony. Thus reducing death rates with little chance of reducing fertility only ensures increased morbidity, social tensions, and all the grim features of the Malthusian specter. Still others note that development assistance constitutes nothing less than interference in the social evolution and historical self-determination of others; this is on the assumption that assistance inherently presupposes superior/inferior relationships and retards equality and mutual respect, whereas in reality "no society, no foreign expert, no multinational organization can provide the guidance for achieving a society that is in any sense superior to or 'more developed' than any that already exists."[3] Finally, there are people who would peg all aid to performance in family planning or human rights. While their concerns may be legitimate, the result is often to introduce impossible conditions, not to mention an additional form of intervention.

The weakness of the noninterventionist argument is that it assumes a possibility of zero intervention in what is inevitably, and in every way, an interventionist or interdependent world—through interlocking economies, trade, communications networks, and environment, not to mention common humanity. Even without aid relationships, there is no way of avoiding these myriad other forms of interventions. The more important point, then, is that aid relationships should not act to reinforce the inevitably negative sides of these interventions—a point on which few would disagree in principle, but one that is also very difficult to define in specific policy terms.[4]

Public opinion polls have been taken in the United States to measure the influence of these thought trends and their more common man-in-the-street manifestations. In 1972—even during U.S. involvement in Vietnam—a poll conducted by the Overseas Development Council found that in spite of a general lack of knowledge about development issues among the U.S. people, "public support for the idea of giving U.S. assistance to underdeveloped countries is at an historic high of 68%, considerably above the 51% and 58% levels recorded, respectively, in 1958 and 1966."[5] By a

---

[3]Avrom and Leah Bendavid Val, "Developed and Underdeveloped: A Radical View of Constructive Relationships," *International Development Review* (March 1974), p. 13.

[4]For a fuller exposition of both sides of the triage, lifeboat, and noninterventionist arguments, see James W. Howe and John W. Sewell, "Triage and Other Challenges to Helping the Poor Countries Develop," in James W. Howe and the staff of the Overseas Development Council, *The U.S. and World Development: Agenda for Action, 1975* (New York: Praeger Publishers, Inc., 1975).

[5]Paul A. Laudicina, *World Poverty and Development: A Survey of American Opinion*, Monograph No. 8 (Washington, D.C.: Overseas Development Council, 1973), p. 4.

proportion of 38-37-25, Americans were sympathetic, uncommitted, or negative, respectively, toward the concerns of poor countries, with the most support coming from young, better-educated, upper-income, and politically liberal Americans. Most supporters of foreign assistance favored aiding poor countries for moral and humanitarian reasons rather than for cold war ones, though there was also a "definite sense that U.S. assistance to underdeveloped countries . . . benefits the United States," albeit in unclear ways. Of significance in the present context was the finding that the expressed support for U.S. overseas assistance was not necessarily translatable into support for the U.S. government aid programs.

> The American public thinks that too much U.S. official aid is wasted in our own bureaucracy, and that U.S. aid does not get to those who need it most in the poor countries. Americans also question the honesty and integrity of the aid bureaucracies of some recipient governments. The public appears to consider voluntary agencies more reliable assistance channels than government aid programs. Public support is strongest to alleviate such basic problems as hunger and malnutrition, disease, and illiteracy. Americans consider aid in these areas to be more direct, its results more visible, and its dispensation less likely to meet with corruption. The public also appears to expect such forms of assistance to do more to strengthen the self-sufficiency of the recipient countries.[6]

A Louis Harris poll conducted in 1974 under the auspices of the Chicago Council on Foreign Relations generally reaffirmed the major ODC findings of two years earlier. Asking its questions somewhat differently, it found that 52 per cent of the American public supported the principle of foreign aid but that 56 per cent wanted its level cut back, while only 10 per cent advocated an increase. Yet "earlier aid efforts are widely regarded as proud moments in U.S. history," with humanitarian and emergency aid particularly approved of and "more public support for economic aid [advocated] when it is clear that it actually helps people in poor countries." All these attitudes are understandably related to aid's impact on the U.S. economy, with 25 per cent of the public thinking it helps the U.S. economy and 63 per cent that it hurts. Indeed, the Chicago study noted that "the principal opposition to foreign economic aid is based on doubts that it helps our national security or our domestic economy."[7] For this reason and because of the understandable fact that people everywhere tend to be most concerned about subjects more visibly close to home, only 37 per cent of a Harris sample poll in 1976 felt that the subject of foreign economic aid should be a major concern and priority at all for the next president of the United States.

---

[6]Ibid., p. 5.
[7]John Reilly, ed., *American Public Opinion and U.S. Foreign Policy 1975* (Chicago: Chicago Council on Foreign Relations, 1975), p. 7.

While teaching and learning about the Third World began to increase dramatically in the United States after the Korean War, especially in the 1960s, economic stringencies in the university world (due to the failure of government funding initiatives) and academic turning inward to domestic concerns have caused a decline again during the 1970s.[8] As an article in the *New York Times* pointed out, "The trend raises the question: Will the current generation be adequately prepared to function in an interdependent world?"[9] According to a study by the American Council on Education that was quoted by the *Times,* "the percentage of college undergraduates studying languages other than English has been dropping steadily since 1963, the rate of decline reaching 15 per cent during the last two years. . . . Language requirements for admission have been dropped at all but 10 per cent of the nation's colleges and universities, and the number of institutions with no foreign-language requirement for graduation has quadrupled since 1966 . . . . Scarcely a fifth of high school graduates now have had even a superficial exposure to any language besides their own." The American Council on Education furthermore estimated that about one in twenty undergraduates enrolls in courses that consider foreign people in any way, while the number of American students in study programs abroad had shrunk by half between 1974 and 1976.

Yet many voluntary agency contributions have significantly increased during the 1970s, suggesting that interest in pursuing knowledge of Third World situations may not be linked to interest in helping suffering people in those countries. Inasmuch as U.S. government contributions to voluntary organizations have held fairly constant, on the average, during the past decade, the significant budget increases have come from the private sector, partly from increasing foundation grants, but partly also from individual contributors.

What Makes Americans Give?

Even a cursory analysis of comparative fund-raising experiences suggests that the most significant factor contributing to increased agency income in the mid-1970s was the world hunger appeals in the face of severe drought throughout much of the world. The main beneficiaries were the relief programs, primarily of the larger agencies such as CARE, Church World Service, and Catholic Relief Services, but also of relatively new groups like Africare and Oxfam-America. This is hardly surprising in view of the tremendous media attention in the United States during the drought, combined with the attention generated by the planning and proceedings of the U.N. World Food Conference in late 1974. "Television," as the ODC public opinion survey noted, "is the American mass public's single most

---

[8] See Adam Yarmolinsky, "Philanthropic Activity in International Affairs," paper prepared for the Commission on Private Philanthropy and Public Needs, 1976.

[9] *New York Times,* April 18, 1976.

important source of information on world problems."[10] C.P. Snow was in this sense proven both right and unnecessarily gloomy when he was once asked if he feared a violent revolution of the hungry poor of the Third World against the overfed rich of the industrial nations; he replied by proclaiming his greater fear—"that we would watch them starve on color TV."

Voluntary agency fund raising is big business, as it would have to be to generate the amounts that have been raised over the years. Agency critics often point to the apparent contradictions between the big business atmosphere that surrounds successful fund-raising efforts and the charitable approach claimed by the agencies for their work overseas.[11] Yet such anomalies are perhaps unavoidable. CARE has developed its fund-raising approach with particular effectiveness from the earliest post-World War II days, when the Advertising Council of America and the national media networks began donating their professional services and time to its cause. Indeed, they were so successful in their promotion that for most Americans, CARE is synonymous with voluntary aid overseas; a 1970 survey showed that only 8 per cent of the general public had never heard of CARE.[12] While responsibly portraying in its public reports what it actually does, CARE also skews its program emphases to particular target audiences. For the general public, it emphasizes the more emotional and relief aspects of its programs; for others deemed more sophisticated, it stresses the more complex, long-range developmental approaches. While distribution of the famous CARE packages has been discontinued as counter to the self-help philosophy, the package is still used, though decreasingly, in its publicity. As CARE executives point out, they are in a situation analogous to that of the 5¢-and-10¢ stores; people know that it is now virtually impossible to buy anything for 5¢ or 10¢, but the symbol is kept for identification purposes.

A more classic case here is that of the Save the Children Federation/Community Development Foundation, clearly a contradictory title in terms of connotations of program philosophy. Save the Children was the organization's original name and represented its initial program approach, whereby sponsors gave cash grants to individual youngsters. As the organization increasingly realized that this approach was not addressing the root causes of poverty, it turned to more fundamental community development approaches. Where children are still being helped, it is in a larger community context. Yet there is understandable reluctance to change the name for fear of losing a faithful constituency that might not understand the significance and value of the program shift. So children in the community continue to write letters to their American sponsors—at some considerable translation,

---

[10]Laudicina, *World Poverty and Development*, p. 5.

[11]See Eugene Linden, *The Alms Race* (New York: Random House, Inc., 1976); and Harvey Katz, *Give: Who Gets Your Charity Dollar?* (New York: Anchor Press/Doubleday, 1975).

[12]*Information, Attitudes, and Motives of CARE Donors and Nondonors*, a nationwide study prepared for CARE (Princeton, N.J.: Response Analysis Corporation, 1970).

secretarial, and postage cost to the organization and its donors. Although the individual child appeal tends to compromise SCF/CDF's broader educational responsibility to its U.S. constituency, the organization feels it is the only realistic option if institutional survival is to be ensured.

The experience of other agencies substantiates this feeling. When Foster Parents Plan once took the tiny step of substituting a photo of a *family* for its famous sad *child* image, it claims to have lost substantial funds over what the traditional photo ad had brought in. When the founder of World Neighbors decided that the proper long-term approach to development was an integrated one appealing to the total person in his total situation, he was told by at least one expert:

> "You'll never raise money for it. It's not emotional enough. No starving babies; no scare approach that says, 'Tomorrow this may be you.' You even make it hard to claim the credit for what you've actually done. Believe me, that's not the kind of thing that separates people from their money!"

> He [the 'expert'] spoke from broad experience. And he knew what he was talking about. What I had in mind was going to be difficult to explain, tough to "package," hard to sell. It lacked neatness, succinctness, pathos and self-gratification. And there were times when, to my embarrassment, we had to "claim the credit" in order to prove to our donors that we had used their investments wisely and well. My idealism was forced to accept the strictures of harsh reality.[13]

If one goes by the testimony of the professional fund-raisers, the American public is sympathetic, but its sympathy is by and large the kind that seeks simple answers and the "fast fix." While agency executives can always cite exceptional cases of hard questions being raised by their donors, the general rule is quite to the contrary. If anything, donor questions focus on the level of overhead expenses and on how much money actually reaches poor people overseas rather than on the form in which it reaches them.

At the same time that SCF/CDF is continuing its individual child appeals, it is in fact trying, through periodic reports, to educate its donors to the reality and higher utility of the more developmental approach. Preliminary results of initial experiments in this direction suggest that donors respond well to SCF/CDF's community approach to development, even though they continue to look for a focus on an individual child. A 1977 Yankelovich survey conducted for the agency showed that projects which address the root causes of problems were deemed the most effective ways to help, whereas the more tactical, palliative approach of giving cash grants directly to children was deemed to be least effective. Encouraged by these results, SCF/CDF is now experimenting with increasingly dignified forms of advertising. One would place emphasis on the local people's own efforts at

---

[13] John L. Peters, *Cry Dignity* (Oklahoma City: World Neighbors, Inc., 1976), p.15.

development: "The spirited people . . . are battling a disease called poverty. They need your help to make a better future for their children." Another would accentuate the positive: "I'm lucky. Good things are happening in our village. Thanks to someone like you who cares."

Because fund-raising practices vary considerably, a few further examples may be illustrative in this context. It is useful to bear in mind, to begin with, that aside from the Jewish agencies, there is not as broad a variation among agencies as one might expect in terms of the number of dollars they raise from the general public. Among the ninety-four agencies registered with the Advisory Committee on Voluntary Foreign Aid, the largest non-Jewish individual fund-raising effort has been that of the Christian Children's Fund, which brought in about $28 million each year during the 1974-1976 period. CARE and Catholic Relief Services are considerably larger and better known agencies, but this is only because of their extensive U.S. government support, especially in the form of commodities and ocean freight reimbursement. In the case of CARE, cash support from individuals totaled about $19 million in fiscal year 1975-76, with U.S. government support accounting for about 78 per cent of its overall $174 million annual budget. The CRS amount during the same time period was $17 million from its individual donors, both directly and through local church campaigns, and U.S. government support amounted to 78 per cent of the $150 million total budget.[14]

Fund raising in the cases of the church umbrella agencies (such as Catholic Relief Services and Church World Service) is complicated by the existence of numerous church entities fulfilling a variety of specialized functions, with some of them overlapping in the area of overseas assistance. The CRS and CWS figures thus give only a partial picture of overall Catholic and Protestant institutional spending. Although Catholic Relief Services is the overseas aid instrumentality of the American Catholic bishops, American Catholics may also contribute to the Society for the Propagation of the Faith, the Pontifical Mission for Palestine, the Catholic Near East Welfare Association, and individual missionary societies; while many of these efforts are aimed at proselytizing, not all of them are exclusively so. Related to CRS is the worldwide Caritas movement, the Catholic welfare agency headquartered in Rome; many European and even American funds may flow through it, if not directly through CRS. To manage these competing overseas claims on limited Catholic constituency funds (not to mention ever increasing domestic claims for parochial schools and other U.S.-based programs), the American bishops have had an agreement dating from 1947 that the proceeds from annual Laetare Sunday Lenten contributions—which have remained essentially fixed until recent

---

[14]Figures supplied by CARE and Catholic Relief Services annual reports. See Annex A, Table 4 for a breakdown of sources of income for various private and voluntary organizations in 1975.

years at roughly $7 million—be allocated for CRS. Because inflation over the last three decades has obviously taken a great toll on this amount, the share required for administrative costs has risen dramatically, with the result that significant program contributions had to come from elsewhere. With the recent and urgent worldwide droughts and famines, however, the U.S. bishops have permitted CRS to compete for more constituency funds through special appeals, thus allowing for both more relief and more development activities as well. Because of the worldwide infrastructure of CRS, which reaches remote dioceses as well as Third World capitals, CRS sometimes also serves as a conduit for other voluntary agency funds—American and European, sectarian and nonsectarian alike. This makes it all the harder to clearly identify which programs are supported by which agency and which constituency.

Church World Service, the ecumenical Protestant counterpart of CRS, represents a partially similar case. Linked with the National Council of Churches in the United States and with the World Council of Churches in Geneva, CWS historically has been composed more of mainstream Protestant denominations than has its NCC umbrella; 40 per cent of its denominational support comes from the Methodist Church, for example, with the United Presbyterians second in scale of support (though the Presbyterians also conduct separate overseas programs relating to development). As a result of increasing discussion within the ecumenical Protestant hierarchies about the proper relationship between mission and service roles, with increased stress now being given to the latter, CWS finds itself in an advantageous position. At the same time, however, it faces increasing demands to help the schools and hospitals that were earlier funded by the religious missions. Contrary to CRS, CWS decided some years ago to substantially scale down its role in U.S. government-supported food distribution programs, with the result that these now comprise a very minor activity—less than 5 per cent of the CWS budget and less than 1 per cent of the total amount of the food that is channeled by the U.S. government through all voluntary organizations.

Where CWS differs from CRS again is in the key role of CROP, its fund-raising and public education affiliate. While the Catholics also have public education activities, CROP is unique in the integral part it plays in both funding the parent CWS (it raised about one third of all CWS private funding in 1975), in raising tithes of harvests from farmers, and in conveying educational messages derived from CWS relief and development programs. During 1976, CROP reassessed its role and the nature of its message to its constituency; the reassessment stemmed from a concern about the tension between the economic and social aspects of development and the extent to which these can be conveyed to an American public as yet relatively unfamiliar with such issues. CROP emerged with the important conclusion that because "the constant criteria and ultimate goal for development is justice for all persons . . . a primary function of development education is to illuminate the root causes of hunger, poverty, underdevelopment and injustice . . . [and] to enable persons to participate in development, their own and [that of] all persons to whom they are linked, theologically and empirically in an increasingly interdependent world."[15] The group defined a number of levels of involvement for Americans on development and justice concerns and ranked them on a scale of increasing activism directed toward social and economic change: apathy, ignorance and misinformation, information, sharing information (incipient advocacy), giving money, self-help within present structures, personal life-style changes, community and national life-style changes, advocacy on human rights, influencing government policy, affecting international structures of cooperation, empowerment for local activism, nonviolent resistance, direct action outside of political processes (changing structures), and finally, support for liberation groups in other countries. The apparent intention was to cause individuals to reflect on the degree to which they were personally abetting the development prospects of the world's poor. While some of these levels represent, by some standards, radical positions, there seems to be a slowly increasing inclination, even among relatively conservative groups, to consider their validity; this is perhaps partly due to increasing frustration with past aid failures.

Perhaps the most unusual church organization in terms of its relationship with a constituency is the Mennonite Central Committee, which embraces fifteen different Mennonite groups. Although there are only some 250,000 Mennonites in the United States and Canada, the Mennonites, after the Jews, appear to be the largest contributors to overseas programs on a per capita basis of any religious denomination in North America. With a 1975 private income of some $9 million for these programs, the average annual per capita contribution amounted to $36.[16] MCC officials offer several possible reasons for this enviable position. First of all, they note that because of alternative service requirements for Mennonite conscientious objectors in times of war, there are as many as 6,000 "alumni" who are thus in a position to spread overseas development information intensively among the 250,000-member constituency. Second, because most U.S. Mennonites are within only three generations of having established themselves in a new country, they remember and are grateful for the fact that many of them or their families were personally helped by MCC during their own difficult moves to the United States; they are thus in a position to better understand the hardships faced by people in other settings. Third, as many as 75 per cent of the supporting constituency are thought to be farmers or one generation removed from farming vocations; the result is that they understand the need for production rather than relief assistance in the Third World and are quicker to give support even without the exclusively relief and sad child

---

[15]"Summary Report of Development Education Consultation," mimeographed (Elkhart, Ind.: CROP/CWS, February 13, 1976).

[16]Although it would be interesting to do so, it is not possible to compare this with equivalent Catholic and other Protestant figures because of the above-noted point that their channels are so much more diverse and the funds thus difficult to count.

appeal. This fact no doubt also accounts for MCC's reputation for effective contributions in the Third World.[17]

In terms of both gross and per capita contributions, the largest fund raisers of all are the Jewish agencies. They have barely been mentioned in this volume because of the highly specialized nature of their cause, which is limited essentially to people either in one country—Israel—or of one faith—Judaism. Yet the Jewish agencies cannot be ignored in the current context because the very magnitude and nature of their appeal offer useful, and possibly even replicable, lessons. Just as in the Catholic and Protestant cases, there is a multiplicity of Jewish voluntary agencies. The major ones are the United Israel Appeal, which aids Israel; the Jewish Joint Distribution Committee, which aids Jewish groups outside Israel; Hadassah, the women's body; the Organization for Rehabilitation and Training (ORT), which conducts vocational training schools and offers technical assistance; and the United Jewish Appeal (UJA), the U.S. fund-raising arm for most of the Jewish groups.[18]

Jewish giving is at such a high dollar level that its fluctuations from year to year significantly affect the overall private American overseas giving figures. Average per capita Jewish giving in the United States was about $56 during the early 1970s. Indeed, the Jewish agencies account on the average for as large a proportion of the overall voluntary agency budget figure—33 per cent—as does the U.S. government. In the year of the 1973 Middle East War, it was nearly double the U.S. government figure. The main explanation for this astonishing outpouring of aid is, in the words of UJA executives, that "we are struggling for survival." As noted earlier, two out of three American Jewish families are said to have lost family members in Europe during the Nazi era, while one out of two are now thought to have family members in Israel. When this personal identification is added to what they point to as a historic concern of Jews for fellow Jews since even before the Christian era, the outpouring becomes more understandable.

Donors know, in addition, that they are giving for clear, well-formulated programs managed by agencies as well organized as the Israeli government itself. They are giving not only for a charity but also for a job that must be done. The United Israel Appeal, for example, unlike most private organizations, is not guided in its programming by the coincidental question of contributions available in any given period. Rather, it defines its program by the immediate requirement and borrows money from the bank when the occasion demands. The result is that in the case of an increase in numbers of immigrants to Israel (as in recent years from Russia, for example), arrangements can be made to settle them immediately on a permanent basis rather than in less costly but debilitating makeshift camps.

---

[17]See Edgar Stoesz, *Thoughts on Development,* Development Monograph Series 1 (Akron, Penn.: Mennonite Central Committee, 1975).

[18]The UJA is guided in its distribution of funds by a fixed, mutually negotiated percentage for each agency, subject to renegotiation in special cases and emergencies.

Proper housing can be immediately constructed, and language and job-training courses conducted, thus speeding the immigrants' ability to be self-sufficient and reducing the relief phase of their transition to a new life. Indeed, this businesslike assessment of need and response is as impressive as the resulting program effectiveness.

Because UJA fund-raising is done by volunteers among their own friends and co-religionists, rather than by professionals, considerable social peer pressure is brought to bear. The same volunteers are also involved in decision making as to how the funds are used, a different situation from the classical CARE or Foster Parents Plan donors who give through a bureaucratic mechanism on the faith that their contributions will be well utilized. The whole ambience of Jewish fund-raising and programming is so unique that on the one hand it appears almost irrelevant here; on the other hand, there may be pertinent lessons for the broader voluntary organization world—a possibility that merits closer study in the future. For as the worldwide Jewish community has its own solidarity, so with increasing global economic interdependence will ways have to be found to break down the more generalized "we/they" dichotomies and establish more just modes of societal interdependence for people everywhere.

Involving the American People

There are some kernels of evidence that Americans are becoming increasingly involved in Third World issues. Some voluntary organizations are endeavoring to come to grips with new and nontraditional definitions of voluntarism that would set them apart from the mainstream of relatively bureaucratic organizations. The leaders of such efforts note that too many of their peer agencies are still acting like "mini-AID programs" rather than exploiting what they see as the special potential of people-based organizations. Rather than simply taking the money of U.S. donors, these new efforts seek to more actively involve Americans with people in other countries. Sometimes efforts that are more political in character are made to link injustice at home with injustice abroad, and vice versa.

Constituency involvement and political approaches appear to be especially well-developed among European voluntary organizations, many of which feel that one of their major aims is to develop at home knowledge about and consciousness of the Third World. This feeling no doubt stems from the particular historical, political, and church-state traditions of Europe alluded to earlier. Indeed, European governments are often keenly aware of voluntary agency roles in molding public opinion. This is in some contrast to the U.S. situation, where the primary emphasis is on helping others, with relatively little emphasis traditionally placed on the need for domestic education and change. There are at least two possible reasons for this difference. One is the historically greater cosmopolitanism of Europe, where different nationalities and cultures have been constantly mixing over the centuries, in contrast to the comparative geographic isolation of the North American continent. Through education systems and through more informal means, the result in Europe has been a constant ebb and flow of information, ideas, and ideologies—as well as what some would call a greater political consciousness and sophistication. The second reason for the difference is related to sheer size alone. The European countries, each one much smaller than the United States, tend to form more compact wholes; thus there is greater unity to their national (indeed, sometimes nationalized) media, where newspapers, radio, and television all impact on an entire country simultaneously, both facilitating and influencing the public education and involvement functions of voluntary organizations.

Whatever the reasons, the constituency activities of several European voluntary organizations are noteworthy. Oxfam and War on Want frequently spread educational and pro-Third World political messages in Britain. Groups on the continent, such as one in Switzerland, sponsor public information campaigns aimed at gaining more just prices for Third World producers of commodities such as bananas and coffee.[19] European groups have a head start in consciousness raising with respect to Third World issues among their own labor groups—the groups that would bear the brunt of any easing of trade restrictions favoring Third World countries.[20] The educationally oriented Commission on the Churches' Participation in Development of the World Council of Churches has drawn far more support from some European churches—especially in Germany—than from U.S. churches.

This is not to say that all European voluntary agencies are advanced in domestic education and political action. Nor is it to say that all U.S. agencies are not. To the extent that some European organizations are automatically funded through church tax systems (as in West Germany, for example), they are also less constrained by the pressures of constituent accountability on how and where they spend their money. If European constituencies have tended to be somewhat more tolerant of domestic public education activites, they—like their American counterparts—have also drawn lines that place limits on how much can be diverted from direct overseas application. In the United States, at the same time, there is an emerging recognition of the larger dimensions of the international development problem and thus of the increasing need for domestic public education and perhaps even political advocacy.

One such cognizant U.S. agency (though political only insofar as it urges greater U.S. concern for Africa) is Africare, the first—and still only—organization run predominantly by black Americans for (and with)

---

[19]See Ivan Ribeiro, *Commodity Campaigns and the Third World—An Evaluation of Education and Action Programmes in Europe* (Rome: Action for Development, Food and Agriculture Organisation, 1974).

[20]See *Workers' Education and the Third World* (Sørmarka, Norway: Action for Development, Food and Agriculture Organisation; and the Workers' Education Branch, International Labour Organisation; May 1973).

black Africans. If American voluntarism is essentially the white middle-class phenomenon that it is said to be, then Africare has begun to break this barrier by persuading black Americans to become involved with the continent of their origin, particularly with the Sahelian region of West Africa. Establishing membership chapters in cities and town throughout the United States, with special attention to schools and colleges, Africare tries to combine fund raising (Muhammad Ali helped in one effort) with education. In short, Africare takes people outside their own parochial range of concerns to identify with others. This new involvement is not limited to the sending of a monthly or yearly check; rather, discussion sessions are encouraged and African art shows and other activities are sponsored.

Oxfam-America tries to carry the concept of an involved constituency a step further. With both a network of community coordinators throughout the United States and a relatively developed public education program, Oxfam-America has promoted World Food Day fasts to call attention to Third World hunger, has sponsored discussion films on development themes such as self-reliance and societal and cultural impediments to family planning, and has conveyed relevant information through its own publications and through special supplements in influential newspapers and journals. Oxfam also has creative contact with a number of local groups in New England that are seeking to develop new life-styles more in keeping with environmental requirements and with a world in which overconsumption at home is difficult to reconcile with gross deprivation abroad.

Concern over gross inequities in the world, combined with demands for more personal involvement, have led to the creation of increasingly significant numbers of communal groups and associations in the United States devoted to these issues; they focus primarily on domestic inequities but in at least a marginal way touch on international issues as well. Some groups originated in the counterculture of the 1960s and some more recently. In a few cities, "people's funds" have been established or planned, in large part as a counter to the more traditional United Way efforts, which mainly support traditional agencies and which aim more at raising money than involving the "whole person," as some of the newer groups would wish. Faced with varying degrees of stability and organizational viability, these groups aim to democratize decision making so that those who contribute can be directly involved in determining the beneficiaries and perhaps in working with them, too. They thus promote a membership concept more than a fundgiving one, an automatic self-tax rather than an ad hoc donation, and assistance to local groups through program-related investments rather than through cash grants alone. While this methodology becomes logistically more problematic on an international scale, some thought has been given to attempting it on a broader plane. The assumption behind such an attempt is that traditional overseas aid-giving isolates the donor from the recipient; reinforces the we/they dichotomy; and invariably leads to paternalism, irrelevance, or outright damage to Third World dignity and self-reliance.

What is needed, rather, is a more genuine people-to-people collaboration—if in no other way than through small-scale, yet personally meaningful, dialogues. Although such efforts still amount to no more than drops in the ocean or dreams, they at least suggest one manifestation of what may in the future become an increasing concern for new definitions of a voluntary approach to human interdependence at home and abroad.

These groups, and other more traditional ones such as the American Friends Service Committee, share a belief that the Third World has as much to teach Americans as it has to learn from Americans. On the U.S. government side, it is a similar belief that has motivated, in part, both the Fulbright program for exchange of scholars and the Peace Corps; one goal of each is to serve as an educational experience for young Americans to attune them more fully to the larger world. If one notes the variety of significant policy positions in which ex-Peace Corps volunteers are now found, one will see, in fact, that that organization has had a significant effect. One can argue that much of the concern for more socially responsible, ecologically sound, and less materialistic life-styles has originated in part in the experiences of these and other young Americans living and traveling in the Third World during the 1960s.

There have been other lessons too. At least one black American leader, the Reverend Jesse Jackson, has pointed to distinguished Third World leaders as models of the self-development that blacks should work harder to pursue in America. "The natural pride of American blacks in the achievement of black leaders abroad is a factor in their own struggle.... The message from there is clear: Through the proper use of money and a positive attitude, we can stimulate self-development and give the people a vision."[21] Jackson also sees a political lesson here. "By virtue of our special empathy for the colored peoples of the third world, and particularly Africa, black Americans can contribute to the foreign-policy debate by exposing the racism at the root of some of our Government's worst domestic and foreign blunders. It would be tragic if our nation lost its potential for true greatness by letting racist legacies deflect it from its proper course."[22]

Racism is only one of the evils that is transnational in scope. Some people cite international arms trade as not only increasing the chances and horror of war but also as deflecting funds badly needed for development. Still others see protectionist trade policies as being unjust for Third World people struggling to make their own way in the world without the need for aid. Agricultural policies aimed primarily at helping the American farmer open new overseas markets for his output may have substantial disincentive effects on farmers in Third World countries, thus encouraging Third World dependency. Some argue that aid itself—being frequently tied to U.S. dollar

---

[21]Jesse L. Jackson, "Give the People a Vision," *New York Times Magazine,* April 18, 1976, p. 13.
[22]Ibid., p. 73.

purchases or to the hiring of U.S. "experts"—does much to perpetuate the system that is seen as the bane of the Third World's poor. In short, the very momentum of the American and Western capitalist system, including the momentum of aid programs, is seen to deprive the same people whom this system then seeks to assist.

Whether one agrees or disagrees with this diagnosis, it is clear that for as powerful a nation as the United States, domestic and international issues are inevitably linked. With the growing recognition of this fact, previously apolitical voluntary agency people are increasingly seeing the need for political responses to the types of issues just noted. Indeed, a number of volunteers have opted to return to the United States to work on U.S. attitudes that affect development, in the belief that the best way to tackle development for the poor majority in the Third World is to improve political decision-making in the United States itself. A number of organizations have been established for this purpose, among them Bread for the World, the Interreligious Task Force on U.S. Food Policy, the Friends Committee on National Legislation, the political action arms of various other church groups, and, at a different level, the broad-based new citizens' lobby called New Directions. The 1970s has also seen a new voluntary agency trend toward participation in the various world conferences held on environmental, population, food, and "habitat" issues. These conferences have served to call world attention to new ways of grappling with development problems; they represent a major opportunity for private and voluntary agency contributions in the larger policymaking arena.[23] The bottom line in all these efforts, like that of the internal Third World efforts themselves, is the recognition that politics is inevitably at the root of development and that voluntary agencies cannot contribute in a sufficiently meaningful way without addressing this fact.

It is because development *is* politics, both at home and abroad, that the need for citizen awareness is so urgent. And it is because the U.S. voluntary organizations are as familiar as any American groups with the grass-roots realities of the Third World that their role is critical. Just as the past tendency to ignore political considerations led to the failure of trickle-down approaches to ameliorate Third World poverty, so too will the failure to realistically present development issues to the American constituency perpetuate this sense of unreality and undermine, in the long run, the agencies' credibility in development. To the extent the simplistic sad child image is promoted, the more likely is the U.S. public to wonder why billions of dollars in past aid commitments have not served to stem the tears. Rather, the public must be honestly told the very long-term nature of the problem, the real impediments to change, and the modest—yet still potentially reward-

---

[23]See Angus Archer, *New Forms of NGO Participation in World Conferences,* Discussion Paper III (New York: UNITAR, October 1976).

ing—progress that has been and can be observed in many areas. Ways must be found to appeal to emotion without sacrificing honesty and affronting Third World dignity. To many in the Third World, the means are as important as the ends employed by the agencies in conducting their programs. While some understand the need to appeal to less sophisticated levels of emotionalism, others, particularly in such parts of the world as Latin America and India, say they would reject any aid procured on the basis of tactics so demeaning to their countries' self-respect. To them, dignity is more valued than a few dollars more or less in voluntary agency assistance.

Voluntary agencies do face one major problem in openly discussing the political ramifications of their efforts with their U.S. constituencies. It is the obvious problem that politics divides, and most organizations—given their need for maximizing income—are reluctant to alienate any potential donor. Thus, just as their programs consist of a mixture of relief and development, so too do their fund-raising and educational messages combine conservative and liberal politics, depending on the particular audience. Occasionally even the most conservative relief and welfare agencies may argue confidentially with their social-change-oriented critics that, indeed, their ultimate goal in feeding or schooling the poor is to make them capable of leading revolution in the future. While there may be some truth to these arguments—for one can never predict the results of such activities—there is also an element of hypocrisy that is both regrettable and unnecessary. It is regrettable because voluntary organizations should be willing to stand up and be counted on their principles, especially where public education is crucial, and unnecessary because the American people are sufficiently sophisticated to appreciate honesty when the facts are properly put before them.

In addition to greater candor on the political issues, the American people must be told more explicitly where their own interests so clearly intersect with those of Third World people, where cooperation and more sensitive assistance could help not only Third World poor but Americans as well through the prospect of a more just global society. Some Americans, primarily the college-educated middle class, may be relatively unexposed to—or threatened by—the needs and injustices in their immediate environment; for them, understanding local realities might be approached through their global awareness concerns. Others, particularly labor groups, for example, are steeped in local problems and need to have the relevance of international circumstances to these problems more sharply drawn.

> As empathy-oriented people learn more and more about situations and problems overseas, they may also begin to register increasing information about local challenges; they may start realizing that many local and overseas problems are similar and that some of them are even interrelated. Similarly, as experience-oriented people learn more and more about situations and problems in their own local environment,

they may begin increasingly to assimilate information about overseas challenges.[24]

The historical trends most certainly lead in the direction of greater mutual understanding and cooperation. Few believe that the world can remain long divided between rich and poor and still avoid a major conflagration. None but the harshest cynic would wish to contemplate the end result of continuing to be a participant—whether knowingly or not—in such an unjust system. Private and voluntary organizations enjoy a comparative advantage in raising the American consciousness to these issues. They can help bring out the best in people everywhere.

---

[24]Jørgen Lissner, *The Politics of Altruism* (Geneva: Lutheran World Federation, 1977), p. 142.

Chapter 9

Beyond Charity

Most people, whether in America or in the Third World, aspire to peace—to the absence of violence. Yet what are the qualities of violence and peace? To most Americans, violence is defined as a *direct physical assault* on people or property. To most people in the Third World, it is seen as a *continuing structural condition* of life and society—a condition that enables some people to be oppressed by others through the erection and maintenance of social, economic, political, and even spiritual and cultural barriers. These differing definitions of violence lead to drastically different interpretations of peace, of life as a whole, and of world politics. They are at the root of Third World demands for a new international order *among* nations. In many places, they are inspiring increasingly vociferous calls for new orders *within* nations.

To illustrate the problem of structural violence, it is useful to examine the case of South Africa, both internally and as a microcosm of the world as a whole. The statistics speak for themselves. Four million South African whites benefit from 80 per cent of the country's gross national product; twenty million nonwhites share 20 per cent of the GNP.[1] In the world as a whole, the major industrialized countries of the West, representing 25 per cent of the global population, control roughly 72 per cent of the global wealth;[2] over a hundred Third World countries, with 67 per cent of the world's population, account for only 14 per cent of the world's wealth. Few Americans would disagree that one of the overarching problems of today's world is this yawning gap between the rich and the poor, the haves and the

---

[1] James P. Grant, "The Changing World Order," in *South Africa: The Next 15 Years: A Microcosm of World Problems* (Johannesburg: South African Institute of Race Relations, 1976), p. 38.
[2] John W. Sewell and the staff of the Overseas Development Council, *The United States and World Development: Agenda 1977* (New York: Praeger Publishers, Inc., 1977), p. 156.

have-nots. Yet few people view the worldwide problem with the same sense of urgency as the more starkly drawn, widely publicized, violence-prone South African analog. To be sure, many of the people engaged in the private and voluntary organizations described in these pages do view the larger problem in this way. Yet many of them, and the Americans who so generously support their efforts, have tended to fight this global structural violence with charity, or at least with forms of assistance that may result in perpetuating dependency rather than encouraging self-reliance, local self-determination, and structural peace. Would they advocate mere charity for black South Africans? Or would they advocate genuine equality of opportunity for all and thus structural and political change?

If the South African example is indeed a microcosm of the world writ large, and if most knowledgeable observers believe that such a stark rich-poor polarity is untenable and a threat to even the American definition of peace over the long run, then it is clear that the worldwide gap, too, must be addressed with structural considerations more sensitively in mind. But how? Because the world, for better or worse, is organized into nation-states, it is considered improper to enter into discussions as to how other countries handle their internal distribution problems. Leadership elites would regard this as gross interference or, in the case of Third World countries, even as a form of neocolonialism. Resistance to change is understandable on their part; change is perceived as a threat. The irony is that many of the Third World spokesmen who advocate redistribution among nations are often the same people who most actively resist—in practice, if not in rhetoric—internal redistribution within their own countries.

Yet just as the world has moved toward greater *economic* interdependence among nations, it is likely that the world's people, too, will move toward increasing *human* interdependence. The worldwide concern over equity problems in South Africa is a case in point. Some people feel that limiting a concern for human rights and equality of opportunity to the plane of national rather than international consideration is illogical and even immoral. Rather, they feel that concern for one's fellow global citizens must transcend such artificial lines. As Dom Helder Camara, the Brazilian Archbishop of Recife and Olinda once put it, "How can there be a new international *economic* order without a new international *social* order?"

One of the difficulties here is in clarifying where the core of the problem exists, whether in the poverty of the poor or in the affluence of the rich. If one accepts the standard American definition of violence, then it is very much the poor who are the problem, for it is their poverty and resultant periodic agitations that disrupt the status quo and the peace. If one accepts the Third World definition, as espoused by Mahatma Gandhi, among others, one must accept the notion that "we," more than "they," are the problem. While the West has earned its wealth through hard work and perseverance, Third World spokesmen are correct in noting that some of it has been earned at their expense. The system today is rigged against them.

To some extent, American private and voluntary organizations have shared in the responsibility for this fact. While they have played a modest but exemplary role in transferring resources from rich nations to poor nations, their effectiveness in reducing the poverty gap within countries has been less notable—largely out of sheer inadvertence. This is because much of their well-intentioned humanitarian aid has been in the form of palliative charity, when what was required was a fair crack at breaking the poverty syndrome and finding access to the self-sustaining process of development. As the Peace Corps summed it up in an advertisement for new volunteers, "If you're not part of the solution, you're part of the problem."

If it is correct to assume that transnational concern for equity will increase rather than decrease in the coming years, one should also assume an increase in the number and power of what one analyst has called "nonterritoral actors";[3] these now include both international governmental organizations, such as those of the U.N. system, and multinational private entities—especially corporations. In the future, different types of multinational private entities are also likely to emerge, including multilateral forms of the private and voluntary organizations described in these pages. While these organizations are now largely based in the industrialized countries of Europe and North America, the locus of power could plausibly begin shifting somewhat, as has already happened with many international governmental organizations. With a more mixed international flavor, such organizations would bring a greater variety of relevant technical skills to bear on development problems. More importantly, they would have the virtue of transcending national partisan politics and of being somewhat less constrained, therefore, in grappling across international boundaries with issues of structural violence. The experiences of such diverse multilateral voices as those of the Red Cross, Amnesty International, and the Society for International Development are cases in point. If one reflects on the accelerating global trend toward collective action in recent history, especially since World War II, still more imaginative modes for expressing global solidarity are not so difficult to imagine. This is not to say that there will be no nationalistic relapses, for these, too, are observable today. It is to say that the trend appears to be otherwise.

Private and Voluntary Aid: A Summary View

What, then, will be the role of U.S. private and voluntary organizations a decade or more hence? Before either gazing into a crystal ball or attempting to formulate recommendations for the transition, it is important to

---

[3]Johan Galtung, "Nonterritorial Actors and the Problem of Peace," in Saul H. Mendlovitz, ed., *On the Creation of a Just World Order* (New York: Free Press, 1975), p. 151.

summarize from the preceding analysis some of these organizations' various strengths and weaknesses. To do this, one must acknowledge the broad range of types, styles, and philosophies within the private sector: the relief and social welfare institutions, the community-development-oriented programs, the relatively hard-headed business and technology approaches, and the more explicitly people-to-people ones. Furthermore, some organizations perform what are effectively contract or consulting roles for both the U.S. government and foreign governments, while others place great emphasis on advancing international understanding between their U.S. constituencies and people in the Third World. Many agencies represent a mix of the two styles. Among the organizations in the former group—those that fill consulting roles—there tends to be a significant difference between private and government organizations. Private groups are usually, though not always, distinguished from their government analogs by their smaller size, greater flexibility, and lower operating costs. Their generally higher level of personalized attention and interest enable them to dispense aid through a less leaky bucket than is typical among the more massive and bureaucratized channels of government. Their localized, sometimes higher-risk initiatives can serve an experimental function that larger governmental sponsors would not themselves attempt, for either political or bureaucratic reasons, until the probability of success was proven. Private organizations that are highly dependent on government funding have been likened to federal grant universities and called "federal grant nongovernmental organizations."[4] Whatever the connotations of this description, such organizations do fulfill important functions, often effectively.

Among the latter group of organizations—those that promote understanding between Americans and people of the Third World—are the smaller church groups, child-sponsorship organizations, and volunteer-sending agencies that place a high premium on personal contacts of one kind or another. By encouraging linkages between their particular constituencies in the United States and abroad, they are doing something that governments cannot do, even though fostering better cross-cultural understanding may well be in the best interest of governments. To the extent that there can be a rationalized, nonpaternalistic, and cumulative thrust to these programs, they, too, constitute a beneficial and also unique role for voluntary organizations.

It is worth emphasizing at this point one general distinction between the traditional and more innovative roles of private and voluntary agencies in the area of grass-roots community development—essentially the distinction between *project* and *process*. Many of the more traditional aid approaches focus on particular *projects* in specific sectors of need, such as agriculture, water resource development, education, or family planning.

---

[4]Alan Pifer, "The Nongovernmental Organization at Bay," reprinted from the 1966 Annual Report, Carnegie Corporation of New York, New York, 1966, p. 7.

Efforts in one domain have sometimes foundered, however, because they have failed to take into account other factors at work within the overall context, usually political, administrative, or larger economic policy considerations. Simple examples of this include the introduction of new crops in the absence of favorable marketing possibilities, the provision of water pumps without maintenance facilities, and the offering of new education or family planning schemes with inadequately institutionalized local administrative or political support for continuity after the outside agency has withdrawn.

However, U.S. private and voluntary agencies tend to have a comparative advantage over other organizations in focusing on the *process* of development. As discussed in Chapter 5, they are often particularly well suited to focusing on broader consciousness-raising efforts. Consciousness raising encourages people to reflect on their own situations and potential and to provide their own impetus toward development. As a strategy, it thus fosters dignity, self-reliance, and continuity, the three qualities most often missing in traditional development approaches. This is not to say that consciousness-raising efforts, in isolation, are sufficient for development; other preconditions for change must also be accessible, including material and institutional resources that may be required once local decisions are made as to how a particular group's development process is to proceed. The important point, however, is one of emphasis and priority. In this context, and on the basis of both theory and development experience to date, consciousness raising should be viewed as a critical precondition for sound development.

While consciousness-raising initiatives often have been equated with politics, they are in fact far enough removed from direct partisan politics to be acceptable as voluntary agency activities. If sensitively handled, they are responsibly and properly defined as educational activities. The dividing line between a liberating education and politics is admittedly a fine one. As one of the Third World's most respected leaders, Tanzanian President Julius Nyerere, has said:

> So development is for Man, by Man, and of Man. The same is true of education. Its purpose is the liberation of Man from the restraints and limitations of ignorance and dependency. Education has to increase men's physical and mental freedom—to increase their control over themselves, their own lives, and the environment in which they live. The ideas imparted by education or released in the mind through education, should therefore be liberating ideas; the skills acquired by education should be liberating skills. Nothing else can properly be called education.[5]

---

[5]Julius K. Nyerere, opening speech at the International Adult Education Conference in Dar es Salaam, Tanzania, June 21, 1976.

To the extent that liberation from oppressive structures is required, the foreigners' role is simply to help set the stage. The larger task is one for the local people themselves, not for the foreigners. Indeed, this is what has happened to a large extent in Nyerere's Africa, where Western church schools served as the training ground for many of the continent's new leaders.[6] Consciousness-raising efforts thus reflect an understanding of the frequent need for structural change while simultaneously gaining local elites' acceptance. Voluntary agencies, more than any other structure for international cooperation, have the potential for espousing this type of liberating approach because of their historical proclivity for relating to people and to the whole person rather than to increasing gross national product alone.

What is needed, then, is a return to the original people-to-people ethos of the voluntary sector. And it is needed not only in the Third World but also in America itself. Consciousness raising is as necessary "here" as it is "there," not only among American poverty groups but among the middle and upper classes as well. There is a need for more understanding of the issues of global interdependence, of the real causes and potential solutions of poverty, of the needs and aspirations of people throughout the world, and of the American stake in their realization. There is a need to build on the basic American sympathy for people of other cultures to render Americans more informed and more constructive within varying value contexts. In all this, voluntary organizations have a unique contribution to make.

For all these existing and potential strengths of the voluntary sector, there are equally worrisome weaknesses. Many Americans are so locked into certain assumptions about charity that they fail to perceive that their very humanitarianism may have inhumane effects. A premium is still placed on good intentions, and the historical American can-do mentality takes over from there. As one observer has commented,

> American optimism spurs an impatience to confront the issues, to get on with the job, to do something, to set things right. In sum, it is the positive and direct action approach. It leads, however, to the uneasy feeling among less activistically-oriented allies that precipitate action may compound the problem rather than resolve it. It precludes opting for no action, which might, in the view of some critics, sometimes lead to more desirable results.[7]

Furthermore, it sometimes appears that something is being bought in return for this charity—sometimes political or economic rewards, sometimes

---

[6]According to a young Zambian politician, "The churches have spread more revolution on this continent than Che Guevera, Lenin, and Mao Tse-tung." Cited in Michael T. Kaufman, "Africa's Churches, Long Scorned as Colonialist, Now Preach Change," *New York Times,* December 20, 1976, p. 1.

[7]Glenn H. Fisher, *Public Diplomacy and the Behavioral Sciences* (Bloomington: Indiana University Press, 1972), p. 145.

psychic pleasure. For example, "some observers believe that Americans have a unique anxiety about being liked, or at least being appreciated for their accomplishments and generosity. These observers say that the United States, although a powerful nation, apparently cannot be content with merely being respected, but requires something more emotionally satisfying to the American mentality tuned to an American style of interpersonal relations."[8] Some would say that Americans actually *need* poverty in order to justify their reaching out.

Another weakness of the U.S. voluntary sector in Third World assistance lies in a perceived element of inconsistency between what appear to be self-confident antipoverty efforts overseas and the weak American record in combating poverty at home. There has been considerable success, to be sure, in raising education and health standards among disadvantaged groups in the United States, along with increasing political power for American minorities. On the other hand, self-sustaining economic power has still eluded these groups. In spite of the very extensive Great Society efforts of the 1960s, the relative gap between American minority groups and whites and between rich and poor is as wide as before. Furthermore, a recent survey by the Organisation for Economic Co-operation and Development showed that, after France, the United States has the highest percentage of population below a standardized poverty line of any OECD industrialized country. Thirteen per cent of the U.S. population is below the poverty line, in contrast to Britain's 7.5 per cent, Sweden's 3.5 per cent, and Germany's 3 per cent.[9] These facts, especially in the face of America's unparalleled affluence, raise certain questions as to American motivations generally, including, by association, those of U.S. private and voluntary organizations. They do not suggest that Americans should cease their efforts in the Third World and clean up their own house first. Rather, they suggest a need for more candor and humility abroad.

Much of the discussion in this volume has revolved around the need for U.S. private and voluntary organizations to respond with more political understanding to poverty in the Third World. If it is a potential strength of the voluntary agencies to be able to grapple with structural problems, at least on local levels, it is also an existing weakness that they do not attempt to do so more often. This is partly a function of wanting to play it safe, since voluntary organizations often feel—usually correctly—that their overseas leverage is limited. The reason for their fear of politics is paradoxical. It relates in large part to the interest of most agencies in having programs in as many countries as possible in order to enhance their reputations and their institutional viability. They are thus generally in the position of having to sell their programs overseas, the mode of initial entry frequently being an

---

[8]Ibid., pp. 149-50.
[9]Wilfred Beckerman, "Are the Poor Always With Us?" *New Statesman*, September 10, 1976, p. 335.

agency representative visiting a given country to solicit an invitation from the local government or from some other group. To sell themselves, they must appear to be cooperative, which in itself encourages close government relations. As one representative in Kenya noted with mixed pride and chagrin, "The Kenyan Government gives us our office, our picture of President Kenyatta, and the nail with which to hang it up." Governments, even if happy enough to welcome the organization and its assistance, do not feel such a commitment to it (as they might to large-scale World Bank aid, for example) that they are willing to tolerate undue political meddling. Yet it is important to note that tolerance thresholds vary widely, as does basic understanding of the long-term results of voluntary agency efforts, whether described as educational or consciousness-raising in nature. On balance, therefore, private and voluntary organizations should persist in their efforts at innovative programming that exploits their full range of potential creativity.

A related political question that constantly rears its head is that of aid to countries governed by totalitarian regimes. In settings such as Haiti and Brazil, the totalitarian nature of the national governments causes constant reflection by the agencies. Is it immoral for an agency to appear to be supporting such a government? Or is it perhaps more moral to encourage poor people, through aid, to gain the wherewithal to ultimately stand up for their democratic rights? Some organization heads say that they do not care who leads the ship of state, but only who is aboard it. Others hope that their aid will cause local people to become more politically astute, for example, by demonstrating to them what their own governments should do. Some thus argue that aid can hasten the necessary or inevitable revolution, while others argue that aid only delays revolution through palliative action. While there can be, of course, no general answer to this dilemma, the important point for a voluntary organization is to see as its primary objective the ability of the poor majority in a given setting to control its own destiny. If local structures exist, or can be rearranged, to fulfill this objective, then outside assistance is justified. If not, then the assistance is more wisely offered elsewhere. Fortunately, national and local elites vary in their perceptions of their own self-interest. Thus much can be accomplished at some levels even in the absence of support from others.

While structural and political issues account for many of the limitations to U.S. private and voluntary effectiveness in the Third World, equally significant obstacles are the inherent sociological and economic difficulties of working with the poor majority. It is far easier to work with better-off groups than to tackle the worst-off. Thus it is hardly surprising that most aid efforts have concentrated first on the path of least resistance and have involved communicating initially through the articulate, Westernized, often English-speaking Third World elites and counting on the trickle-down principle of development to do the rest. How does one respond to local superstition—to Sahelian farmers who believe that if new irrigation facilities bring water to their plots at "the wrong time of year," God will punish them by causing them to sink irretrievably into the muddy mire thus created? How does one encourage new practices among people whose eyes have never been opened to the possibility of change and among people too poor to risk what little they may have on some unbelievable vision imported from outside? How does one penetrate the inertia of traditional societies? The foreigner attempting to do this often risks either doing too much himself in order to "complete the project," or not doing enough, in which case nothing may happen. Because of this inherent difficulty of the development process, and in particular because of the lack of human and physical absorptive capacity in the poorest areas of the world, the number of good voluntary agency projects is limited.

This leads to a further problem: rampant competition among organizations for the privilege and prestige of supporting one or another among the relatively few local groups and local leaders effectively grappling with development at the grass-roots level. Unpopular though it is to say so, the problem is frequently one of too many dollars chasing too few opportunities for their wise expenditure. In such a situation there are three alternatives. One is to spend the larger sums required for more welfare-oriented approaches, the way most frequently chosen. Another is to recognize that self-sustaining development efforts, by definition, require less money in specific situations, and thus to reduce agency support; this is an unpopular alternative because many individuals and institutions still hold that "big is beautiful." The third alternative (which may enjoy a certain complementarity with the second) is to seek creative new ways to respond to the poor majority, for instance, by guaranteeing low-interest, no-collateral bank loans, and through consciousness-raising approaches.

One inhibition to pursuing such creative approaches—at least for the largest voluntary organizations—has been the U.S. government's preference for channeling food rather than cash aid through the agencies. While earlier discussion has pointed to the constructive uses of food for development programs, the fact is that it is more difficult to use food creatively for longer-term goals of structural change than it is to use cash. For the consciousness-raising efforts that constitute a critical prerequisite to development, there is no substitute for cash that can be used to fund the hiring of local people as catalysts. Yet cash resources are sometimes scarce, and many U.S. private and voluntary organizations have policies against using them to pay continuing salaries or other recurring costs; they prefer instead to contribute only to the initial capital costs of projects. The result is thus a built-in bias toward grants of physical objects such as schools or jeeps, without provision for the recurring costs of consciousness-raising teachers to staff the schools or gasoline to run the jeeps. Policies against funding recurring costs are understandable, given the need for self-help contributions from local groups and the fact that foreign funds are most logically devoted to purposes requiring foreign exchange. Yet the irony is that if structural change is required to enable equality of opportunity for the poor majority, then consciousness-raising methods are also required; and for them, continuing cash resources—which may not always be locally available—are indispensable.

This need for flexible cash resources raises again the problem of how U.S. private and voluntary organizations are themselves supported. It is a serious and urgent problem of legitimate concern to some of the most effective development agencies. The U.S. public, as discussed in Chapter 8, responds more magnanimously to appeals for relief than for development aid. The public has been reinforced in this direction, no doubt, by the relief-oriented nature of agency advertising. Also playing a role is America's history and isolated continental geography that has until recently furnished relatively little opportunity for exposure to larger Third World realities. While the American public is becoming increasingly aware of these realities, and thus of the need for long-term, more explicitly developmental approaches, constituency contributions are likely to remain an insufficient source of support during the immediate transition future.

Private U.S. foundations and corporate donations are also not as forthcoming as they might be. With a few exceptions, these groups have tended to concentrate on funding domestic U.S. activities that they can monitor more conveniently and understand better. Except for the large Ford and Rockefeller Foundations, which have their own operating networks, most foundations and corporations that have funded Third World activities have tended to support cultural and scientific exchanges rather than explicit antipoverty efforts. Others, especially from business philanthropy, have tended to support educational and health projects benefiting the relative elites from which they draw their customers and workers, rather than the poor.[10] These are regrettable limitations, given the potential impact that even the smaller foundations and corporations could have. By supporting selected U.S. voluntary agencies in their overseas efforts—perhaps concentrating intensively on support to one or two based in the same town or state as the foundation or corporation itself—they could make a much-needed Third World contribution, encourage local internationally minded U.S. groups, and still be able to monitor progress through the U.S. headquarters and constituencies of the particular agency concerned.

Another potential resource for U.S. voluntary organizations—in intellectual, if not monetary terms—is the university community. While U.S. foundations and government aid programs have made considerable use of university services, the voluntary sector has rarely done so. This is partly because the university ethos is quite different from their own and partly

---

[10]See James R. Basche, Jr., *U.S. Business Support for International Public Service Activities,* 2 parts [New York: Conference Board, Inc., 1973 (Part I, "Support from U.S. Headquarters") and 1974-75 (Part II, "Support from Foreign Affiliates," in 5 vols. covering Brazil, Mexico, Argentina, Colombia, and the Philippines)]; and *Information Bulletin No. 6* (a study update), April 1976.

because university service costs are high. Yet increased partnership would be useful for both sides. The voluntary agencies would have the benefit of intelligent and objective analyses of their programs, and the universities would gain opportunities for field research for their better understanding of both Third World development problems and U.S. responses to them. Such collaboration should be possible on a relatively low-cost basis if, for example, relevant university specialists were increasingly invited to serve on the boards of directors of voluntary agencies and if academic research topics were selected from among voluntary organization program experiences.

It is to a large extent because of the inadequacy of these various existing support structures that U.S. government assistance has come to be as important as it has for so many voluntary organizations. The problems inherent in this situation have been described at some length already. They are especially pronounced if one takes consciousness rasing to be an important voluntary agency role. Quite aside from the political and bureaucratic ramifications, the government's more rigidly time-bound project framework can be an impediment to the continuing process of development implied in consciousness-raising activities. Such activities are clearly not as measurable in their results as are well-digging or the introduction of new crops or even literacy instruction. Accountability thus becomes a problem.

Indeed, accountability constitutes a very serious problem. To whom *are* private and voluntary organizations accountable? In this connection, the foundations have been the subject of periodic congressional criticism and investigation, culminating in the more stringent controls imposed in the tax reform legislation of 1969. Voluntary organizations are generally assumed to be accountable to their supporters—to government and foundation donors and in some loose way to their contributors among the general public. Yet the public appears more concerned with agency overheads remaining low and the bulk of the income going directly to Third World recipients who need it than with the form and quality of that aid. It is thus legitimate to ask whether the ultimate accountability ought not be to the Third World poor themselves. Small steps in this direction have occasionally been taken by agencies giving block grants designed to be distributed and accounted for by local private organizations. This technique, along with the establishment of voluntary agency local advisory panels, brings the level of accountability significantly closer to those ultimately affected by the aid. In other cases, Third World governments have wanted to exercise coordinating roles over project approval and implementation, a desire that the U.S. agencies have generally resented as unnecessarily stultifying interference. Given the bureaucratic, political, and elitist pressures often exerted by governments or other controlling elites, this resentment is often quite understandable. Yet whatever the mechanism, there must be accountability to the particular Third World groups being aided at the local level. It is they—more than the agency, the agency's donors, or the host government—who are being affected, for better or for worse, by the assistance.

Trends and Options for the Future

Emerging from an analysis of the strengths and weaknesses of the admittedly diverse private sector and of the various issues thus raised, one can identify certain clear trends in the field of private and voluntary assistance. *First*, there is a clear movement to supplement the more narrowly defined relief programs with longer-term development efforts. This does not necessarily mean, for all groups, a change in the high priority they attach to relief and welfare.[11] On the other hand, organizations that earlier were engaged primarily in curative health care, for example, are now shifting to preventative care and to training programs for Third World medical personnel. Others that disbursed food are increasingly facilitating farmers' access to seeds to grow their own food, or adding to fishermen's capabilities to catch more fish. The most far-sighted organizations are applying to their development programs an amended version of the well-known fishing aphorism: It is one thing to give a person a fish and another to teach him to fish for himself; but it is still better, in the long run, to teach him to *breed* fish.

A *second* trend is primarily methodological, but it has important substantive implications as well. Voluntary agencies, on the one hand, are more frequently playing professional consulting roles, and, on the other hand, are increasingly filling mini-foundation roles by providing grants to local intermediary groups. The first of these roles may seem to place the concerned organizations more in competition with regular consulting firms, while the latter may have them supplementing traditional foundation roles. Yet this dual trend should not be cause for excessive concern. The fact that the Third World is increasingly asking for professional foreigners rather than American B.A. generalists to provide development assistance is a sign of Third World progress in both self-confidence and development as a whole. The fact that foreign grants are in many areas becoming more acceptable than programs operated by foreigners fits the same pattern. Even though both trends may tend to reduce the opportunities for people-to-people contact and understanding, they are in keeping with increasing nationalism, growing demands for internal control and accountability, and increasing awareness of the importance of cultural integrity and values. While highly sensitive outside catalysts can play important roles in a consciousness-raising process, direct action is generally best implemented by local intermediary groups, usually Third World voluntary organizations. All these advantages notwithstanding, the possible reduction in opportunities for interpersonal communication could represent an important loss in the equation.

---

[11]For example, in 1976 a few agencies appeared willing to sacrifice U.S. government *development* funds in favor of lobbying for higher ocean freight allotments for shipping surplus food commodities for their feeding programs.

A *third* trend is the increasing recognition that development education is important in America itself. In the past, the few educational efforts that existed tended to center around fund-raising appeals or suggestions for higher government aid budgets that might also (if incidentally) benefit voluntary agency programs themselves. More recently, prompted by the dire world food shortages of the 1970s, new and different types of groups have formed to take up more broadly policy-oriented educational efforts, encompassing issues such as the need for trade, monetary, and arms policy reforms. These groups have supplemented the roles of older organizations such as the United Nations Association and the Foreign Policy Association. U.S. voluntary agencies with Third World programs have yet, by and large, to figure out how to translate their theoretical belief in the need for development education into actual practice. Communicating greater realism as to the slow and complex progress of development is too often seen as potentially counterproductive to their public relations and fund-raising demands. Yet the trend in terms of new kernels of interest in development education must be noted. It is likely that new ways will be found in the future to reconcile what now often appear to be competing interests between too much and too little knowledge on the part of the U.S. public.

It is not an exaggeration to say that U.S. private and voluntary organizations are today at a crossroads in their collective history. The world has changed all around them, and they too—to some extent—have changed. Yet they will have to undergo more rapid transitions than heretofore if they are to maintain their unique advantages as flexible, sensitive, and human organisms for international development and understanding. Some observers, noting that U.S. private organizations account for only some $1 billion out of $17 billion in annual development aid to the Third World, wonder whether it would make any difference if these agencies were to go out of business altogether. In terms of Third World gross national product, it would not matter very much, for the influence of these private organizations is small when measured against the larger resources and processes of history. Yet measured at individual family and community levels, their withdrawal from the scene could make a big difference. Experience has shown that even small influences, carefully planned and thoughtfully implemented, can have disproportionately large effects, whether on crop production, marketing, education, or health. Small influences can also have leverage effects by attracting larger-scale resources from Third World and outside donors.

Voluntary organizations have several options for the future. One is to continue along existing trend lines. If this were done, voluntary agencies would probably continue to make contributions for several years to come. They would supplement the various governmental and multilateral development efforts and fill useful complementary roles. But they would no longer serve as pioneers, as so many of them did during their early years. Nor would they fill a preeminent role. Just as in the United States the government has assumed a dramatically increased share in financing the domestic education and health sectors that were once largely supported by private organizations, so too have governments both in the West generally and in the Third World expanded and improved their relative contributions to Third World development. Foundations and voluntary organizations would still be able to perform many roles more effectively than could the larger governmental entities. However, Third World voluntary agency analogs are coming increasingly to the fore, and the tendency already is to place increasing reliance on them. Over the long run, therefore, the comparative advantage of the U.S. private agencies would be likely to diminish further. Some would probably go out of existence while others would muddle through from year to year, suffering financial woes and contributing less than their potential to the development process.

A second option is more promising. U.S. private and voluntary organizations could strike out more clearly in new directions, capitalizing on a new sense of comparative advantage. They could do this by keeping paramount in their programs the goal of equality of opportunity for members of the poor majority—a goal that is significantly absent in many organizations' current formulations of objectives. While some groups are already pursuing this objective in an evolutionary way, the majority of organizations do not always ask the hard questions relevant to it: Who is benefiting from the outside aid? Does the aid promote genuine equality of opportunity? Are the benefits likely to be self-sustaining after the foreign group withdraws? Does the local group feel able to determine its own future through a sense of dignity and full participation in the development process? Satisfactory answers to these types of questions have not often emerged from voluntary agency efforts of the past. Nor are the new directions suggested in this volume to elicit them either unrealistic or revolutionary. The main point is to keep the larger objectives constantly in view. Voluntary organizations should not be diverted by "projectitis"—that is, by the more intermediate questions relating to the *means* of development (for instance, how many new schools should be built)—away from the larger (and not necessarily compatible) *ends* of development.

Perhaps the major role of private and voluntary organizations a decade hence will be in the area of social prophecy—not prophecy in the mystical sense, but rather in the sense of promoting new patterns for human interaction in an increasingly interdependent world. If voluntary agencies were to take the lead today in this direction, they would truly distinguish themselves both from other kinds of organizations and from their current roles. They would become forces for raising the consciousness of people not only in the Third World but also at home in America. In partnership with the voluntary associations of Europe and other countries, they could contribute to multinational perceptions of the common aspirations of people everywhere—aspirations to minimum physical needs for food, shelter, clothing, and health care, and to higher orders of cultural and spiritual needs. Voluntary organizations, being composed of freely motivated and well-intentioned individuals, are particularly well suited to developing and propounding a new ethos for human cohabitation of the earth.

Recommendations

Skeptics may feel that the vision for American voluntary organizations suggested in this book is overly idealistic. Proponents of the voluntary sector may find the criticisms of hindsight too harsh. Thus it is important to concretize the conclusions of this study with specific recommendations that will clarify both the objectives suggested and the means by which they might be realized. If these recommendations are followed, the private and voluntary organizations of the United States—and the American people as a whole—should be able to further enrich both their own lives and those of the world's poorest billion people.

1. At a general level, the private and voluntary organizations need to recognize and be more forthright about their full range of motivations for doing what they do. The belief that good intentions automatically lead to good deeds and then to good results has been shown to be illusory. However commendable charitable motives may be, they too often have taken the form of arrogance on the one hand or misguided philanthropy on the other—the kind of philanthropy that creates dependency rather than self-reliance among aided groups. What is needed, therefore, is a recognition that donors stand as much to gain as much as recipients by their involvement in development efforts; this is true both in a psychological sense and in the sense that a narrowed gap between rich and poor means a more just and thus a more peaceful world for rich and poor alike. Once this interdependence of needs is more honestly faced and accepted, then, too, should relationships become smoother and richer for all.

2. Development efforts undertaken in the Third World must be efforts of *self*-development. This means that the *process* becomes inherently more important than the *project*, a critical distinction if results are to endure after the foreign contribution has come to an end. A focus on process is particularly critical if the structural obstacles to equitable development are to be removed, for this can happen only by the action of local people exercising their own rights and demands. The rule of thumb for the foreigner must be to avoid taking too dominant a role in particular development efforts. Such dominence is often too easy to assume either through locally expressed preferences or through defaults in local initiative. The supportive or catalytic role—which is at the root of nearly every voluntary agency's *theoretical* policy, if not always reflected in its actual practice—is what is needed. Indeed, if an aid recipient is an appropriate one in the first place, he should then be deemed an appropriate *partner*. The foreigner should thus defer to local control and be accountable to it. This does not necessitate agreeing on every point with local leadership; rather, it necessitates a process of free, frank, and equal exchange among all parties. This, after all, is the essence of partnership.

3. Private and voluntary organizations should seek ways to overcome their traditional tendency to act alone and instead collaborate more constructively both with each other and with local organizations in recipient countries. The American custom of decentralizing and proliferating agencies and associations has resulted in a myriad of private and voluntary organizations operating overseas. Dealing with such a number of groups can be confusing for many Third World people and time-consuming for their government officials. Some of the latter feel it a sign of arrogance, as well as inconvenience, that so many small-agency representatives presume on their time to compete for favored projects. In this connection, existing models of interagency collaboration should be carefully examined and emulated. Such models include Private Agencies Collaborating Together (PACT), whose member agencies formulate joint programs and negotiate them as integrated packages in various Third World countries; Church World Service, the ecumenical Protestant collaborative agency for both relief and development assistance; and the Church World Service/Lutheran World Relief collaborative effort, which has been established in some areas for purposes of better joint programming and less costly administration. Collaborations between voluntary organizations and local organizations in the Third World have proven similarly beneficial and should also be encouraged. Existing examples of these include Action for Food Production (AFPRO), an Indian agency that gives technical support to rural development projects and that is funded by various Western church groups; the Calcutta Bustee Development Organization, supported primarily by European church groups for Calcutta slum development; and local consortia in Bangladesh and Niger, organized by Western voluntary agencies to facilitate their in-country program collaboration and to offer stronger representation vis-à-vis local governments. Experience has shown that all such collaborative arrangements, whether of U.S. or Third World groups, suffer from a variety of defects. Often these are rooted in the problems of individual institutional egos, deriving, in turn, from the felt need of each group to demonstrate to its supporters that it is unique and thus worthy of support. Still, the consortia constitute a step in the right direction. In situations of increasing Third World economic stringencies and demands for professional talent, such collaborative arrangements can provide both higher-quality and lower-cost assistance.

4. Beyond the level of specific programming collaboration, improved structures are needed for interagency reflection, forward planning, and perhaps self-policing. Some observers have proposed the equivalent of a bar association for voluntary agencies, while others have suggested a peer accreditation system. These would maintain standards not only in bookkeeping practices but also in promoting truthfulness and wisdom in fund-raising techniques and in the quality and sophistication of development programming overall. While there has been understandable resistance to an association with such a broad mandate to judge among peers, there is clearly a need for a considerably more active forum than currently exists for

bringing together members of the broadest possible spectrum of agencies for meaningful reflection, discussion, and forward thinking. Indeed, the only existing channel at present is the Committee on Development Assistance of the American Council of Voluntary Agencies; it represents only a limited membership, however, and has not yet demonstrated a long-term commitment to grappling with substantive development issues. With the private and voluntary organizations at a particularly important crossroads today, active attention should be given either to restructuring and strengthening the Council and its development committee or to establishing a new forum for this purpose.

5. There is an urgent need for private and voluntary organizations to take new initiatives to ensure greater funding stability. The sense of financial stability, however, should fall short of that which induces total complacency. If current trends continue, the voluntary sector may be left to muddle through a series of financial crises. Inflation and other problems that face domestic U.S. philanthropy could increasingly thwart the international organizations as well; indeed, the particularly high costs of implementing programs overseas would take a special toll.

Several initiatives should be pursued here. First, the U.S. government should be encouraged to establish an endowed international development institute along the lines suggested in Chapter 7. Such an institute would provide a source of flexible non-State Department, multiyear funds for innovative programming, not only by private and voluntary agencies but by U.S. government groups as well. As a short-term solution, and as also suggested in Chapter 7, AID procedures should be substantially streamlined to facilitate cooperation between the private and voluntary sector and the U.S. government. Second, U.S. private foundations and corporate philanthropies should be made more aware of the emerging implications of global interdependence and of the need for their more enlightened participation in the kinds of private and voluntary organization efforts described here. A national commission of distinguished Americans should be formed to give strong leadership in this direction. Third, private and voluntary organizations should explore various types of entrepreneurial activities that would generate funds internally, either to support agency budgets in an ongoing way or to create endowments for future earnings and budget support. There are precedents for this in the business ventures of some Latin American Caritas organizations, in the Oxfam model of shops selling Third World products and locally contributed used clothing in Britain, in similar U.S. thrift shop experiences of the Foundation for the Peoples of the South Pacific, and in various plans considered by Nigerian church groups to construct buildings in order to earn rental income. Surely the American entrepreneurial spirit can devise many other variants relevant in the United States.

6. A new relationship with the American people must be evolved. Here, too, many of the voluntary organizations are at a turning point. Some have found that their appeal lies heavily among older people who remember well

the post-World War II relief period when CARE and the big church groups first made their names; other organizations (far fewer) enjoy a significant response from younger donors. In any case, new appeals are now needed, appeals both to hearts and to minds. An end must be declared to the "sad child" syndrome and to its unnecessarily damaging separation of mankind into the poor and pitiable on the one hand and the rich and charitable on the other. There is thus a need for development education and for experimenting with new techniques of combining fund-raising demands with these concerns for dignity and human solidarity. There is also a need to go beyond this, to pioneer new ways in which people who live in both affluent and poor countries can become personally involved with each other in ways other than through giving and receiving money. Cultural and educational exchanges and "reverse Peace Corps" initiatives are only some of the ways to do this. Americans have already learned much about alternative life-styles and philosophies derived from Asia, Africa, and Latin America. The opportunities for this kind of learning and understanding must be developed much further, so that interdependence comes to mean equality of opportunity in a larger, more human sense.

Over the years, the contributions of the American private and voluntary organizations overseas, and of the people who support them, have been significant. It is for this reason that one continues to expect so much of them now. Yet in a world undergoing more rapid change than ever before, what is to be their role in the future? Some broad trends are clear. One of these is the trend toward inevitably increasing human interdependence. The other is the growing demand for equality of opportunity and human rights—political and economic—for all people everywhere. Both trends are of primary concern to American private and voluntary organizations. Current evolution in the private sector as a whole, and the degree to which critical issues are being thoughtfully discussed, lead one to be optimistic for the future. The question is to what extent the implications of these trends and demands are being thoroughly and dispassionately analyzed and to what extent appropriate programming adjustments are being made, not just for tomorrow, but for 1980, 1990, and the year 2000.

In 1776, out of "a decent respect to the opinions of mankind," a new nation announced to the world that "all men are created equal, that they are endowed by their Creator with certain inalienable rights, that among these are life, liberty, and the pursuit of happiness." The issue is still one of implementation. To whom are these basic rights to be applied? And for whom is mere charity to suffice?

Annex A

Facts of Interest about the Private and Voluntary Organizations

Table 1. Net Flow of Private and Voluntary Assistance from Selected Countries, 1970 and 1975 ($ millions, $, and percentages)

Countries Listed by 1975 Rank[a]	Total Contribution ($ millions) 1970	1975	Per Capita Contribution ($) 1970	1975	Contribution as Percentage of GNP 1970	1975
Switzerland	11	32	1.74	5.01	.05	.06
Sweden	25	39	3.13	4.73	.08	.06
United States	**598**	**804**	**2.92**	**3.76**	**.06**	**.05**
Germany	78	205	1.28	3.32	.04	.05
Canada	52	67	2.42	2.91	.06	.04
Australia	16	34	1.26	2.50	.05	.04
Netherlands	5	24	.40	1.72	.02	.03
United Kingdom	34	53	.61	.95	.03	.02
France	6	15	.12	.29	.004	.005
Japan	3	10	.03	.09	.002	.002
Italy	5	3	.09	.05	.009	.002

[a]Rank according to 1975 grants by voluntary agencies as a percentage of 1975 GNP.

NOTE: The eleven countries cited represent 96 per cent of the private assistance of all members of the Development Advisory Committee (DAC) of the Organisation for Economic Co-Operation and Development to the Third World in 1975.

SOURCES: Based on Report by the Chairman of the Development Assistance Committee, *Development Co-operation, 1975 Review* (Paris: OECD, 1975), pp. 206-17; and Report by the Chairman of the Development Assistance Committee, *Development Co-operation, 1976 Review* (Paris: OECD, 1976), Tables 10 and 44.

Table 2. U.S. Private and Voluntary Assistance to the Third World, 1919-1975 ($ millions)

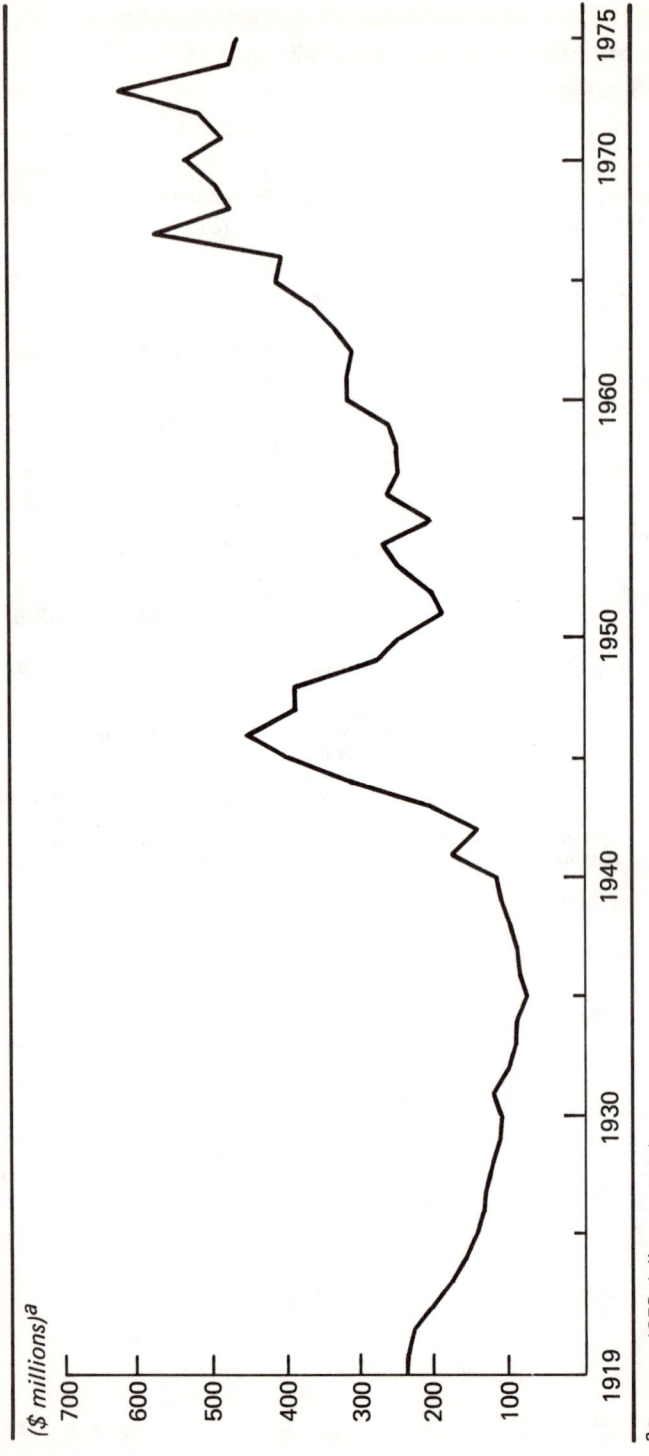

[a]Constant 1958 dollars.

NOTE: The sharp rise and subsequent decline of U.S. private and voluntary assistance during the early 1970s is due to unusually high United Israel Appeal fund raising during the 1973 Middle East War.

SOURCE: Figures for 1919-1959 are from Merle Curti, *American Philanthropy Abroad* (New Brunswick, N.J.: Rutgers University Press, 1963), pp. 506-7. Figures for 1960-1975 are from the Balance of Payments Division, Bureau of Economic Analysis, U.S. Department of Commerce.

Table 3. U.S. Foundations Making Largest Grants for Third World Activities[a] ($ millions)

	Total Annual Grant Amounts ($ millions)	Amount of which for Third World ($ millions)
Ford Foundation	185.2	46.9
Rockefeller Foundation	43.1	23.9
Lilly Endowment, Inc.	44.6	3.8
W.K. Kellogg Foundation	23.9	2.6
Edna McConnell Clark Foundation	10.3	2.0
China Medical Board of New York	1.9	1.9
Rockefeller Brothers Fund	10.5	1.0
Carnegie Corporation of New York	13.8	0.9

[a] All amounts are averaged from figures provided by the respective foundations for fiscal years ending in 1973 through 1976. Definitions of grants benefiting Third World countries, as opposed to grants for international purposes generally, may vary somewhat from one foundation to another. Additional variations may occur depending on whether commitments or actual disbursements are counted.

Table 4. Incomes of U.S. Voluntary Agencies[a]
(U.S. dollar value)

	Total Income	From U.S. Government Sources				From Private Sources	
		Overseas Freight Paid by U.S. Govt.	U.S. Govt. Excess Property	Donated Food (Incl. P.L.-480)	Grants and Contracts	Donations of Supplies and Equipment	Cash Contributions and Other Income
Agricultural Missions Foundation	71,341	—	—	—	—	—	71,341
Aid for International Medicine	166,943	—	—	—	—	142,216	24,727
American Bureau for Medical Aid to China	1,002,523	—	—	—	702,379	400	299,744
American Committee for Shaare Zedek Hospital in Jerusalem	4,362,994	57,617	—	—	299,493	—	4,005,884
American Dentists for Foreign Service	208,386	—	—	—	—	177,555	30,831
American Foundation for Overseas Blind	638,062	—	—	—	—	—	638,062
American Freedom from Hunger Foundation	267,857	—	—	—	—	—	267,857
American Friends Service Committee	10,381,752	—	—	—	266,293	195,311	9,920,148
American Fund for Czechoslovak Refugees	386,051	—	—	—	299,158	—	86,893
American Institute for Free Labor Development	5,726,252	—	—	—	5,432,848	—	293,404
American Jewish Joint Distribution Committee	32,407,100	45,500	—	123,200	1,526,500	—	30,711,900
American Kor-Asian Foundation	1,900,948	21,176	509,022	—	—	175,200	1,195,550
American Mission to Greeks	1,886,540	—	—	—	—	45,720	1,820,820

American Mizrachi Women	1,780,324	—	—	—	—	1,780,324
American National Committee to Aid Homeless Armenians	73,199	—	—	—	—	73,199
American Near East Refugee Aid (AMER-A Division of ANERA)	294,963	—	—	—	53,950	241,013
American ORT Federation	7,572,992	10,160	—	557,717	6,175	6,915,330
Asian-American Free Labor Institute	2,039,105	—	83,610	1,949,972	—	89,133
Assemblies of God, Foreign Service Committee	367,342	—	—	—	15,056	352,286
Boys' Towns of Italy	1,015,549	—	—	—	—	1,015,549
Catholic Relief Services, U.S. Catholic Conference	169,979,828	25,912,799	315,047	87,951,791	14,117,063	23,558,739	18,124,389
Children's Medical Relief International	705,554	—	—	—	257,799	—	447,755
Christian Children's Fund	28,842,015	—	—	—	13,647	—	28,828,368
Christian Reformed World Relief Committee	1,644,586	—	—	—	—	493,795	1,150,791
Church World Service	26,333,190	1,771,182	—	2,003,231	34,570	10,647,622	11,876,585
CODEL (Coordination in Development), Inc.	309,384	—	—	—	78,811	—	230,573
Community Development Foundation	978,108	—	—	—	290,845	—	687,263
CARE (Cooperative for American Relief Everywhere)	170,062,924	35,221,554	—	91,160,601	8,466,636	14,894,616	20,319,517
Cooperative League Fund	163,810	—	—	—	—	—	163,810
Direct Relief Foundation	1,790,849	—	—	—	—	1,511,309	279,540
Docare International	5,326	—	—	—	—	—	5,326
The Thomas A. Dooley Foundation	862,087	19,755	—	—	—	236,799	605,533
Foster Parents Plan	13,949,756	—	—	—	22,088	—	13,927,668
Foundation for the Peoples of the South Pacific	160,611	—	—	—	—	—	160,611
Franklin Book Programs	14,668,107	—	—	—	12,333,298	—	2,334,809
Friends of Children	42,939	—	—	—	—	—	42,939

Table 4. (continued)

	Total Income	From U.S. Government Sources				From Private Sources	
		Overseas Freight Paid by U.S. Govt.	U.S. Govt. Excess Property	Donated Food (Incl. P.L.-480)	Grants and Contracts	Donations of Supplies and Equipment	Cash Contributions and Other Income
Friends of the United States of Latin America	1,150	—	—	—	—	—	1,150
HADASSAH	27,825,950	107,398	—	—	545,977	—	27,172,575
Heifer Project International	1,564,326	7,905	—	—	—	470,704	1,085,717
HIAS	4,078,991	—	—	—	870,446	—	3,208,545
Holt Adoption Program	2,567,626	7,394	—	—	173,534	—	2,386,698
International Development Foundation	250,279	—	—	—	71,254	—	179,025
International Educational Development	227,531	23,117	—	—	89,089	—	115,325
International Eye Foundation	618,601	—	—	—	171,307	83,100	364,194
International Institute of Rural Reconstruction	395,340	116	—	—	—	—	395,224
International Rescue Committee	3,884,494	—	—	—	2,227,350	—	1,657,144
International Voluntary Services	871,535	—	—	—	719,818	—	151,717
Iran Foundation	141,161	400	—	—	—	—	140,761
Laubach Literacy	1,072,142	—	—	—	—	—	1,072,142
Lutheran World Relief	8,912,322	989,521	—	1,241,258	—	4,598,789	2,082,754
Meals for Millions Foundation	486,544	—	—	—	—	31,785	454,759
Medical Assistance Programs	8,106,314	118,216	—	—	117,795	5,772,443	2,097,860
Mennonite Central Committee	9,475,911	180,000	—	—	338,890	3,721,950	5,235,071
Missions Health Foundation	27,082	—	—	—	—	—	27,082
National Association of the Partners of the Alliance	10,821,624	—	—	—	—	1,003,165	9,818,459

Near East Foundation	1,494,171	—	—	925,669	—	568,502
Oxfam-America	912,194	—	—	—	—	912,194
Pan American Development Foundation	1,322,235	74,968	—	—	567,148	680,119
Pathfinder Fund	4,694,375	—	—	4,349,025	—	345,350
People-to-People Health Foundation (Project HOPE)	8,327,932	78,333	—	1,734,189	304,981	6,210,429
Polish American Immigration and Relief Committee	80,413	—	—	35,000	—	45,413
Project Concern	2,355,945	—	—	176,021	140,665	2,039,259
Refuge des Petits	57,819	—	—	—	—	57,819
Dr. Jose P. Rizal, Gen. Douglas MacArthur Memorial Foundation	100,659	—	—	—	85,900	14,759
Salvation Army National Headquarters	1,985,420	—	—	—	—	1,985,420
Save the Children Federation	7,091,257	—	—	198,113	29,969	6,863,175
Albert Schweitzer Fellowship	262,682	—	—	—	—	262,682
Seventh-Day Adventist World Service	3,585,063	550,026	1,437,781	—	1,275,156	322,100
Shoeshine Boys Foundation	183,257	—	—	—	—	183,257
Stelios M. Stelson Foundation	6,275	—	—	—	3,000	3,275
Summer Institute of Linguistics	11,890,616	14,531	—	10,951	8,142	11,856,992
Tolstoy Foundation	1,763,377	—	—	827,663	9,000	926,714
Travelers Aid, International Social Service of America	1,045,471	—	—	2,438	—	1,043,033
Unitarian Universalist Service Committee	593,883	—	—	—	—	593,883
United Israel Appeal	303,620,532	45,490	1,306,472	40,500,000	—	261,768,570
United Lithuanian Relief Fund of America	111,373	—	—	—	7,750	103,623
United States Foundation for International Scouting	642,132	—	—	—	—	642,132

Table 4. (continued)

	Total Income	From U.S. Government Sources				From Private Sources		
		Overseas Freight Paid by U.S. Govt.	U.S. Govt. Excess Property	Donated Food (Incl. P.L.-480)	Grants and Contracts	Donations of Supplies and Equipment	Cash Contributions and Other Income
United Ukrainian American Relief Committee	70,154	—	—	—	—	—	70,154
VITA (Volunteers in Technical Assistance)	491,186	—	—	—	—	—	491,186
Volunteer Border Relief	4,529	—	—	—	—	—	4,529
World Education	1,182,661	—	—	—	1,033,599	—	149,062
World Neighbors	1,860,031	—	—	—	—	2,025	1,858,006
World Relief Commission, National Association of Evangelicals	2,507,714	108,525	—	—	—	715,686	1,683,503
World University Service	97,510	—	—	—	—	—	97,510
World Vision Relief Organization	4,088,960	137,252	—	1,255	—	3,739,874	210,579
YMCA International Committee	3,719,146	—	—	—	184,560	—	3,534,586
World Relations Unit, National Board of the YWCA of the USA	266,984	—	—	—	—	—	266,984
Total, All Agencies	$950,774,176	$65,502,935	$2,214,151	$183,919,117	$101,951,805	$74,725,695	$522,460,473

[a]This list is comprised of those agencies registered with, and having reported to, the Advisory Committee on Voluntary Foreign Aid in 1975. For each agency, data represent the 12-month period of the fiscal year that ended during, or just prior to, calendar year 1975; fiscal years vary from agency to agency.

SOURCE: U.S. Agency for International Development, Bureau for Population and Humanitarian Assistance, Office of Private and Voluntary Cooperation, "Voluntary Foreign Aid Programs," 1975, pp. 12-15.

Table 5. Recipients of U.S. Overseas Voluntary Aid by Region, FYs 1946, 1960, and 1975 (percentages)

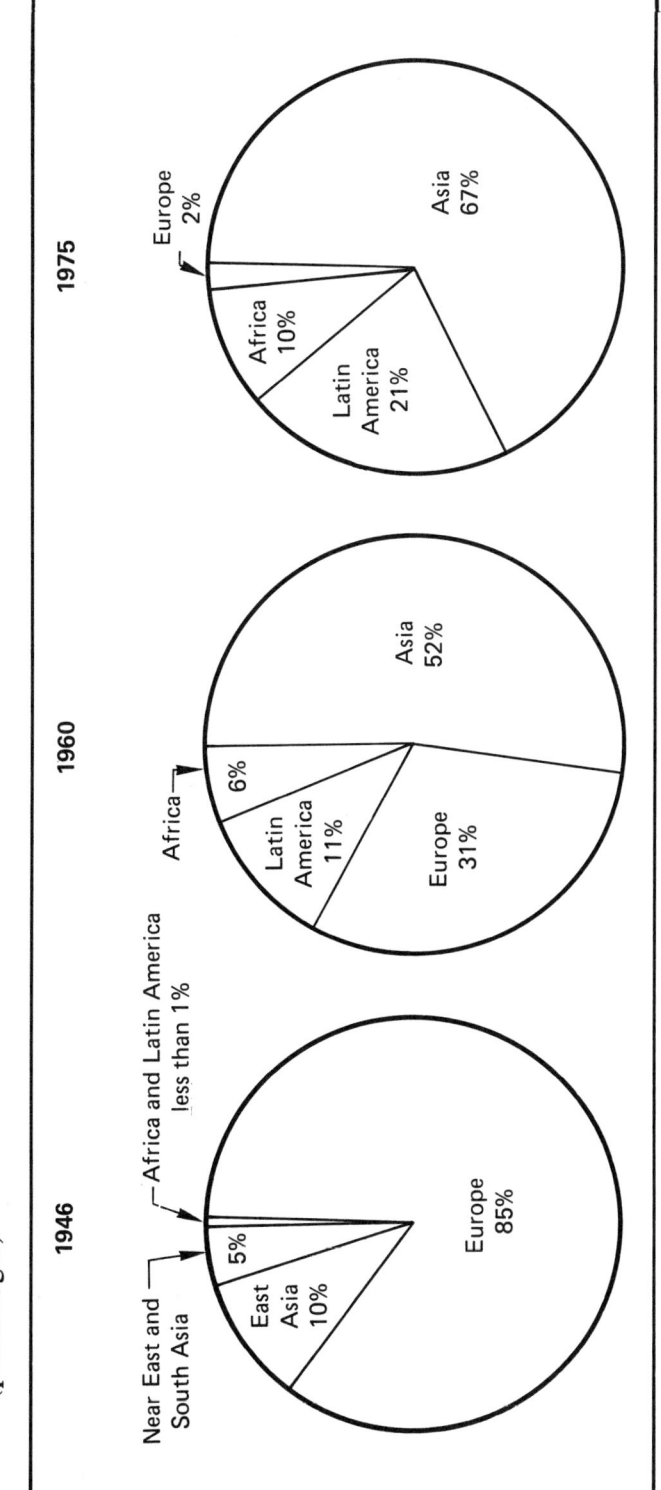

1946

- Near East and South Asia: 5%
- East Asia: 10%
- Africa and Latin America: less than 1%
- Europe: 85%

1960

- Africa: 6%
- Latin America: 11%
- Europe: 31%
- Asia: 52%

1975

- Europe: 2%
- Africa: 10%
- Latin America: 21%
- Asia: 67%

NOTE: Data based on contributions of those agencies registered with, and having reported to, the Advisory Committee on Voluntary Foreign Aid.

SOURCE: U.S. Agency for International Development, Bureau for Population and Humanitarian Assistance, Office of Private and Voluntary Cooperation, "Voluntary Foreign Aid Programs," 1975, p. 19.

Annex B

Private and Voluntary Organization Program Criteria

Annex B

Private and Voluntary Organization Program Criteria

The following statement was drawn up by executives from a number of leading U.S. private and voluntary agencies at a meeting on new roles for private organizations in overseas development. Sponsored by the Overseas Development Council, the meeting was held at the Belmont Conference Center in Elkridge, Maryland, September 14-16, 1975. In January 1976, the participants agreed to the slightly revised version of the statement given below.

The meeting participants were: C. Payne Lucas, Executive Director, Africare; Leon Marion, Executive Director, American Council of Voluntary Agencies for Foreign Service; Richard Redder, Special Assistant, Catholic Relief Services; Paul McCleary, Executive Director, Church World Service; Louis Samia, Deputy Executive Director, CARE; Allie Felder, Vice-President, The Cooperative League of the USA; James MacCracken, Executive Director, Coordination in Development; Anthony Lake, Executive Director, International Voluntary Services; Bernard Confer, Executive Secretary, Lutheran World Relief; John Thomas, Harvard University and Chairman, Oxfam-America; Robert O'Brien, Executive Director, Private Agencies Collaborating Together; Charles MacCormack, Program Director, Save the Children Federation; and Thomas Fox, Executive Director, Volunteers in Technical Assistance. Also participating were representatives of the U.S. Agency for International Development, U.S. House of Representatives International Relations Committee, Inter-American Foundation, Christian Action for Development in the Caribbean, New World Coalition, Lilly Endowment, Aspen Institute for Humanistic Studies, and Overseas Development Council.

No private voluntary organization [PVO] working in international development can meet all of the following criteria in all of its activities. But every PVO should at least question and judge its program in the light of these criteria. Many of them boil down to one injunction: the means used in development activities should be consistent with the ends. Private voluntary organizations seek to promote human advancement and to confront human suffering and its root causes. The criteria which follow and by which our programs should be judged—by ourselves and by others—are consistent with this broad purpose.

I. *Our programs must be of demonstrable benefit, on a small or large scale, to a group that is part of the so-called "poor majority."* ("Group" is a deliberately broad term here.)

The program must enhance the ability of that group to participate in the production of its own goods and services, and thus increase income, raise health and literacy levels, lower death and birth rates, or other such specific accomplishments.

The group must be able to sustain and improve on that progress after the program is completed. Short-term relief efforts should be explicitly tied to longer-term development programs.

The program should have the consequence of increasing—or at the very least not diminishing—the power of the group within its own local or national system.

The PVO should make itself actively accountable to the local group, sharing power over the program with that group.

II. *A program must take due account of the needs, aspirations, and operational constraints of the local group as well as the program criteria of the PVO.*

The local group must define its own needs and then have the major responsibility to decide with the PVO the terms and conditions of the program.

The program itself must be designed flexibly and realistically, in particular with respect to the time frame of the program. Similarly, we would expect that the program would evolve as the PVO and the local group learned from mistakes and from each other.

The program should also be designed to affect positively all segments of the local "poor majority," and certainly women.

The local group must participate fully and increasingly throughout the implementation of the program, both in decision making and in contributions of materials and personnel.

The PVO should work in a manner that respects the primacy of local cultural values, while at the same time not violating its own cultural standards.

The PVO must openly state to the local group its own motivation, goals, and evaluation criteria for the program.

The programs should be susceptible to continuing evaluation, in quantifiable and/or nonquantifiable terms. Evaluations should be made, or at the least shared, with local groups.

The local group must be as aware as the PVO of the political, cultural, and economic implications of embarking on the program. Local groups should be aware that "experimental" programs are experimental.

The power of the local group vis-à-vis the PVO should grow during the course of the program.

The program should either reach the "poor majority" of the community directly and/or seek out and work through those groups, organizations, or institutions—including government structures—which offer the best opportunity to reach the "poor majority."

III. *PVO programs should help build and inform an American constituency for development as well as seek its support.*

PVOs should openly share their thinking on development with the American public and government.

Funds raised for a specific program (or needy individual) should be spent only on that program.

PVOs should make available to donors its program assessments and regular, detailed, audited financial reports. Donors should be made aware of the availability of these reports.

A PVO program should provide for a means for those supporting it financially to participate in the identification of objectives and implementation of the program and to learn about and from the local group abroad.

PVO fund-raising appeals should present a fair picture of Third World societies, conveying the aspirations and dignity of groups and individuals abroad.

IV. *PVOs have an obligation to share resources and results with other development agencies, to their mutual benefit.*

PVOs should seek programs that can be replicated by other development agencies—private and public, national and international. Especially when innovations are attempted, as they should be, funds and resources should be limited to levels replicable elsewhere.

PVOs should emphasize programs in which they combine their efforts, thus reducing individual overheads while increasing the marginal effectiveness of each. Such combinations and collaborations can also facilitate communications with institutions and local groups in individual countries.

PVOs should judge programs on their merit and in terms of the criteria here listed, not because they serve or do not serve the policies of any government.

About the Overseas Development Council and the Author

The Overseas Development Council is an independent, nonprofit organization established in 1969 to increase American understanding of the economic and social problems confronting the developing countries, and of the importance of these countries to the United States in an increasingly interdependent world. The ODC seeks to promote consideration of development issues by the American public, policymakers, specialists, educators, and the media through its research, conferences, publications, and liaison with U.S. mass membership organizations interested in U.S. relations with the developing world. The ODC's program is funded by foundations, corporations, and private individuals; its policies are determined by its Board of Directors. Theodore M. Hesburgh, C.S.C., is Chairman of the Board, and Davidson Sommers is its Vice Chairman. The Council's President is James P. Grant.

John G. Sommer is a Fellow with the Overseas Development Council. His past experience with private and voluntary organizations includes six years with the Ford Foundation, for most of which he served as its assistant representative in New Delhi, India (1970–1975). Prior to that (1963–1967), he was a volunteer and then a staff member with International Voluntary Services in South Vietnam. He has also served as a consultant to the U.S. Senate Subcommittee on Refugees, the U.S. Department of State, the U.S. Agency for International Development, and the United Methodist Church Board of Social Concerns. He is coauthor of the book *Viet-Nam: The Unheard Voices* (with Don Luce, 1969) and author of various articles and papers relating to U.S. overseas assistance. In connection with the present study of voluntary agencies, he has traveled widely in Asia, Africa, Latin America, and Europe.

Selected ODC Publications

■ Books

The United States and World Development: Agenda 1977, by John W. Sewell and the staff of the Overseas Development Council. Published for the Council by Praeger Publishers, March 1977. 272 pp. $4.95. (A hardback edition is available for $16.50.) *Agenda 1977* includes a description of the context and background for major policy questions facing the new Administration, an analysis of options open to President Carter, and a series of policy recommendations on a variety of development issues. The Statistical Annexes include over 90 pages of current data on issues affecting U.S.-Third World relationships.

Employment, Growth and Basic Needs: A One-World Problem, prepared by the ILO International Labour Office for the 1976 World Employment Conference. Published for the Council in cooperation with the ILO by Praeger Publishers, March 1977. 256 pp. $3.95. (A hardback edition is available for $16.50.) This volume is the U.S. edition of the International Labour Office's comprehensive blueprint of national and international "basic needs" development strategies—strategies aiming more directly than those of the past to ensure certain minimum levels of personal consumption and access to social services.

Women and World Development, edited by Irene Tinker and Michèle Bo Bramsen (May 1976, 240 pp., $3.50), and *Women and World Development: An Annotated Bibliography*, prepared by Mayra Buvinić (May 1976, 176 pp., $2.50). When ordered at the same time, these two publications are available as a set for $5.00. (A hardback edition entitled *Women and World Development*, which combines the two volumes, was published by Praeger Publishers and is available for $21.50.)

The first volume of this set includes essays on selected issues in this field by Margaret Mead, Rae Lesser Blumberg, Irene Tinker, Fatima Mernissi, Teresa Orrego de Figueroa, Hanna Papanek, Nadia H. Youssef, Kenneth Little, Mary Elmendorf, Mallica Vajrathon, Ulla Olin, and Erskine Childers. Also included are summaries of the proceedings and recommendations of the Seminar's workshops on food production and small technology; education and communication; health, nutrition, and family planning; urban affairs; and women's associations.

The second volume of the set consists of an introductory overview and annotations of over 400 published and unpublished studies in this field, arranged according to subject categories and geographic focus.

Beyond Dependency: The Developing World Speaks Out, edited by Guy F. Erb and Valeriana Kallab, with essays by Mahbub ul Haq, Ali A. Mazrui, Samuel L. Parmar, Félix Peña, Krishna Roy, Soedjatmoko, Soumana Traoré, Constantine V. Vaitsos, and Bension Varon. September 1975. 268 pp. $3.95. (A hardback edition is available for $17.50.)

The ten essays in this volume offer the private views of developing-country experts on a number of subjects of longer-term North-South contention. Among the issues discussed from a "southern" perspective are multinational corporations, foreign investment and technology transfer, oceans use, population policy, and the effectiveness of different development strategies. Other chapters discuss the costs of continued confrontation and suggest global "bargains" whereby all could gain. The appendices include the major nongovernmental statements and official declarations documenting the current debate.

Global Justice and Development: The Report of the Aspen Interreligious Consultation (May 1975, 175 pp., $2.50).

The report of the meeting in June 1974 of over one hundred American religious leaders to discuss issues of global poverty and justice contains addresses on various aspects of interdependence, the "Statement of Conscience by Christians and Jews" issued at the end of that meeting, and summaries of the workshop sessions. Also included are annexes containing statements of concern by various religious groups since the Consultation, resource materials, films, organizations, and a compilation of background facts on global poverty.

The Uncertain Promise: Value Conflicts in Technology Transfer, by Denis Goulet (September 1977, 320 pp., $5.95). (A hardback edition is available for $10.95.)

Focusing on technology transfers between transnational corporations based in rich countries and firms and governments in the developing countries, this volume demonstrates (with case-study illustrations) how confusions over basic values and social priorities can often lead to the uncritical purchase of technologies that ultimately prove totally inappropriate—if not absolutely counter—to development.

■ Development Papers

Accelerating Population through Social and Economic Progress, by Robert S. McNamara, No. 24, September 1977 (64 pp., $1.50).

Managing Interdependence: Restructuring the U.S. Government, by Robert H. Johnson, No. 23, February 1977 (32 pp., $1.25).

The Third World and the International Economic Order, by Mahbub ul Haq, No. 22, September 1976 (54 pp., $1.50).

World Interdependence: Verbal Smokescreen or New Ethic?, by Denis Goulet, No. 21, March 1976 (36 pp., $1.00).

U.S. Voluntary Aid to the Third World: What Is Its Future?, by John G. Sommer, No. 20, December 1975 (68 pp., $1.50).

Growth from Below: A People-Oriented Development Strategy, by James P. Grant, No. 16, December 1973 (29 pp., $.50). Reprinted from *Foreign Policy*.

A catalogue of ODC publications in print is available upon request.

Board of Directors

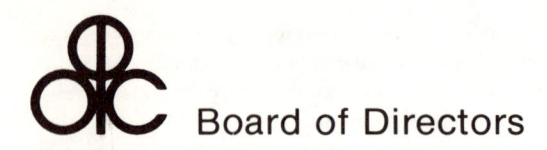

Chairman: Theodore M. Hesburgh, C.S.C.
Vice-Chairman: Davidson Sommers

Robert O. Anderson
William Attwood
Eugene R. Black
Harrison Brown
Lester R. Brown
John Bullitt
John F. Burlingame
John T. Caldwell
Anne Campbell
Wallace Campbell
Thomas P. Carney
Robert A. Charpie
Mrs. Wm. M. Christopherson
Frank M. Coffin
Owen Cooper
Richard H. Demuth
Charles S. Dennison
John Diebold
*Thomas L. Farmer
Roger Fisher
Luther H. Foster
*J. Wayne Fredericks
*Orville L. Freeman
*William S. Gaud
Philip L. Geyelin
*Lester E. Gordon
*Lincoln Gordon
*James P. Grant (ex officio)
*Edward K. Hamilton
J. George Harrar
Samuel P. Hayes
*Theodore M. Hesburgh, C.S.C.
*Ruth J. Hinerfeld
Donald Hornig
Vernon Jordan
Nicholas deB. Katzenbach
*Tom Killefer

Peter F. Krogh
*Anne O. Krueger
*William J. Lawless
Walter J. Levy
*John P. Lewis
David E. Lilienthal
C. Payne Lucas
*Harald B. Malmgren
*Louis E. Martin
Edward S. Mason
C. Peter McColough
Lawrence C. McQuade
*Alfred F. Miossi
Thomas A. Murphy
*Randolph Nugent
William S. Ogden
F. Taylor Ostrander
James A. Perkins
Hart Perry
John Petty
Samuel D. Proctor
*Andrew E. Rice
Charles W. Robinson
James D. Robinson, III
Bruce W. Rohrbacher
William D. Rogers
David H. Shepard
Joseph E. Slater
**Davidson Sommers
Lauren K. Soth
*Stephen Stamas
Richard L. Thomas
Raymond Vernon
*C. M. van Vlierden
Clifton R. Wharton, Jr.
Charles W. Yost
*Barry Zorthian

*Member of Executive Committee
**Chairman of Executive Committee